A YOUNG PEOPLE'S
HISTORY
of the UNITED STATES

D0981748

A YOUNG PEOPLE'S
HISTORY
of the UNITED STATES

COLUMBUS
to the
WAR ON TERROR

HOWARD
ZINN

Adapted by
REBECCA STEFOFF

7

SEVEN STORIES PRESS
New York

Copyright © 2007, 2009 by Howard Zinn

Previously published as a two volume set

A Triangle Square *books for young readers* edition,
published by Seven Stories Press.

All rights reserved. No part of this book may be reproduced, stored
in a retrieval system, or transmitted in any form or by any means, including
mechanical, electric, photocopying, recording, or otherwise, without the
prior written permission of the publisher.

SEVEN STORIES PRESS
140 Watts Street, New York, NY 10013
www.sevenstories.com

College professors may order examination copies of
Seven Stories Press titles for a free six-month trial period.
To order, visit http://www.sevenstories.com/textbook
or send a fax on school letterhead to (212) 226-1411.

Library of Congress Cataloging-in-Publication Data

Stefoff, Rebecca, 1951-
A young people's history of the United States / Howard Zinn ; adapted by
Rebecca Stefoff.—Seven Stories Press 1st ed.
p. cm.
Previously published in 2 volumes: 2007.
Includes Indexes.
ISBN 978-1-58322-886-9 (hardcover, single volume)—
ISBN 978-1-58322-869-2 (pbk., single volume)
1. United States--History--Juvenile literature. I. Zinn, Howard, 1922- People's
history of the United States. II. Title.
E178.3.S735 2009
2009006055

Design by Pollen, New York
Printed in the United States of America

15 17 19 20 18 16

Contents

PART TWO

*To all the parents and teachers over the years who
have asked for a people's history for young people,
and to the younger generation, who we hope will
use their talents to make a better world.*

❖

Thanks to Dan Simon, of Seven Stories Press,
for initiating this *Young People's History* and
to Theresa Noll of Seven Stories Press,
for steering the project so carefully
through its various stages.

❖

A special appreciation to Rebecca Stefoff,
who undertook the heroic job of adapting
A People's History for young readers.

Introduction

EVER SINCE my book *A People's History of the
United States* was published twenty-five years ago,
parents and teachers have been asking me about an
edition that would be attractive to youngsters. So I
am very pleased that Seven Stories Press and
Rebecca Stefoff have undertaken the heroic job of
adapting my book for younger readers.

Over the years, some people have asked me:
"Do you think that your history, which is radically
different than the usual histories of the United
States, is suitable for young people? Won't it create
disillusionment with our country? Is it right to be
so critical of the government's policies? Is it right
to take down the traditional heroes of the nation,
like Christopher Columbus, Andrew Jackson,
Theodore Roosevelt? Isn't it unpatriotic to empha-

size slavery and racism, the massacres of Indians, the exploitation of working people, the ruthless expansion of the United States at the expense of the Indians and people in other countries?

I wonder why some people think it is all right for adults to hear such a radical, critical point of view, but not teenagers or sub-teenagers? Do they think that young people are not able to deal with such matters? It seems to me it is wrong to treat young readers as if they are not mature enough to look at their nation's policies honestly. Yes, it's a matter of being honest. Just as we must, as individuals, be honest about our own failures in order to correct them, it seems to me we must do the same when evaluating our national policies.

Patriotism, in my view, does not mean unquestioning acceptance of whatever the government does. To go along with whatever your government does is not a characteristic of democracy. I remember in my own early education we were taught that it was a sign of a totalitarian state, of a dictatorship, when people did not question what their government did. If you live in a democratic state, it means you have the right to criticize your government's policies.

The basic principles of democracy are laid out in the Declaration of Independence, which was adopted in 1776 to explain why the colonies were no longer willing to accept British rule. The Declaration makes it clear that governments are not holy, not beyond criticism, because they are artificial creations, set up by the people to protect the equal right of everyone to "life, liberty, and the pursuit of happiness." And when governments do not fulfill this obligation, the Declaration says that "it is the right of the people to alter or abolish the government."

And, if it is the right of the people to "alter or abolish" the government, then surely it is their right to criticize it.

I am not worried about disillusioning young people by pointing to the flaws in the traditional heroes. We should be able to tell the truth about people whom we have been taught to look upon as heroes, but who really don't deserve that admiration. Why should we think it heroic to do as Columbus did, arrive in this hemisphere and carry on a rampage of violence, in order to find gold? Why should we think it heroic for Andrew Jackson to drive Indians out of their land? Why should we think of Theodore Roosevelt as a hero because he fought in the Spanish-American War, driving Spain out of Cuba, but also paving the way for the United States to take control of Cuba?

Yes, we all need heroes, people to admire, to see as examples of how human beings should live. But I prefer to see Bartolomé de Las Casas as a hero, for exposing Columbus's violent behavior against the Indians he encountered in the Bahamas. I prefer to see the Cherokee Indians as heroes, for resisting their removal from the lands on which they lived. To me, it is Mark Twain who is a hero, because he denounced President Theodore Roosevelt after Roosevelt had praised an American general who had massacred hundreds of people in the Philippines. I consider Helen Keller a hero because she protested against President Woodrow Wilson's decision to send young Americans into the slaughterhouse of the First World War.

My point of view, which is critical of war, racism, and economic injustice, carries over to the situation we face in the United States today.

More than five years have elapsed since the most recent edition of *A People's History*, and this young people's edition gives me an opportunity, in the final chapter of Volume Two, to bring the story up to date, to the end of 2006, halfway through the second administration of George W. Bush, and three and a half years after the start of the U.S. invasion of Iraq.

A YOUNG PEOPLE'S
HISTORY
of the UNITED STATES

PART ONE

COLUMBUS
to
THE AMERICAN EMPIRE

CHAPTER ONE

COLUMBUS
AND THE INDIANS

ARAWAK MEN AND WOMEN CAME OUT OF their villages onto the beaches. Full of wonder, they swam out to get a closer look at the strange big boat. When Christopher Columbus and his soldiers came ashore, carrying swords, the Arawaks ran to greet them. Columbus later wrote about the Indians in his ship's log:

> They . . . brought us parrots and balls of cotton and spears and many other things, which they exchanged for the glass beads and hawks' bells. They willingly traded everything they owned. . . . They were well-built, with good bodies and handsome features. . . . They do not bear arms, and do not know them, for I showed them a sword, they took it by the edge and cut themselves out of ignorance. They had no iron. Their spears are made of cane. . . . They would make fine servants. . . . With fifty men we could subjugate [over-power] them and make them do whatever we want.

(*left, detail*)
Captain Mason's attack on the Pequots' fortified village, 1637.

The Arawaks lived in the Bahama Islands. Like Indians on the American mainland, they believed in hospitality and in sharing. But Columbus, the first messenger to the Americas from the civilization of western Europe, was hungry for money. As soon as he arrived in the islands, he seized some Arawaks by force so that he could get information from them. The information that Columbus wanted was this: Where is the gold?

Columbus had talked the king and queen of Spain into paying for his expedition. Like other European states, Spain wanted gold. There was gold in the Indies, as the people of Europe called India and southeastern Asia. The Indies had other valuable goods, too, such as silks and spices. But traveling by land from Europe to Asia was a long and dangerous journey, so the nations of Europe were searching for a way to reach the Indies by sea. Spain decided to gamble on Columbus. In return for bringing back gold and spices, Columbus would get 10 percent of the profits. He would be made governor of any newly discovered lands, and he would win the title Admiral of the Ocean Sea. He set out with three ships, hoping to become the first

European to reach Asia by sailing across the Atlantic Ocean.

Like other informed people of his time, Columbus knew that the world was round. This meant that he could sail west from Europe to reach the East. The world Columbus imagined, however, was small. He would never have made it to Asia, which was thousands of miles farther away than he thought. But he was lucky. One-fourth of the way there he came upon an unknown land between Europe and Asia.

Thirty-three days after leaving waters known to Europeans, Columbus and his men saw branches floating in the water and flocks of birds in the air. These were signs of land. Then, on October 12, 1492, a sailor called Rodrigo saw the moon shining on white sands, and cried out. It was an island in the Bahamas, in the Caribbean Sea. The first man to sight land was supposed to get a large reward, but Rodrigo never got it. Columbus claimed that he had seen a light the evening before. He got the reward.

CHILD SAILORS

LIKE MOST HISTORIANS, I WRITE ABOUT COLUMBUS and his "men," but many of those who sailed with Columbus in 1492—on the Niña, the Pinta, and the Santa Maria—were children. One of those children was twelve-year-old Diego Bermúdez, a page who sailed with Columbus on the Santa Maria. Of the ninety sailors who sailed on the three ships, nearly twenty were boys!

The children who sailed with Columbus worked in their bare feet, took showers by dumping buckets of seawater over their heads, and used a toilet that stuck out from the ships' decks over the sea. And even the youngest boys drank strong white wine with their food.

Older boys, called "criados," assisted ships' officers, or apprenticed as "gromets," climbing ropes high above to trim the sails. Gromets became expert at tying different kinds of knots. They hung lengths of rope from their belts and carried knives at all times to help them in their work. Younger boys like

Diego worked as "pages," who cooked and scrubbed the decks, though their most important job was to tell time. There were no clocks on board, so they kept time by using an ampolleta, which was a half-hour glass filled with sand. As soon as all the sand ran out, the page turned it over and ran to the poop deck, where he rang a bell and sang out a prayer to signify that another half-hour had passed. Pages had to learn sixteen different prayers by heart, each one for a different half-hour of the working day. Here is one of them:

> Blessed be the hour God came to earth,
> Holy Mary who gave him birth,
> And St. John who saw his worth.
> The guard is posted,
> The watchglass filling,
> We'll have a good voyage,
> If God be willing.

Source: Hoose, Phillip. *We Were There, Too!: Young People in U.S. History*. New York: Farrar Straus Giroux, 2001.

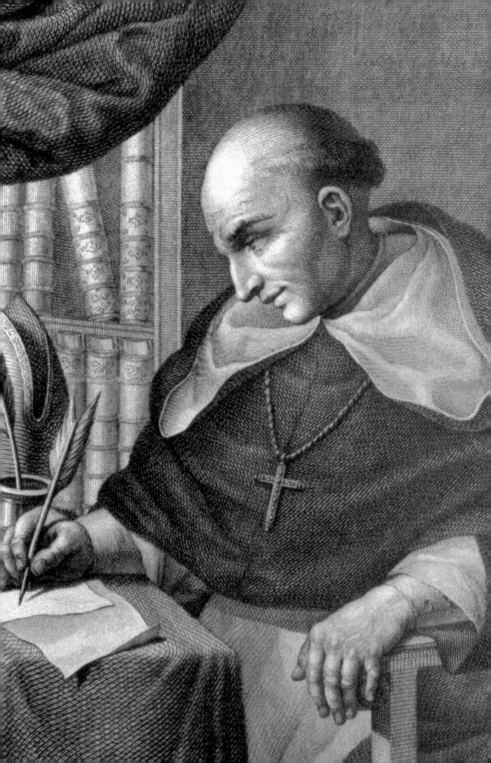

The Arawaks' Impossible Task

THE ARAWAK INDIANS who greeted Columbus lived in villages and practiced agriculture. Unlike the Europeans, they had no horses or other work animals, and they had no iron. What they did have was tiny gold ornaments in their ears.

Those little ornaments shaped history. Because of them, Columbus started his relationship with the Indians by taking prisoners, thinking that they could lead him to the source of the gold. He sailed to several other Caribbean islands, including Hispaniola, an island now divided between two countries, Haiti and the Dominican Republic. After one of Columbus's ships ran aground, he used wood from the wreck to build a fort in Haiti. Then he sailed back to Spain with news of his discovery, leaving thirty-nine crewmen at the fort. Their orders were to find and store the gold.

The report Columbus made to the royal Spanish court was part fact, part fiction. He claimed to have reached Asia, and he called the Arawaks "Indians," meaning people of the Indies. The islands Columbus had visited must be off the coast of China, he said. They were full of riches:

(*left*)
Bartolomé de Las Casas, 1791.

Hispaniola is a miracle. Mountains and hills, plains and pastures, are both fertile and beautiful . . . the harbors are unbelievably good and there are many wide rivers of which the majority contain gold. . . . There are many spices, and great mines of gold and other metals. . .

If the king and queen would give him just a little more help, Columbus said, he would make another voyage. This time he would come back to Spain with "as much gold as they need . . . and as many slaves as they ask."

Columbus's promises won him seventeen ships and more than 1,200 men for his second expedition. The aim was clear: slaves and gold. They went from island to island in the Caribbean, capturing Indians. But as word spread among the Indians, the Spaniards found more and more empty villages. When they got to Haiti, they found that the sailors left behind at the fort were dead. The sailors had roamed the island in gangs looking for gold, taking women and children as slaves, until the Indians had killed them in a battle.

Columbus's men searched Haiti for gold, with no success. They had to fill up the ships returning to Spain with something, so in 1495 they went on a great slave raid. Afterward, they picked five hundred captives to send to Spain. Two hundred of the Indians died on the voyage. The rest arrived alive in Spain and were put up for sale by a local church official. Columbus, who was full of religious talk, later wrote, "Let us in the name of the Holy Trinity go on sending all the slaves that can be sold."

But too many slaves died in captivity. Columbus was desperate to show a profit on his voyages. He had to make good on his promises to fill the ships with gold. In a part of Haiti where Columbus and his men imagined there was much gold, they ordered everyone over the age of thirteen to collect gold for them. Indians who did not give gold to the Spaniards had their hands cut off and bled to death.

The Indians had been given an impossible task. The only gold around was bits of gold dust in streams. So they ran away. The Spaniards hunted them down with dogs and killed them. When they took prisoners, they hanged them or burned them to death. Unable to fight against the Spanish soldiers' guns, swords, armor, and horses, the Arawaks began to commit mass suicide with poison. When the Spanish search for gold began, there were a quarter of a million Indians on Haiti.

In two years, through murder or suicide, half them were dead.

When it was clear that there was no gold left, the Indians were enslaved on the Spaniards' huge estates. They were overworked and mistreated, and they died by the thousands. By 1550, only five hundred Indians remained. A century later, no Arawaks were left on the island.

Telling Columbus's Story

WE KNOW WHAT HAPPENED ON THE Caribbean islands after Columbus came because of Bartolomé de Las Casas. He was a young priest who helped the Spanish conquer Cuba. For a while he owned a plantation where Indian slaves worked. But then Las Casas gave up his plantation and spoke out against Spanish cruelty.

Las Casas made a copy of Columbus's journal, and he also wrote a book called *History of the Indies*. In this book, he described the Indians' society and their customs. He also told how the

Spaniards treated the Indians:

> As for the newly born, they died early because their
> mothers, overworked and famished [starving], had no
> milk to nurse them, and for this reason, while I was in
> Cuba, 7,000 children died in three months. Some
> mothers even drowned their babies from sheer desper-
> ation. . . . In this way, husbands died in the mines,
> wives died at work, and children died from lack of
> milk. . . . My eyes have seen these acts so foreign to
> human nature, and now I tremble as I write. . . .

This was the start of the history of Europeans
in the Americas. It was a history of conquest, slavery, and death. But for a long time, the history
books given to children in the United States told a
different story—a tale of heroic adventure, not
bloodshed. The way the story is taught to young
people is just beginning to change.

The story of Columbus and the Indians shows
us something about how history gets written. One
of the most famous historians to write about
Columbus was Samuel Eliot Morison. He even
sailed across the Atlantic Ocean himself, retracing
Columbus's route. In 1954 Morison published a
popular book called *Christopher Columbus, Mariner.*
He said that cruel treatment by Columbus and the

Europeans who came after him caused the "complete genocide" of the Indians. *Genocide* is a harsh word. It is the name of a terrible crime—the deliberate killing of an entire ethnic or cultural group.

Morison did not lie about Columbus. He did not leave out the mass murder. But he mentioned the truth quickly and then went on to other things. By burying the fact of genocide in a lot of other information, he seemed to be saying that the mass murder wasn't very important in the big picture. By making genocide seem like a small part of the story, he took away its power to make us think differently about Columbus. At the end of the book, Morison summed up his idea of Columbus as a great man. Columbus's most important quality, Morison said, was his seamanship.

A historian must pick and choose among facts, deciding which ones to put into his or her work, which ones to leave out, and which ones to place at the center of the story. Every historian's own ideas and beliefs go into the way he or she writes history. In turn, the way history is written can shape the ideas and beliefs of the people who read it. A view of history like Morison's, a picture of the past that sees Columbus and others like him as great sailors and discoverers, but says almost nothing about their genocide, can make it seem as though what they did was right.

People who write and read history have gotten used to seeing terrible things such as conquest and murder as the price of progress. This is because many of them think that history is the story of governments, conquerors, and leaders. In this way of looking at the past, history is what happens to states, or nations. The actors in history are kings, presidents, and generals. But what about factory workers, farmers, people of color, women, and children? They make history, too.

The story of any country includes fierce conflicts between conquerors and the conquered, masters and slaves, people with power and those without power. Writing history is always a matter of taking sides. For example, I choose to tell the story of the discovery of America from the point of view of the Arawaks. I will tell the story of the U.S. Constitution from the point of view of the slaves, and the story of the Civil War from the point of view of the Irish in New York City.

I believe that history can help us imagine new possibilities for the future. One way it can do this

is by letting us see the hidden parts of the past, the times when people showed that they could resist the powerful, or join together. Maybe our future can be found in the past's moments of kindness and courage rather than its centuries of warfare. That is my approach to the history of the United States, which started with the meeting between Columbus and the Arawaks.

More Meetings, More Fighting

The tragedy of Columbus and the Arawaks happened over and over again. Spanish conquerors Hernan Cortés and Francisco Pizarro destroyed the Aztecs of Mexico and the Incas of South America. When English settlers reached Virginia and Massachusetts, they did the same thing to the Indians they met.

Jamestown, Virginia, was the first permanent English settlement in the Americas. It was built inside a territory governed by an Indian chief named Powhatan. He watched the English settle

(left)
Captain Mason's attack on the Pequots' fortified village, 1637.

on his land but did not attack. In 1607, Powhatan spoke to John Smith, one of the leaders at Jamestown. The statement that has come down to us may not truly be Powhatan's words, but it sounds a lot like what other Indians said and wrote at later times. We can read Powhatan's statement as the spirit of what he thought as he watched the white men enter his territory:

> I know the difference between peace and war better than any man in my country. Why will you take by force what you may have quietly by love? Why will you destroy us who supply you with food? What can you get by war? Why are you jealous of us? We are unarmed, and willing to give you what you ask, if you come in a friendly manner, and not so simple as not to know that it is much better to eat good meat, sleep comfortably, live quietly with my wives and children, laugh and be merry with the English, and trade for their copper and hatchets, than to run away from them, and to lie cold in the woods, and feed on acorns, roots, and such trash, and be so hunted that I can neither eat nor sleep.

In the winter of 1609–1610, the English at Jamestown went through a terrible food shortage they called the "starving time." They roamed the woods looking for nuts and berries, and they dug up graves to eat the corpses. Out of five hundred colonists, all but sixty died.

Some of the colonists ran off to join the Indians, where they would at least be fed. The next summer, the governor of the colony asked Powhatan to send them back. When he refused, the colonists destroyed an Indian settlement. They kidnapped the queen of the tribe, threw her children into the water and shot them, and then stabbed her.

Twelve years later, the Indians tried to get rid of the growing English settlements. They massacred 347 men, women, and children. From then on it was total war. The English could not enslave the Indians, and they would not live with them, so they decided to wipe them out.

To the north, the Pilgrims settled in New England. Like the Jamestown colonists, they came to Indian land. The Pequot tribe lived in southern Connecticut and Rhode Island. The colonists wanted this land, so the war with the Pequots began. Massacres took place on both sides. The English used a form of warfare that Cortés had used in Mexico. To fill the enemy with terror, they attacked civilians, people who were not warriors.

"WHITE INDIANS"

ENGLISH COLONISTS CAPTURED IN BATTLE
by Native Americans who found that they preferred
life in Native American communities over their own
were referred to as "white Indians." Eunice Williams
was one such example. She was seven years old
when she was taken prisoner by the Kahnawake
Mohawks. Her mother and two of her brothers were
among those killed. Her other two brothers were
also captured. Two and a half years later, her father,
Reverend John Williams, negotiated the return of
Eunice and her brothers, but Eunice refused to leave
the Native American community. As a Mohawk, she
converted to Catholicism and married another
Mohawk.

It was said that the Mohawks were kinder to children and that females were respected as the equals
of males. Where European parents considered physical punishment essential, the Native Americans

believed that children should be "reproved with gentle words," and that corporal punishment would weaken character and make children submissive. In Native American cultures, the goal was to imbue children with independence and courage.

Benjamin Franklin wrote in 1753, "When white persons of either sex have been taken prisoners young by the Indians, and lived awhile among them, tho' ransomed by their Friends, and treated with all imaginable tenderness to prevail with them to stay among the English, yet in a Short time they become disgusted with our manner of life, and the care and pains that are necessary to support it, and take the first good Opportunity of escaping again into the woods, from whence there is no reclaiming them."

Source: Mintz, Steven. *Huck's Raft: A History of American Childhood.* Boston: Harvard University Press, 2004, p. 7, 8, 15, 35.

They set fire to wigwams, and as the Indians ran out to escape the flames, the English cut them to bits with their swords.

When Columbus came to the Americas, 10 million Indians lived north of what is now Mexico. After the Europeans began taking that land, the number of Indians was reduced until, in time, fewer than a million remained. Many Indians died from diseases brought by the whites.

Who were these Indians? Who were the people who came out onto the beaches with presents for Columbus and his crew and who peered out of the forests at the first white settlers of Virginia and Massachusetts?

As many as 75 million Indians lived throughout the Americas before Columbus. They had hundreds of different tribal cultures and about two thousand languages. Many tribes were nomads, wanderers who lived by hunting and gathering food. Others, were expert farmers and lived in settled communities. Among the Iroquois, the most powerful of the northeastern tribes, land did not belong to individuals. It belonged to the entire community. People shared the work of farming and hunting, and they also shared food.

Women were important and respected in Iroquois society, and the sexes shared power. Children were taught to be independent. Not only the Iroquois but other Indian tribes behaved in similar ways.

So Columbus and the Europeans who followed him did not come to an empty wilderness. They came to a world that was, in some places, as crowded as Europe. The Indians had their own history, laws, and poetry. They lived in greater equality than people in Europe did. Was "progress" enough of a reason to decimate their population and wipe out their societies? The fate of the Indians reminds us to look at history as something more than just a story of conquerors and leaders.

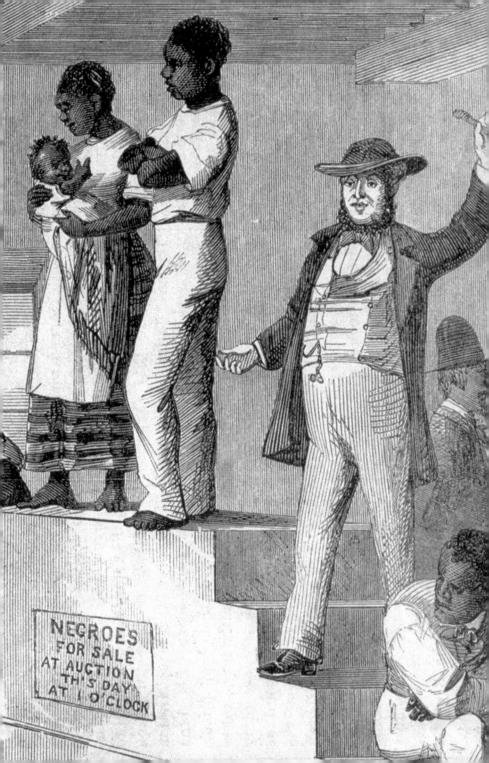

CHAPTER TWO

BLACK AND WHITE

IN THE HISTORY OF THE WORLD, THERE IS
no country where racism has been more important
than in the United States. How did this racism
start? How might it end? Another way of asking the
question might be: Is racism natural?

Maybe history can help answer these questions. If so, the history of slavery in North
America could hold some clues, because we can
trace the coming of the first white people and the
first black people to this continent.

In North America, slavery became a widespread substitute for paid labor. At the same
time, whites came to believe that blacks were
not their equals. For 350 years, blacks would
suffer inhumane treatment in American society
because of racism, which combines ideas about

(*left, detail*)
A slave auction
in Virginia, 1861.

23

black inferiority with the unequal treatment of
black people.

Why Turn to Slavery?

EVERYTHING THAT HAPPENED TO THE FIRST
white settlers pushed them toward the enslavement of blacks. In Virginia, the settlers who had
survived the "starving time" of 1609–1610 were
joined by new arrivals. They were desperate for
labor to grow enough food to stay alive. But they
wanted to grow more than corn. The Virginia settlers had learned from the Indians how to grow
tobacco, and in 1617 they sent the first cargo to
England. The tobacco brought a high price. Even
though some people thought smoking was sinful,
the planters were not going to let such thoughts get
in the way of making a profit. They would supply
England with tobacco.

But who would do the hard work of growing
the tobacco and preparing it for sale? The settlers
couldn't force the Indians to work for them. The

Indians outnumbered the settlers. Even though the settlers could kill Indians with their guns, other Indians would massacre settlers in return. The settlers couldn't capture Indians and make them into slaves, either. The Indians were tough and defiant. And while the North American woods seemed strange and hostile to the settlers, the Indians were at home there. They could avoid the settlers—or escape from them.

Maybe the Virginians were angry that they couldn't control the Indians. Maybe they envied the way the Indians could take care of themselves better than the whites did, even though the whites thought that they themselves were civilized and that the Indians were savages. In his book *American Slavery, American Freedom,* historian Edmund Morgan imagines how the colonists felt about their failure to live better than the Indians, or to control them:

> The Indians, keeping to themselves, laughed at your superior methods and lived from the land more abundantly and with less labor than you did. . . . And when your own people starting deserting in order to live with them, it was too much. . . . So you killed the Indians, tortured them, burned their villages, burned their cornfields. . . . But you still did not grow much corn.

Maybe those feelings of envy and anger made the settlers especially ready to become the masters of slaves. It was profitable to the Virginians to import blacks as slave labor. After all, other colonies in the Americas were already doing it.

By 1619, a million blacks had been forcibly brought from Africa to work as slaves in the mines and sugar plantations of the Portuguese and Spanish colonies in South America and the Caribbean islands. Even earlier, fifty years before Columbus, the slave trade started when ten Africans were taken to Portugal and sold. So that in 1619, when the first twenty blacks were brought by force to Jamestown and sold to settlers, white people had been thinking of Africans as slave labor for a long time.

The Africans' having been torn from their land and their cultures made enslavement easier. The Indians were on their own land. The whites were in a new continent, but they had brought their English culture with them. But the blacks had been torn from their land and their culture. They were forced into a situation where their heritage—languages, clothes, customs, and family life—was wiped out bit by bit. Only with amazing strength of will could blacks hold on to pieces of this heritage.

Was African culture easy to destroy because it was inferior to European culture? African civilization was in some ways more advanced than that of Europe. It was a civilization of 100 million people. They built large cities, they used iron tools, and they were skilled at farming, weaving, pottery making, and sculpture. Europeans who traveled in Africa in the sixteenth century were impressed with the kingdoms of Timbuktu and Mali. These African states were stable and organized, at a time when European states were just beginning to develop into modern nations.

Slavery existed in Africa, and Europeans sometimes pointed to that fact to excuse their own slave trade. But although slaves in Africa had a harsh life, they also had rights that those brought to America did not have. American slavery was the most cruel form of slavery in history because of two things. First, American slavery was driven by a frenzy for limitless profit. Second, it was based on racial hatred, a view that saw whites as masters and blacks as slaves. For these reasons, American slavery treated slaves as less than human.

The inhuman treatment began in Africa,

(overleaf)
A Slave Auction in Virginia, 1861.

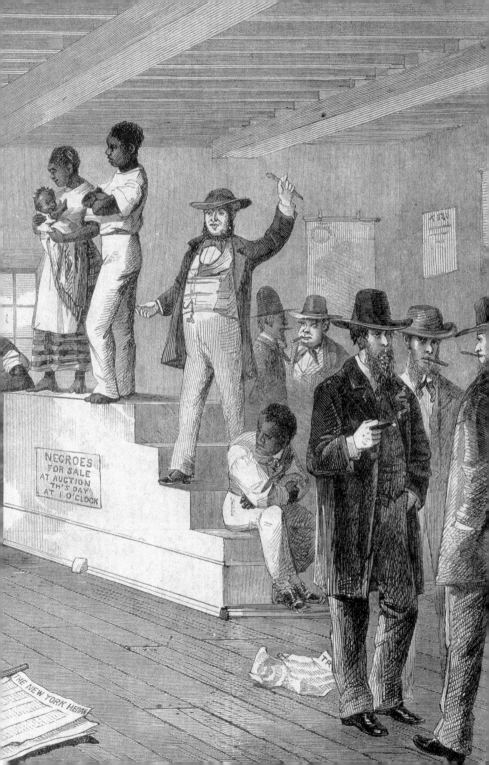

where captured slaves were chained together and forced to walk to the coast, sometimes for a thousand miles. For every five blacks captured, two died during these death marches. When the survivors reached the coast they were kept in cages until they were sold.

Then they were packed aboard the slave ships, chained together in the dark, in spaces not much bigger than coffins. Some died for lack of air in the crowded, dirty cargo holds of the ships. Others jumped overboard to end their suffering. As many as a third of all the Africans shipped overseas may have died during the journey. But the trade was profitable, so merchants crammed the blacks into the holds of the slave ships like fish.

At first, the Dutch were the main slave traders. Later the English led the trade. Some Americans in New England entered the business, too. In 1637 the first American slave ship sailed from Massachusetts. Its holds were divided into racks two feet wide and six feet long, with leg irons to hold the captives in place.

By 1800, somewhere between 10 million and 15 million black Africans had been brought to the Americas. In all, Africa may have lost as many as

(*left*)
African captives leaping off a slave ship off the coast of Africa, 1700s.

50 million human beings to death and slavery during the centuries that we call the beginnings of modern civilization.

Slavery got started in the American colonies because the Jamestown settlers were desperate for labor. They couldn't use Indians, and it would have been hard to use whites. But blacks were available in growing numbers, thanks to profit-seeking dealers in human flesh. And the terrible treatment Africans suffered after being captured left many of them in a state of helplessness. All of these things led to the enslavement of the blacks.

Fear and Racism

WERE ALL BLACKS SLAVES? MAYBE THE SETTLERS considered some blacks to be servants, not slaves. The settlers had white servants, too. Would they have treated white servants differently from black ones?

A case from colonial Virginia shows that whites and blacks received very different treatment. In 1640, six white servants and one black started to run away. They were caught. The black man, named Emanuel in the court record, received thirty blows with a whip. He was also branded on one cheek and sentenced to work in shackles for a year or longer. The whites received lighter sentences.

This unequal treatment was racism, which showed itself in feelings and in actions. The whites felt superior to the blacks, and they looked at blacks with contempt. They also treated the blacks more harshly and oppressively than they treated each other. Was this racism "natural"? Did the whites dislike and mistreat the blacks because of some instinct born into them? Or was racism the result of certain conditions that can be removed?

One way to answer those questions is to find out whether any whites in the American colonies viewed blacks as their equals. And evidence shows that they did. At times when whites and blacks found themselves sharing the same problems and the same work, with the same master as their enemy, they treated each other as equals.

We don't have to talk about "natural" racial dislike to explain why slavery became established on the plantations of the American colonies. The

need for labor is enough of a reason. The number
of whites who came to the colonies was just not
enough to meet the needs of the plantations, so
the settlers turned to slaves to meet those needs.
And the needs kept rising. In 1700, Virginia had
six thousand slaves, one-twelfth of the colony's
population. By 1763, there were 170,000 slaves,
about half the population.

From the beginning, black men and women
resisted their enslavement. Through resistance, they
showed their dignity as human beings, if only to
themselves and their brothers and sisters. Often they
used methods that were hard to identify and punish,
such as working slowly or secretly destroying white
property. Another form of resistance was running
away. Slaves just arrived from Africa, still holding on
to the heritage of village life, would run away in
groups and try to set up communities in the wilderness. Enslaved people born in America were more
likely to run off alone and try to pass as free.

Runaway slaves risked pain and death. If they
were caught even planning to escape, they could
be punished in terrible ways. Slaves were burned,
mutilated, and killed. Whites believed that severe
punishments would keep other slaves from

becoming rebellious.

White settlers were terrified of organized black uprisings. Fear of slave revolts, it seems, was a fact of plantation life. A Virginia planter named William Byrd wrote in 1736 that if a bold slave leader arose, "a man of desperate fortune," he might start a war that would "tinge our rivers wide as they are with blood."

Such rebellions did take place—not many, but enough to create constant fear among the planters. In 1720 a settler in South Carolina wrote to London about a planned slave uprising that had been caught just in time:

> I am now to acquaint you that very lately we have had a very wicked and barbarous plot of the . . . negroes rising with a designe to destroy all the white people in the country and then to take Charles Town . . . but it pleased God it was discovered and many of them taken prisoners and some burnt and some hang'd and some banish'd.

We know of about 250 cases in which ten or more slaves joined in a revolt or plot. But not all rebellions involved slaves alone. From time to time, whites were involved in the slave resistance. As early as 1663, white servants and black slaves in Virginia formed a conspiracy to rebel and gain their freedom. The plot was betrayed and ended with executions.

In 1741, New York had ten thousand white and two thousand black slaves. After a hard winter brought much misery to poor people of both races, mysterious fires broke out. Blacks and whites were accused of conspiring together. The trial was full of high emotion and wild claims. Some people made confessions under force. Eventually two white men and two white women were executed, eighteen slaves were hanged, and thirteen slaves were burned alive.

Only one fear in the American colonies was greater than the fear of black rebellion. That was the fear that whites who were unhappy with the state of things might join with blacks to overthrow the social order. Especially in the early years of slavery, before racism was well established, some white servants were treated as badly as slaves. There was a chance that the two groups might work together.

To keep that from happening, the leaders of the colonies took steps. They gave a few new rights and benefits to poor whites. For example, in 1705

Virginia passed a law that said that masters had to give white servants some money and corn when their term of service ended. Newly freed servants would also receive some land. This made white people of the servant class less unhappy with their place in society—and less likely to side with the black slaves against the white masters.

A web of historical threads trapped blacks in American slavery. These threads were the desperation of the starving settlers, the helplessness of Africans torn from their homeland, the high profits available to slave traders and tobacco growers, and the laws and customs that allowed masters to punish rebellious slaves. Finally, to keep whites and blacks from joining together as equals, the leaders of the colonies gave poor whites small benefits and gifts of status.

The threads of this web are not "natural." They are historical, created by special circumstances. This does not mean that they would be easy to untangle. But it does mean that there is a possibility for blacks and whites to live together in a different way, under different historical circumstances.

CHAPTER THREE

WHO WERE THE COLONISTS?

A HUNDRED YEARS BEFORE THE AMERICAN Revolution, a rebellion broke out in Virginia. Angry colonists set Jamestown, their capital, on fire. The governor fled the burning town, and England shipped a thousand soldiers across the Atlantic, hoping to keep control of the forty thousand colonists.

This was Bacon's Rebellion. It was not a war of American colonists against the British. Instead, Bacon's Rebellion was an uprising of angry, poor colonists against two groups they saw as their enemies. One was the Indians. The other was the colonists' own rich and privileged leaders.

Bacon's Rebellion brought together groups from the lower classes. White frontiersmen started the uprising because they were angry

(left)
Nathaniel Bacon and his followers burning Jamestown, Virginia, 1676.

39

about the way the colony was being run. Then white servants and black slaves joined the rebellion. They were angry, too—mostly about the huge gap between rich and poor in Virginia.

Nathaniel Bacon and the Rebellion

BACON'S REBELLION STARTED WITH TROUBLE on Virginia's western frontier. By the 1670s rich landowners controlled most of eastern Virginia. As a result, many ordinary people felt that they were pushed toward the frontier. Life was more dangerous there. The settlers had problems with Native Americans. They wanted the colony's leaders to fight the Indians, but the politicians and big landowners who ran the colony wouldn't fight— maybe because they were using some of the Indians as spies and allies against the others.

The frontiersmen felt that the colonial government had let them down. They were angry, and they weren't the only ones. Times were hard. Many Virginians scraped out a living in poverty or worked as servants in terrible conditions. In 1676, these unhappy Virginians found a leader in Nathaniel Bacon.

A British government report explained how Bacon appealed to his followers:

> He seduced the Vulgar and most ignorant people to believe . . . that their whole hearts and hopes were now set on Bacon. Next he charges the Governour as negligent [neglectful] and wicked, treacherous and incapable, the Lawes and Taxes as unjust and oppressive. . . .

Bacon owned a good bit of land. He probably cared more about fighting Indians than about helping the poor. Still, the common people of Virginia felt that he was on their side. They elected Bacon to the colonial government, called the House of Burgesses. Bacon was ready to send armed militias, or armed groups of citizens, to fight the Indians. These militias would act outside government control. This alarmed William Berkeley, the governor of the colony. Berkeley called Bacon a rebel and had him captured.

After two thousand of Bacon's supporters marched into Jamestown, the governor let Bacon go, in return for an apology. But as soon as Bacon was free, he gathered his militia and began raiding the Indians. The rebellion was under way.

Bacon gave his reasons for the rebellion in a paper called "Declaration of the People." It blended the frontiersmen's hatred of the Indians with the common people's anger toward the rich. Bacon accused the Berkeley government of wrongdoing, including unfair taxes and not protecting the western farmers from the Indians.

A few months later, Bacon fell sick and died at the age of twenty-nine. The rebellion didn't last long after that. A ship armed with thirty guns cruised the York River, one of the main waterways of the colony, to restore order. Its captain, Thomas Grantham, used force and tricks to disarm the last rebel bands. At the rebellion's main stronghold, Grantham found four hundred armed whites and blacks— freemen, servants, and slaves. He promised to pardon them and to free the servants and slaves. Instead, he turned his boat's guns on the rebels and took their weapons. Then he returned the servants and slaves to their masters. Eventually, twenty-three rebel leaders were hanged.

Bacon's Rebellion came about because of a chain of oppression in Virginia. The Indians had their lands seized by white frontiersmen. The frontiersmen were taxed and controlled by the rich upper classes in Jamestown. And the whole colony, rich and poor, was being used by England. The colonists grew tobacco to sell to England, but the English set the price. Each year, the king of England made a large profit from the Virginia colony.

Most people in Virginia had supported the rebellion. One member of Governor Berkeley's council said that the rebels wanted to take the colony out of the king's hands and into their own. Another said that the Indian problem was the original cause of Bacon's Rebellion, but that poor people had joined because they wanted to seize and share the wealth of the rich. Who were these rebels?

The Underclass

THE SERVANTS WHO JOINED BACON'S Rebellion were part of a large underclass of miserably poor whites. They came to the North American colonies from English and European cities whose governments wanted to get rid of them. In England, for example, changes in land laws had driven many farmers into poverty and homelessness in the cities. New laws were passed to punish the poor, imprison them in workhouses, or send them out of the country. So some of the poor were forced to leave their homes for America. Others were drawn to America by hope—or by promises and lies about the good lives they would have there.

Many poor people bound for America became indentured servants. They signed an agreement called an indenture that said that they would repay the cost of their journey to America by working for a master for five or seven years. Often they were imprisoned after signing the indenture, so that they couldn't run away before their ship sailed.

The voyage to America from England or Europe lasted from eight to twelve weeks. If the weather was bad, the trip could take even longer, and passengers could run out of food. Poor people crossing the ocean to work as servants in the American colonies were crammed into crowded, dirty quarters. Not all of them survived the journey. Gottlieb Mittelberger, a musician who sailed from Germany to America around 1750, wrote about the terrible trip:

> During the journey the ship is full of pitiful signs of distress—smells, fumes, horrors, vomiting, various kinds of sea-sickness, fever, dysentery, headaches, heat, constipation, boils, scurvy, cancer, mouth-rot. . . . Add to that shortage of food, hunger, thirst, frost, heat, dampness, fear, misery, vexation, and lamentation as well as other troubles. . . . On board our ship, on a day on which we had a great storm, a woman about to give birth and unable to deliver under the circumstances, was pushed through one of the portholes into the sea. . . .

Once they arrived in America, indentured servants were bought and sold like slaves. On March 28, 1771, the *Virginia Gazette* reported: "Just arrived . . . the Ship Justitia, with about one Hundred Healthy Servants, Men Women & Boys. . . . The Sale will commence on Tuesday the 2nd of April."

More than half the colonists who came to North America came as servants. They were mostly English in the seventeenth century, Irish and German in the eighteenth century. Many of them found that life in the American colonies was worse than they had imagined.

Beatings and whippings were common. Servant women were raped. Masters had other means of control. Strangers had to show papers to prove that they were freemen, not runaway servants. The colonial governments agreed among themselves that servants who escaped from one colony to another must be returned. (This later became part of the U.S. Constitution.)

Masters lived in fear of servants' rebellions. After Bacon's Rebellion, English soldiers stayed in Virginia to guard against future trouble. One report at the time said, "Virginia is at present poor and more populous than ever." The writer added that many people were afraid of an uprising by servants who needed basic necessities, such as clothes.

Escape was easier than rebellion. Historian Richard Morris, who wrote a book called *Government and Labor in Early America,* studied colonial newspapers and found many reports of white servants running away, sometimes in groups. Other servants went on strike and refused to work. In 1663, a Maryland master complained to the court that his servants would not do "their ordinary labor." The servants said that they were too weak to work, because the master fed them only beans and bread. The court ordered the servants to receive thirty lashes with a whip.

More and more, as servants ran away or finished their indentures, slaves replaced them. What happened to the servants after they became free? Cheerful stories tell of former servants who rose to wealth, owned land, and became important people. But in his book *Colonists in Bondage,* historian Abbot Smith reported that almost none of the wealthy, important men in the colonies had been indentured servants, and only a few of them were descended from servants.

Rich and Poor

CLASS LINES HARDENED DURING THE colonial period. The difference between rich and poor grew sharper. At the very beginning of the Massachusetts Bay Colony, in 1630, Governor John Winthrop showed the thinking of colonial

(*detail*)
Nathaniel Bacon
and his followers
burning Jamestown,
Virginia, 1676.

leaders when he said that "in all times some must be rich, some poore." The leaders of the colonies were men of money and status. They wanted society in North America to mirror England, where a small number of people controlled the best land and much of the wealth.

The colonies grew fast in the eighteenth century. Between 1700 and 1760, their population rose from one-quarter of a million people to more than a million and a half. Agriculture, shipping, and trading grew. Small factories developed. Boston, New York, Philadelphia, and Charleston doubled and tripled in size.

Through all that growth, the upper class got most of the benefit and held most of the political power. For example, in Boston in 1770, the top 1 percent of property owners had 44 percent of the wealth.

Rich colonial merchants built mansions. People of the upper classes had their portraits painted and traveled in coaches or in chairs carried by servants or slaves. Meanwhile, the poor struggled to stay alive, to keep from freezing in cold weather. And their numbers kept rising. By the 1730s, people demanded institutions to hold the "many Beggarly people daily suffered to wander about the Streets."

The cities built poorhouses for old people, widows, cripples, and orphans, and also for unemployed people and new immigrants. The poorhouses quickly became overcrowded. A Philadelphia citizen wrote in 1748, "It is remarkable what an increase of the number of Beggars there is about town this winter." Nine years later, Boston officials spoke of "a great number of Poor" who found it hard to feed their families.

Traditional histories of the colonies make it seem that the colonists were united in the struggle against England, their outside enemy. But there was much conflict within the colonies. Slave and free, servant and master, tenant and landlord, poor and rich—disorder broke out along these lines of tension.

In 1713, Boston suffered a severe food shortage. In spite of the city's hunger, a wealthy merchant named Andrew Belcher shipped grain to the Caribbean islands, because the profit was greater there. A mob of two hundred people rioted, broke into Belcher's warehouses looking for food, and shot the lieutenant governor of the colony when he tried to stop them. Later, another Boston mob beat up the sheriff and surrounded the governor's house to protest impressment, or forced service in the navy. In 1747, poor Bostonians felt that Thomas Hutchinson, a rich merchant and official, had discriminated against them. His house mysteriously burned, while a crowd watched and cheered.

In New Jersey in the 1740s and 1750s, poor farmers clashed with rich landowners. Both groups claimed they owned the land, and the farmers rioted when the landowners demanded rent. During this time, England fought several wars that brought wealth to a few colonial shipbuilders and merchants. But to the mass of colonists, England's wars brought high taxes, unemployment, and poverty—and more anger against the rich and powerful.

How to Rule

BY THE 1760S, THE WEALTHY ELITE that controlled the British colonies in North America had three big fears: Indian hostility, the danger of slave revolts, and the growing class anger of poor whites. What if these three groups should join together?

Bacon's Rebellion had shown the colonial leaders that it was risky to ignore the Indians, because that infuriated the white people living near the frontier. Better to make war on the Indians and gain the support of the whites. By turning the poor against the Indians, authorities might head off possible class conflict between poor and rich.

Could blacks join the Indians against the whites? This was a real threat. In the Carolinas in the 1750s, twenty-five thousand whites were outnumbered by forty thousand black slaves and sixty thousand Native Americans. Authorities decided to turn blacks and Indians against each other. They bribed Indians to return runaway slaves, and they also made it illegal for free blacks to travel in Indian country. Indian villages did shelter hundreds of runaway slaves, but blacks and Indians never united on a large scale.

The greatest fear of wealthy southern planters was that black slaves and poor whites would combine in another uprising like Bacon's

Rebellion. One tool to keep blacks and whites from uniting was racism. Edmund Morgan, a historian of slavery in Virginia, wrote in his *American Slavery, American Freedom* that racism was not a "natural" feeling about the differences between black and white. Instead, white leaders encouraged a negative view of blacks. If poor whites felt contempt for African Americans, they were less likely to join with them in rebellion.

As the colonies grew, the ruling class found another way of keeping control. Along with the very rich and the very poor, a white middle class was developing. It was made up of small planters, independent farmers, and craft workers in cities and towns. If these middle-class colonists joined forces with the merchants and big planters, they would be a solid buffer against the frontier Indians, the black slaves, and the poor whites.

The upper classes had to win the loyalty of the middle class. This meant that they had to give the middle class something, but how could they do this without damaging their own wealth or power? In the 1760s and 1770s, the ruling group found a wonderfully useful tool. That tool was the language of liberty and equality. It could unite just enough whites to fight a revolution against England—without ending slavery or inequality.

CHAPTER FOUR

TYRANNY IS TYRANNY

AROUND 1776, SOME IMPORTANT PEOPLE
in the British colonies of North America made a
discovery. They found that by creating a nation
and a symbol called the United States, they could
take over land, wealth, and political power from
other people who had been ruling the colonies for
Great Britain.

When we look at the American Revolution this
way, it was a work of genius. The Founding
Fathers created a new system of national control
that has worked very well for more than two hundred years.

Control was desperately needed. The colonies
boiled with discontent. By 1760 there had been
eighteen uprisings aimed at overthrowing the government of one or more colonies. There were also

(*left*)
Bonfire at the Bowling
Green to protest the
Stamp Act, New York City,
1765.

six black rebellions, from South Carolina to New York, and forty other riots.

But by the 1760s the colonies also had people we call local elites. These were political and social leaders in their city, town, or colony. Most of them were educated people, such as lawyers, doctors, and writers. Their thoughts carried weight. Some of these elite colonists were close to the ruling circles, made up of governors, tax collectors, and other officials who represented Great Britain. Other elite colonists were outside the ruling circles, but their fellow colonists looked up to them anyway.

These local elites were disturbed by the rising disorder. They feared that if the social order of the colonies were overturned, their own property and importance could be harmed. Then the elites saw a way to protect themselves and their positions. They could turn the rebellious energy of the colonists against Britain and its officials. This discovery was not a plan or a simple decision. Instead, it took shape over a few years as the elites faced one crisis after another.

Anger and Violence

IN 1763 THE BRITISH DEFEATED FRANCE
in the Seven Years' War (called the French and
Indian War in the colonies). France no longer
threatened Britain's colonies in North America.
But after the war, the British government tight-
ened its control over those colonies, because they
were valuable. Britain needed taxes from the
colonists to help pay for the war. Also, trade with
the colonies brought large profits to Great Britain
every year.

But unemployment and poverty were rising in
the colonies. Poor people wandered the streets,
begging. At the same time, the richest colonists
controlled fortunes worth millions in today's dollars. There were many very poor people but only a
few very rich people.

Hardship made some colonists restless, even
rebellious. In the countryside, where most people
lived, poor and rich came into conflict. From the
1740s to the 1760s, tenants rioted and rebelled
against landlords in New York and New Jersey.

White farmers in North Carolina formed a
"Regulator Movement" in 1766. The Regulators
called themselves poor peasants and laborers. They

claimed to stand for the common people against rich, powerful officials who governed unfairly. The Regulators were angry about high taxes. They also resented lawyers and merchants taking poor people to court over debts. When Regulators organized to keep taxes from being collected, the governor used military force against them. In May 1771, an army with cannon defeated several thousand Regulators. Six Regulators were hanged.

In Boston, the lower classes started using town meetings to air their complaints. One governor of Massachusetts wrote that Boston's poor people and common folk came regularly to the meetings. There were so many of them that they outvoted the "Gentlemen" and other Bostonians close to the ruling circle.

Something important was happening in Boston. It started with men like James Otis and Samuel Adams. They belonged to the local elite, but they were not part of the ruling group that was tied to Britain. Otis, Adams, and other local leaders recognized the feelings of the poorer Bostonians. Through powerful speeches and written articles, they stirred up those angry feelings and called the lower classes into action.

The Boston mob showed what it could do after the British government passed the Stamp Act of 1765. This law taxed the colonists to pay for the Seven Years' War. Colonists had already suffered during the war, and now they didn't want to pay for it. Crowds destroyed the homes of a rich merchant and of Thomas Hutchinson, one of those who ruled in the name of Britain. They smashed Hutchinson's house with axes, drank his wine, and carried off his furniture and other belongings.

Officials reported to Britain that the destruction of Hutchinson's property was part of a plan to attack other rich people. It was to be "a War of Plunder, of general levelling and taking away the Distinction of rich and poor." But such outbursts worried local leaders like James Otis. They wanted the class hatred of the poor to be turned only against the rich who served the British—not against themselves.

A group of Boston merchants, shipowners, and master craftsmen formed a political group called the Loyal Nine. They set up a march to protest the Stamp Act. The Loyal Nine belonged to the upper and middle classes, but they encouraged lower-class people such as shipworkers, apprentices, and craftsmen to join their protest (but they did not include blacks). Two or three thousand people demonstrated outside a local official's home. But after the "gentlemen" who planned and organized the protest left, the crowd went further and destroyed some of the official's property. Later, the leaders said that the violence was wrong. They turned against the crowd and cut all ties with the rioters.

The next time the British government tried to tax the colonies, the colonial elites called for more demonstrations. But this time leaders like Samuel Adams and James Otis insisted, "No Mobs—No Confusions—No Tumults." (A "tumult" was a riot.) They wanted the people to show their anger against Britain, but they also wanted "Persons and Properties" to remain safe.

Revolution in the Air

AS TIME WENT ON, FEELING AGAINST the British grew stronger. After 1768, two thousand British troops were stationed in Boston. At

COMMON SENSE:
ADDRESSED TO THE
INHABITANTS
OF
AMERICA.
On the following interesting
SUBJECTS.

e Origin and Design of Government in general, h concise Remarks on the English Constitution.

Monarchy and Hereditary Succession.

ghts on the present State of American Affairs.

e present Ability of America, with some miscellaneous flections.

itten by an ENGLISHMAN.
y Thomas Paine

n knows no Master save creating HEAVEN,
those whom choice and common good ordain.
THOMSON.

PHILADELPHIA, Printed
Sold by R. BELL, in Third-Street, 1776.

a time when jobs were scarce, these soldiers began taking the jobs of working people. On March 5, 1770, conflict between local workers and British soldiers broke into a tumult called the Boston Massacre.

Soldiers fired their guns at a crowd of demonstrators. They killed a mixed-race worker named Crispus Attucks, and then others. Colonist John Adams, a lawyer, defended the eight British soldiers at their trial. Adams called the crowd at the massacre "a motley rabble" and described it in scornful terms. Two of the soldiers were discharged from the army. The other six were found not guilty, which made some Bostonians even angrier. Britain took its troops out of the city, hoping things would quiet down.

But the colonists' anger did not go away. Political and social leaders in Boston formed a Committee of Correspondence to plan actions against the British. One of their actions was the Boston Tea Party of 1773. To protest the tax on tea, a group of colonists seized the cargo from a British ship and dumped it into Boston Harbor.

Britain's answer to the Boston Tea Party was a set of new, stricter laws. The British closed the port in Boston, broke up the colonial government, and sent in troops. Colonists held mass meetings of protest.

What about the other colonies? In Virginia, the educated elite wanted to turn the anger of the lower orders against Britain. They found a way in the speechmaking talents of Patrick Henry. In inspiring words, Henry told the colonists why they should be angry at Britain. At the same time, he avoided stirring up class conflict among the colonists. His words fed a feeling of patriotism, a growing resistance against Britain.

Other inspiring words helped turn the resistance movement toward independence. In 1776 Thomas Paine published a pamphlet, or short book, called *Common Sense*. It boldly made the first claim that the colonies should be free of British control.

Paine argued that sticking to Great Britain would do the colonists no good and that separating from Britain would do them no harm. He reminded his readers of all the wars that Britain had dragged them into—and of the lives and money those wars had cost them. Finally he made a thundering statement:

Everything that is right or reasonable p
tion. The blood of the slain, the weepin
cries, 'TIS TIME TO PART.'

Common Sense was the most
phlet in colonial America. But it
alarm in elite colonists like John
elites supported the patriot caus
ence from Britain, but they didn
far toward democracy. Rule by th
be kept within limits, Adams tho
the masses made hasty, foolish d

Thomas Paine did not belong
He came to America as a poor em
England. But once the Revolution
rated himself from the crowd acti
classes. Still, Paine's words in *Con*
became part of the myth of the Re
was the movement of a united peo

Whose Independence?

EVERY HARSH ACT OF BRITISH CONTROL made the colonists more rebellious. By 1774 they had set up the Continental Congress. It was an illegal political body, but it was also a step toward independent government.

The first military clash between colonists and British troops came at Lexington and Concord in April 1775. Afterward, the Continental Congress decided on separation from Great Britain. Thomas Jefferson wrote a Declaration of Independence. The Congress adopted it on July 2, 1776, and announced it two days later.

Throughout the colonies, there was already a strong feeling for independence. The opening words of the Declaration gave shape to that feeling:

> We hold these truths to be self-evident, that all men are created equal, that they are endowed by their Creator with certain unalienable Rights, that among these are Life, Liberty and the pursuit of Happiness—That to secure these rights, Governments are instituted among Men, deriving their just powers from the consent of the governed—That whenever any Form of Government becomes destructive of these ends, it is the Right of the People to alter or to abolish it, and to institute new Government. . . .

(*left*)
Title page of Thomas Paine's revolutionary pamphlet "Common Sense," 1776.

Next, the Declaration listed the unjust or harmful acts of the British king. It described his rule as tyranny, or oppression—that is, rule by force, without fairness. The Declaration called for the people to control their government. It reminded them of the burdens and difficulties Britain had caused them. This language was well suited to bring various groups of colonists together. It could even make those who were at odds with each other turn against Britain.

But the Declaration did not include Indians, enslaved blacks, or women. As for the Indians, just twenty years earlier the government of Massachusetts had called them "rebels, enemies and traitors" and offered cash for each Indian scalp.

Black slaves were a problem for the author of the Declaration. At first, Jefferson's Declaration blamed the king for sending slaves to America, and also for not letting the colonies limit the slave trade. Maybe this statement grew out of moral feelings against slavery. Maybe it came from the fear of slave revolts. But the Continental Congress removed it from the Declaration of Independence because slaveholders in the colonies disagreed among themselves about whether or not to end slavery. So

Jefferson's gesture toward the enslaved black was left out of the Revolution's statement of freedom.

"All men are created equal," claimed the Declaration. Jefferson probably didn't use the word "men" on purpose, to leave out women. He just didn't think of including them. Women were invisible in politics. They had no political rights and no claim to equality.

By its own language, the Declaration of Independence limited life, liberty, and happiness to white males. But the makers and signers of the Declaration were like other people of their time. Their ideas grew out of the ordinary thinking of their age. We don't study the Declaration of Independence so that we can point out its moral failures. We study it so we can see how the Declaration drew certain groups of Americans into action while it ignored others. In our time, inspiring words are still used to get large numbers of people to support a cause, even while the same language covers up serious conflicts among people or leaves out whole parts of the human race.

The reality behind the Declaration of Independence was that a rising class of important people in the colonies needed enough support to defeat England. At the same time, they didn't want to disturb too much of the settled order of wealth and power. In fact, the makers of independence were part of that settled order. More than two-thirds of the men who signed the Declaration had served as colonial officials under the British.

When the fiery Declaration of Independence was read from Boston's town hall, the reader was Thomas Crafts. He was one of the Loyal Nine, who had opposed militant action against the British. Four days later, Boston's Committee of Correspondence ordered the town's men to show up to be drafted into a new patriot army. But the rich, it turned out, could avoid the draft. They could pay someone else to serve in the army for them. The poor had no choice but to serve. This led to rioting and shouting: "Tyranny is tyranny, let it come from whom it may."

CHAPTER FIVE

REVOLUTIONS

THE REVOLUTIONARY WAR WAS FOUGHT between Great Britain and its colonies in North America. But other rebellions took place during the revolutionary years. Soldiers turned against their officers, Indians sided with their old enemies, and poor farmers in Massachusetts took up arms against their brand-new American government.

War and Mutiny

JOHN ADAMS, THE MASSACHUSETTS lawyer who defended the soldiers who had fired in the Boston Massacre, believed that only a third of

the people in the colonies supported the Revolution. A modern historian named John Shy, who studied the Revolutionary Army, thinks that only about a fifth of the total population actively turned against Britain.

But just about every white male in the colonies had a gun and could shoot. The leaders of the Revolution distrusted mobs of the poor, but they needed their help if they were going to beat Britain. How could the Revolutionary leaders win more people to their cause? One way to win support was by offering the rewards of military service. Men from the lower classes joined the army hoping to rise in rank, gain some money, and move up in society.

Historian Shy found that poor people "did much of the actual fighting and suffering" in the Revolution. Not all of them were volunteers. Just a few years earlier, colonists had rioted against the British practice of impressment, seizing men and forcing them to serve in the navy. But by 1779, in the middle of the Revolution, the American navy was doing the same thing.

The Americans lost the first battles of the war, at Bunker Hill and Brooklyn Heights. They won

(left)
Blacksmith being served a tax writ, 1786.

small battles at Trenton and Princeton, then a big battle at Saratoga, New York, in 1777. While George Washington's frozen army hung on at Valley Forge, Pennsylvania, Benjamin Franklin was in France, looking for help. Britain had defeated France in the Seven Years' War, and the French were hungry for revenge. They joined the war on the American side.

The war moved to the South. The British won victory after victory, until British and American armies met at Yorktown, Virginia, in 1781. With the help of a large French army, and with the French navy blocking the British from getting more men or supplies, the Americans won this final victory, and the war was over.

Throughout the war, rich and poor Americans came into conflict. Rich men led the Continental Congress, which governed the colonies. These men were connected to each other by marriage and family relationships, and also by business ties. They looked out for each other.

The Congress voted that army officers who stuck to the end of the war would receive half their military pay for the rest of their lives. This ignored the common soldiers, who were not getting paid.

On New Year's Day, 1781, some Pennsylvania
troops mutinied. They killed one of their captains,
wounded others, and marched with cannon
toward Philadelphia and the Congress. George
Washington, commander of the army, made peace
with the rebellious soldiers.

Soon afterward, when soldiers mutinied in
New Jersey, Washington took a sterner stand. He
ordered two of the ringleaders shot by firing
squads made up of their friends, who cried as they
pulled the triggers. It was "an example,"
Washington said.

Soldiers' mutinies were rare. Rebellion was
easier for people who were not in the army. Civil
disorder flared up in half a dozen colonies, even
while the colonies were fighting against Great
Britain.

In the southern colonies, the lower classes did
not want to join the Revolution. They thought the
war had nothing to do with them. Whether or not
the colonies won independence from Britain, they
would still be ruled by a political elite.

Nathanael Greene, Washington's general in the
South, wrote a letter to Thomas Jefferson telling
how his troops dealt with some Loyalists, colonists

who had remained loyal to Britain. Greene wrote that "upwards of one hundred were killed and most of the rest cut to pieces." He added that this action had a "happy effect" on people in the area who had held back from supporting the Revolution.

Tenant farmers became a threatening force during the war. These farmers paid rent to land-lords who owned huge estates. When they stopped paying rent, the Revolutionary government feared a rebellion. So the government seized Loyalists' land and sold some of it to tenants. These new landholders no longer had to pay rent—but now they had to pay the banks that had loaned them money to buy land.

Much property taken from Loyalists went to enrich the Revolutionary leaders and their friends. The Revolution gave these colonial elites a chance to seize power and property from those who had been loyal to Britain. The war also gave some ben-efits to small landholders. But for most poor white working people and tenant farmers, the Revolution brought little change.

Indians and Blacks in the Revolution

IN THE SEVEN YEARS' WAR BETWEEN
Britain and France, many of the Indians of
North America had fought on the side of
France. The French were traders who did not
try to take over Indian lands, but the British
wanted living space.

After the Seven Years' War, the French ignored
their Indian allies and gave French territory in the
Ohio Valley to the British. There the Indians
attacked British forts, and the British fought back.
One of their weapons was biological warfare.
They gave the Indians blankets from a hospital,
hoping to spread the deadly disease smallpox
among the tribes.

But the British could not destroy the will of the
Indians, so in 1763 they made peace. Britain
declared that the land west of the Appalachian
Mountains was Indian territory. Colonists were
forbidden to settle there. This angered the
colonists and gave them another reason to turn
against Britain. It also explains why many Indians
fought on the side of the British, their old enemies, during the Revolution. After the war, with
the British out of the way, the Americans could

begin pushing the Indians off their lands, killing them if they fought back.

Black slaves also fought in the Revolution—on both sides. Blacks seeking freedom offered to fight in the Revolutionary Army. George Washington turned them down. In the end, though, about five thousand blacks served with the Revolutionaries. Thousands more fought for the British.

The Revolution encouraged some blacks to demand more from white society. In 1780, for example, seven blacks in Massachusetts asked the legislature for the right to vote. They pointed out that Americans had just been fighting a war for the right to govern themselves, and they reminded lawmakers that many "of our Colour" had fought for the Revolutionary cause.

After the war, slavery ended in the northern states—but slowly. In 1810 about thirty thousand people remained enslaved in the North. By 1840 there were still a thousand slaves. In the lower South, slavery expanded with the growth of rice and cotton plantations.

(left)
Revolutionary War
soldiers, 1780.

Farmers in Revolt

BY THE TIME OF THE REVOLUTION, certain patterns were already set in the American colonies. Indians had no place in the new society. Blacks were not treated as the equals of whites. The rich and powerful ran things. After the war, the Revolutionary leaders could make those patterns into the law of the new nation.

A group of leaders met in Philadelphia in 1787 to write the United States Constitution. Hanging over them was the fear of revolt. The year before, a farmers' uprising called Shays' Rebellion had turned western Massachusetts into a battleground.

Massachusetts had passed state laws that raised the property qualifications for voting. People couldn't vote if they didn't own enough land. In addition, only the very wealthy could hold state office. Farmers who could not pay their debts were angry that the state lawmakers did nothing to help them.

A countryman named Plough Jogger spoke up at a meeting to say how the government had mistreated him—and what he wanted to do about it:

> I have been greatly abused, have been obliged to do more
> than my part in the war; have been loaded with class rates

[taxes], town rates, province rates, Continental rates and all
rates . . . been pulled and hauled by sheriffs, constables
and [tax] collectors, and had my cattle sold for less than
they were worth. . . . The great men are going to get all we
have and I think it is time for us to rise up and put a stop
to it, and have no more courts, nor sheriffs, nor collectors
nor lawyers. . . .

Some of the discontented farmers were veterans of the Continental Army. They had fought for
the Revolutionary cause, but when the war ended,
they did not receive their pay in cash. They were in
debt, but they had no money. When the courts
met to take away their cattle and land, the farmers
protested. Large, armed groups marched to courthouse steps, keeping the courts from carrying out
their actions. Farmers' mobs also broke into jails
to free imprisoned debtors.

The political leaders of Massachusetts became
alarmed. Samuel Adams, who had acted against
the British government in Boston, now insisted
that people stay within the law. People in the town
of Greenwich answered back. They said: You in
Boston have the money. We don't. And didn't you
act illegally yourselves in the Revolution?

Daniel Shays was a poor farm hand when the

Revolution broke out. He joined the army and fought at Lexington, Bunker Hill, and Saratoga. In 1780 he quit the army because he had not been paid. Back home, he found himself in court because he couldn't pay his debts. He saw the same thing happening to others. One sick woman, unable to pay, had her bed taken from under her.

When the Massachusetts Supreme Court charged leaders of the farmers' rebellion with crimes, Shays organized seven hundred armed farmers, mostly veterans. As they marched toward Springfield and the court, others joined them. The judges cut the court session short.

The farmers kept up the pressure, but winter snows began to interfere with their trips to the courthouses. When Shays marched a thousand men toward Boston, a storm forced them back, and one man froze to death. Then Boston merchants raised money to pay for an army to take the field against the farmers. The rebels were outnumbered and on the run. Shays fled to Vermont. Some of his followers surrendered. A few died in battle. Others carried out desperate acts of violence against authority, such as burning barns or killing a general's horse.

Captured rebels were put on trial. Although Shays was later pardoned, a dozen were sentenced to die. Sam Adams claimed that there was a difference between rebelling against a king, as he had done, and the farmers' uprising. Treason against a king might be pardoned, Adams said, "but the man who dares rebel against the laws of a republic ought to suffer death."

Thomas Jefferson felt differently. He thought that such uprisings were healthy for society. Jefferson wrote, "I hold it that a little rebellion now and then is a good thing. . . . It is a medicine necessary for the sound health of government."

But the political and economic leaders of the new nation did not share Jefferson's view. They feared that revolt would spread, and that the poor would demand a share of the rich people's property. These fears were in the minds of those who wrote the U.S. Constitution.

The Constitution—Business as Usual

MANY AMERICANS HAVE SEEN THE
Constitution as a work of genius, put together by
wise men who created a legal framework for
democracy and equality. But there is another way
to look at it.

In 1935, historian Charles Beard put forward a
view of the Constitution that angered some people.
Beard studied the fifty-five men who met to write
the Constitution. He found that most were wealthy.
Half of them were moneylenders, and many were
lawyers. They had reasons to create a strong federal,
or central, government that could protect the economic system that they understood and were part
of. Beard also noted that no women, blacks, indentured servants, or people without property helped
write the Constitution. So the Constitution did not
reflect the interests of those groups.

The Constitution said that each state's lawmakers would elect the senators who would represent
that state in the federal Congress. The state lawmakers would also choose electors, who would
elect the president. The president would name the
members of the Supreme Court. The only part of
the government that the people would elect

directly was the U.S. House of Representatives. Even in those elections, each state set its own voting requirements. Women, Indians, and slaves could not vote. In almost every state, men without property could not vote, either.

The problem of democracy went deeper than the Constitution's limits on voting. It lay in the division of society into rich and poor. Some people had great wealth and power. They owned and controlled the land, the money, the newspapers, the churches, and the educational system. How could voting cut into such power?

The time came for the states to ratify the Constitution—to accept it and make it the new national law. Some people wanted the Constitution and its strong central government. Others felt that the thirteen states should remain independent or loosely connected.

In New York, debate over ratification was intense. Supporters of the Constitution were called Federalists. One of the leading Federalists was Alexander Hamilton, who believed that society was naturally divided into classes. In Hamilton's view, the upper class should run things, because true democracy was dangerous:

All communities divide themselves into the few and the many. The first are the rich and well-born, the other the mass of the people. . . . The people are turbulent and changing; they seldom judge or determine right. Give therefore to the first class a distinct permanent share in the government. . . . Nothing but a permanent body can check the imprudence of democracy. . . .

The Federalists published papers explaining the advantages of a central government. One advantage, said James Madison, was that riots, revolts, and civil disorder would be less likely to arise in "a large nation ranging over thirteen states" than in a single state. People's desire for such "wicked" things as "an equal division of property" might overcome a state government, but not a federal one.

About a third of the people in the United States owned some property. Most of them owned only small amounts of land. Still, one-third of the population felt they had something that a strong, stable government could protect. In addition, crafts workers in the cities wanted a central government that could protect their jobs by taxing imported goods. This was a larger base of support for government than anywhere else in the world at the end of the eighteenth century.

The Constitution served the interests of a wealthy elite. But it also did enough for small property owners and middle-income workers and farmers to win their support. The Constitution became even more acceptable after Congress passed the amendments, or changes, known as the Bill of Rights. The Bill of Rights seemed to make the new government a protector of people's liberties. It guaranteed the right to speak, to publish, to worship, to be tried fairly, and so on. It also guaranteed the right of habeas corpus, which means that no one can be imprisoned without a hearing. But the First Amendment shows how quickly liberty could be taken away.

The First Amendment says that Congress will make no law that limits freedom of speech or of the press. But in 1798, just seven years after the Bill of Rights was added to the Constitution, Congress passed a law that clearly limited the right of free speech.

That law was the Sedition Act, which made it a crime to say anything "false, scandalous and malicious" against the federal government. Criticism that might turn the people against the government was forbidden. The Sedition Act seemed to violate the First Amendment, but ten people went to prison for saying things against the government.

Congress also passed new taxes to pay for war bonds. Although society's richest people owned most of the bonds, ordinary people had to pay the taxes. One law, the Whiskey Tax, hurt small farmers who made whiskey to sell. When farmers took up arms against the tax in 1794, the government sent troops to put down the rebellion. Even in the early years of the Constitution, some parts of it, such as the First Amendment, could be treated lightly. Other parts, such as the power to tax, were powerfully enforced.

Were the Founding Fathers wise and just men trying to create a balance of power? They did not want a balance, except one that kept things as they were. They certainly did not want an equal balance between slave and master, rich and poor, or Indian and white. Half the people in the country were not even considered by the Founding Fathers. These "invisible" citizens were the women of early America.

CHAPTER SIX

THE WOMEN
OF EARLY AMERICA

SOME HISTORY BOOKS MAKE IT LOOK
as if half the people in America never even
existed. History books talk about explorers, merchants, politicians, and generals—but these are all
men. In early America, women couldn't hold any
of those jobs. They were invisible to history.

For the European people who settled the
Americas, law and social customs said clearly that
women were not the equals of men. Fathers and
husbands had the right to control women. Women
were oppressed, which means that they could not
control their own lives. The oppression of women
would be hard to uproot.

How Women Were Treated

THE FIRST SETTLEMENTS IN THE AMERICAN colonies were made up almost completely of men. Women were brought in to be wives, childbearers, and companions. In 1619, a ship arrived at the colony of Jamestown, Virginia, carrying ninety women. They had agreed to come to the colony to marry men they had never met, in exchange for the cost of their passage across the Atlantic Ocean.

Many women and teenaged girls came to the colonies as indentured servants. Their lives were not very different from slaves' lives, except that their service had an end. While they were servants, they had to obey their masters and mistresses, and they sometimes experienced sexual abuse. Female servants "were poorly paid and often treated rudely and harshly," according to a history called *America's Working Women*.

Black women suffered doubly. They were oppressed as blacks *and* as women. A slave trader reported on the terrible conditions they endured crossing the Atlantic:

> I saw pregnant women giving birth to babies while chained to corpses which our drunken overseers had not removed. . . . On board the ship was a young negro

woman chained to the deck, who had lost her senses soon after she was purchased and taken on board.

Even free white women faced hardships. Giving birth and raising children were difficult in a time when medical care was poor and disease was common. Eighteen married women came to America on the *Mayflower*, the Pilgrims' ship. Three were pregnant. Less than a year later, only four of the women were alive. Childbirth and sickness had taken the others.

Laws and ideas carried over from England were another burden for women. Under the law, when a woman married, her husband became her master. Husbands had the legal right to control their wives in every way. A man could physically punish his wife (although he could not kill her or give her a permanent injury). Her property and possessions became his. If she earned money, that was his, too.

Advice to a Daughter was a bestselling English book. It claimed that "Inequality in Sexes" was a fact of life. Many Americans read this book, which said that men were meant to be the lawgivers and that they had more power of reason—more thinking ability—than did women. But in spite of powerful

messages that women were inferior to men, some women found ways to show their independence.

Independent Women

ANNE HUTCHINSON WAS A RELIGIOUS woman in the early years of the Massachusetts Bay Colony. She stood up to the church fathers by insisting that she could read the Bible and figure out its meaning for herself, and so could other ordinary people.

Hutchinson went to trial twice. The church put her on trial for heresy, the crime of holding beliefs that were not approved by the religious leaders. The government of the colony put her on trial for standing up against its authority.

Hutchinson was ordered to leave the Massachusetts Bay Colony. When she left for Rhode Island in 1638, thirty-five other families followed her. Later Hutchinson went to Long Island. Indians there thought that she was one of the enemies who had cheated them out of their land, and they killed

(left)
"Anne Hutchinson Preaches," 20th Century.

her and her family. Another woman in the Massachusetts Bay Colony, Mary Dyer, was hanged because of her "rebellious" beliefs and behavior.

Few women took part in public affairs such as politics. But during the American Revolution, the pressures of war brought some women into public life. Women formed patriotic groups, carried out anti-British actions, and wrote articles for independence.

In 1777, women even had their own version of the Boston Tea Party. Abigail Adams described it in a letter to her husband John Adams, a lawyer and one of the Founding Fathers. When a rich merchant refused to sell coffee at a fair price, a band of women marched to his warehouse. After one of the women threw the merchant into a cart, he handed over his keys, and the women helped themselves to the coffee and left. Abigail Adams wrote, "A large concourse of men stood amazed, silent spectators of the whole transaction."

On the frontier, when skill and labor were in short supply, some women had the chance to prove that they were equal to men. Before and after the Revolution, they worked at important jobs, such as publishing newspapers, running shops, and managing inns. Other women—and children, too—worked in their homes, spinning thread for local plants to weave into cloth.

When industry started to be an important part of the economy, women were pulled out of the home and into factory jobs. But at the same time, there was pressure for women to stay at home where they could be more easily controlled.

What some claimed to be the perfect woman began to appear in sermons and books. Her job was to keep the home cheerful, religious, and patriotic. She was supposed to be her family's nurse, cook, cleaner, seamstress, teacher, and flower arranger. She shouldn't read too much— and certain books must be avoided. Above all, a woman's role was to meet her husband's needs.

Women at Work

WHILE PREACHERS AND WRITERS WERE PRAISING proper "womanly" behavior, women started pushing against the limits that society set on what they

Striking Women, 1860.

could do. They couldn't vote or own property. They couldn't go to college or study law and medicine. If they worked, their wages would be much less than men's, for the same jobs.

But women *were* going to work. In the nineteenth century many of them found jobs in textile, or clothmaking factories, where they operated new industrial machines such as power looms. Out of every ten textile workers, eight or nine were women. Most of those women were between fifteen and thirty years old.

These working women led some of the first industrial strikes. They walked off their jobs in the textile mills to demand higher wages and better working conditions. The earliest known strike of female factory workers came in 1824, in Pawtucket, Rhode Island. Ten years later, when a young woman was fired from her job in Lowell, Massachusetts, other young women left their looms in protest. One of them climbed onto the town pump and made a fiery speech about the rights of women.

Catherine Beecher was in Lowell at that time. Beecher later became a reformer who worked to improve education for women. She wrote about the mill system that inspired the women's revolt:

> I was there in mid-winter, and every morning I was awakened at five, by the bells calling to labor. . . . Then half an hour only allowed for dinner, from which the time for going and returning was deducted. Then back to the mills, to work till seven o'clock. . . . [I]t must be remembered that all the hours of labor are spent in rooms where oil lamps, together with from 40 to 80 persons, are exhausting the healthful principle of the air . . . and where the air is loaded with particles of cotton thrown from thousands of cards, spindles, and looms.

Rights for Women?

THE TEXTILE MILLS WEREN'T THE ONLY places where people were talking about women's rights. The place of women in society was beginning, slowly, to change.

Middle-class women couldn't go to college, but they could become teachers in primary schools. They began to take over that profession. As teachers, they read more and communicated more.

Girls and women started to knock more loudly on the doors of higher education.

In 1821, Emma Willard founded the first school specially for girls. Twenty-eight years later, Elizabeth Blackwell became a pioneer when she managed to earn a medical degree.

Women also began to write for magazines, and they even started some women's magazines. Between 1780 and 1840, the percentage of American women who could read and write doubled. Women joined religious organizations and became health reformers. Some of the most powerful of them joined the antislavery movement.

Through all of these activities, women gained experience in organizing, giving speeches, and taking action for causes. Soon they would use that experience in a new cause: women's rights.

Lucy Stone was a lecturer for the American Anti-Slavery Society. She was a firm speaker who wasn't afraid to voice ideas that were unpopular. During her speeches Stone was soaked with cold water, struck by a thrown book, and attacked by mobs. Still, she started lecturing about women's rights in 1847, in a church in Massachusetts where her brother was a minister.

Angelina Grimké was another antislavery activist who turned to the cause of women's rights. She believed that if the United States could "lift up millions of slaves of both sexes from the dust, and turn them into men and women," then it could also take "millions of females from their knees and set them on their feet."

All over the country, women did an enormous amount of work for the antislavery societies. This helped inspire a movement for women's equality that raced alongside the movement against slavery. An important starting point for the women's rights movement was a World's Anti-Slavery Convention in London, England, in 1840.

The organizers of the meeting almost kept women from attending it at all, because it wasn't "proper" for women to go to public conventions. In the end, women were allowed to attend—but only if they sat behind a curtain. American abolitionist William Lloyd Garrison, who supported the rights of women as well as the end of slavery, sat with them.

Being treated as second-class members of the antislavery movement angered women such as Elizabeth Cady Stanton and Lucretia Mott. They were antislavery activists who became deeply concerned with the roles and rights of women in society.

Stanton and Mott organized the first women's rights convention in history. It took place in Stanton's hometown of Seneca Falls, New York, in 1848. Three hundred women came to the meeting. So did some men who were in favor of women's rights.

At the end of the convention, a hundred people signed a Declaration of Principles that used some of the language of Thomas Jefferson's Declaration of Independence—but changed to include women. The Declaration of Principles said that "all men and women are created equal." It described the unfair treatment of women and outlined steps toward greater equality.

But true equality would mean more than giving rights to women. It would mean treating black women equally with white women. In 1851, at a meeting in support of women's rights, an elderly black woman sat listening to some male ministers. They were doing most of the talking. Then she rose to her feet. Tall and thin, wearing a gray dress and a white turban, this former slave named Sojourner Truth told about her life as a black woman:

That man over there says that woman needs to be helped into carriages and lifted over ditches. . . . Nobody ever helps me into carriages, or over mud-puddles or gives me any best place. And a'nt I a woman?

Look at my arm! I have ploughed, and planted, and gathered into barns, and no man could head me! And a'nt I a woman?

I would work as much and eat as much as a man, when I could get it, and bear the lash as well. And a'nt I a woman?

I have born thirteen children and seen em most all sold off to slavery, and when I cried out with my mother's grief, none but Jesus heard me! And a'nt I a woman?

As other women held conventions around the country, the movement gained strength. Women were fighting back against those who wanted to keep them in "a woman's place." They took part in all sorts of movements—not just for women's rights but for prison reform, health care, and the end of slavery.

In the middle of all these movements, a new urge seized the United States. It was the urge to expand, to become larger. Americans wanted more land. They would take it from the Indians, as they had done from the start.

IN THE REVOLUTIONARY WAR, ALMOST every important Indian nation fought on the side of the British. They knew that if the British lost the war, there would be no holding back the Americans. Settlers would pour across the Appalachian Mountains into Indian territory.

The Indians were right. By the time Thomas Jefferson became president in 1800, about 700,000 white settlers were already living west of the mountains. Americans were eager to fill up the land between the Appalachians and the Mississippi River. They wanted to cut forests, plant cotton and grain, and build roads, cities, and canals. In time, they came to think that their nation should reach all the way across North America to the Pacific Ocean.

The Indians stood in the way of these plans. So the United States government came up with the idea of "Indian removal" to clear the land so that whites could use it. This "removal" cost a great deal in lives and suffering. It is hard for historians to measure this huge loss.

CHAPTER SEVEN

AS LONG AS GRASS GROWS OR WATER RUNS

From Indian Fighter to President

AFTER THE REVOLUTION, RICH AMERICANS bought up huge pieces of land on the frontier. They planned to sell it later for great profits. This was called speculating. Some of the speculators were Founding Fathers, including George Washington and Patrick Henry.

Another land speculator was also a merchant, slave trader, soldier, and future president. He was Andrew Jackson, the harshest enemy of the Indians in early American history.

Jackson became famous during the War of 1812. Textbooks usually say that the war was a struggle against Britain for America's survival, but it was more than that. It was also a war for territory. It allowed the United States to expand into

Canada, into Florida (which was owned by Spain), and into Indian territory.

Jackson's first Indian wars were against the Creeks, who lived in most of Georgia, Alabama, and Mississippi. In the midst of the war, Creek warriors massacred 250 whites at an Alabama fort. Jackson's troops took revenge by burning down a Creek village, killing women and children as well as men. A year later, in 1814, Jackson became a national hero when he fought the Battle of Horseshoe Bend against a thousand Creeks. He killed eight hundred of them, with few deaths on his side. Jackson owed his victory to Cherokees who fought on his side because the government had promised to treat them well if they joined the war. Jackson's white troops failed in an attack on the Creeks, but the Cherokees swam a river, came up behind the Creeks, and won the battle for Jackson.

When the war ended, Jackson and his friends started buying up Creek lands. Jackson got himself put in charge of treaties. In 1814 he wrote a treaty that took away half the land of the Creek nation.

This treaty started something new and important. The Indians had never thought that land belonged to individual owners. As a Shawnee chieftain named Tecumseh said, "The land belongs to all, for the use of each. . . ." But Jackson's treaty gave the Indians individual ownership of land and broke up their shared landholdings. The treaty turned Indian against Indian, bribing some of them with land and leaving others out.

Over the next ten years, Jackson was involved in many more treaties with the southern Indians. Through force, bribery, and tricks, he helped whites takes over three-fourths of Alabama and Florida, a third of Tennessee, and parts of four other states. These land grabs became the basis for the cotton kingdom of the South, where slaves labored on white-owned plantations.

Soon white settlement reached the edge of Spanish Florida, home of the Seminole Indians and some escaped black slaves. Jackson claimed that the United States had to control Florida in order to defend itself—just what modern nations often say before starting a war of conquest in some other country's territory.

Jackson started making raids into Florida, burning Seminole villages and seizing Spanish forts. As a result of these attacks, Spain agreed to

sell Florida to the United States. Jackson became governor of the new territory. He also gave his friends and relatives advice on buying slaves and speculating in land.

In 1828, Americans elected Jackson president. Under Jackson and Martin Van Buren, the man he chose to follow him as president, the U.S. government removed seventy thousand Indians from their homelands east of the Mississippi River. A government official named Lewis Cass explained the removal by saying that "savages" could not live "in contact with a civilized community."

Cass had taken millions of acres from the Indians when he was governor of the Michigan Territory. In 1825, at a treaty meeting with the Shawnees and Cherokees, he had promised them that if they moved west, across the Mississippi River, "The United States will never ask for your land there." The land beyond the river, Cass declared, would remain Indian territory forever.

(left)
Jackson & Weatherford,
19th century.

The Trail of Tears, 1838.

The Terrible Choice

FOR A FEW YEARS IN THE 1820S, BEFORE Jackson became president, the southern Indians and whites had settled down. They lived in peace, often close to one another. White men visited Indian communities, and Indians were guests in white homes. Frontier figures like Davy Crockett and Sam Houston came out of this setting. Both of them—unlike Andrew Jackson—were friends of the Indians.

Pressure to remove the Indians from the land came from politicians, business interests, land speculators, and population growth that demanded new railroads and cities. These pressures might push poor white frontiersmen into the first violent clashes with the Indians, but the frontiersmen who were neighbors of the Indians did not lead the movement to get rid of them.

Just *how* did the government remove the Indians from Georgia, Alabama, Mississippi, and other places? The answer lies in the difference between federal (or national) laws and state laws. Federal laws, like treaties between the federal government and the tribes, put the U.S. Congress in charge of Indian affairs. But the states passed their own laws that gave away Indian land to whites.

As president, Jackson was supposed to enforce the federal laws. Instead he ignored them, letting the states do what they wanted. This put the Indians in a terrible position. They would not be "forced" to go west. But if they stayed, they would have to obey state laws, which destroyed their rights. They would suffer endless trouble from whites who wanted their land.

On the other hand, if the Indians agreed to leave, the federal government would help them with money and give them land west of the Mississippi. Jackson told the Choctaws and Cherokees that if they left their old lands peacefully, they would be given new lands, and the government would leave them alone. He sent them this message:

> Say to the chiefs and warriors that I am their friend . . . but they must, by removing from the limits of the States of Mississippi and Alabama and by being settled on the lands I offer them, put it in my power to be such—There, beyond the limits of any State, in possession of land of their own, which they shall possess as long as Grass grows or water runs. I am and will protect them and be their friend and father.

Now the pressures began on the tribes, one by one. The Choctaws didn't want to leave, but after fifty members of the tribe were bribed with money and land, they signed a treaty that gave up Choctaw lands east of the Mississippi. In return, the Choctaws were supposed to get financial help for the journey west. Thirteen thousand of them began that journey in late 1831, migrating to a land and climate completely different from everything they knew. The army was supposed to organize their trip, but it failed miserably. Indians died by the thousands from hunger, cold, and disease. The seven thousand Choctaws still in Mississippi refused to follow them. Some of their descendants still live in Mississippi.

After Jackson was re-elected to the presidency in 1832, he speeded up what was called the Indian removal. By this time, Alabama's twenty-two thousand Creeks lived on a tiny portion of their former territory. They agreed to leave in exchange for the federal government's promise that some of that land would be given to individual Creeks, who could either sell it or stay on it with federal protection.

The government immediately broke its promise. It didn't protect Creeks from whites who swarmed onto their land. An army officer wrote that the Creeks were "brow beat, and cowed, and imposed upon, and depressed with the feeling that they have no adequate protection in the United States. . . ."

Speckled Snake was a man of the Creek nation. During his long life, he saw the white American government cheat and mistreat the Indians over and over again. When he was more than a hundred years old, he told a story about how the white man had betrayed the Indian:

> Brothers! I have listened to many talks from our great white father. When he first came over the wide waters, he was but a little man . . . very little. His legs were cramped by sitting long in his big boat, and he begged for a little land to light his fire on. . . . But when the white man had warmed himself before the Indians' fire and filled himself with their hominy, he became very large. With a step he bestrode the mountains, and his feet covered the plains and the valleys. His hand grasped the eastern and the western sea, and his head rested on the moon. Then he became our Great Father. He loved his red children, and he said, "Get a little further, lest I tread on thee."

After some desperate Creeks attacked white settlers, the government claimed that this "war" had broken the treaty. Now the U.S. Army could use force to make the Creeks go west. Soldiers invaded Creek communities and marched the people westward in groups of two or three thousand. The government was supposed to supply things like food, shelter, and blankets to the marchers, but again it failed. Starvation and sickness killed hundreds as the Creeks were carried across the Mississippi on old, rotting boats. More than three hundred Indians died when one boat sank.

Fighting for Freedom

IN DECEMBER 1835 A GOVERNMENT OFFICIAL ordered the Seminoles of Florida to gather at a meeting place to begin their journey west. No one showed up. The Seminoles had decided to fight.

They started making surprise attacks on white settlements along the coast, striking quickly from hideouts in the interior. They murdered white families, captured slaves, and destroyed property. General Winfield Scott led U.S. troops into Florida to fight the Seminoles, but they found no one. Two-thirds of Scott's officers resigned from the army, worn out by mud, swamps, heat, and disease.

The war lasted eight years and cost $20 million and 1,500 American lives. But the Seminoles were a tiny force fighting a huge nation that had great resources. Finally, in the 1840s, they got tired. The Seminoles asked for a truce but were arrested. Their leader, Osceola, died in prison, and the war died out.

In Georgia, the Cherokees were fighting back in their own way, without violence. They tried to fit into the white man's world by becoming farmers, blacksmiths, and carpenters. They set up a governing council and welcomed Christianity and white missionaries. After their chief, Sequoyah, invented a written form of their language, they printed a newspaper in both English and Cherokee. But although the Cherokees were taking up the ways of white society, the whites still wanted their land.

Georgia passed laws that stripped the Cherokees of their land and outlawed the tribal government, meetings, and newspaper. Any Indian who encouraged others to stay in the

a	D	ka	Ꮺ		e	Ꭱ
ga	Ꮪ				ge	Ꮨ
ha	Ꮧ				he	Ꮄ
la	W				le	Ꮣ
ma	Ꮯ				me	Ꭴ

Writing Cherokee

PHILLIP HOOSE, IN HIS WONDERFUL BOOK
We Were There, Too!, argues that it wasn't Cherokee
chief Sequoyah alone, but also his six-year-old
daughter Anyokah, who brought a written language
to the Cherokee people and found a way to prove its
importance to the tribal elders.

First, father and daughter tried to make a list of
every sound in the spoken language of the Cherokee
people and to draw a picture for each sound. Then
they made a list of all the spoken syllables. They
came up with about two hundred, but were able to
narrow down the list to eighty-six distinct syllables,
each with its own written expression.

By now Anyokah was ten years old. It was 1821.
Sequoyah and Anyokah rode to the Cherokee Tribal
Council to present their idea. At first, the Council
laughed because they couldn't see how writing down

i	T		o	ꮞ	u	Ꮎ	v	i
	y		go	A	gu	J	gv	Ꭼ
	Ә		ho	Ꮖ	hu	Ꮆ	hv	Ꮣ
	P		lo	Ꮐ	lu	Ꮇ	lv	ꮧ
i	H		mo	Ꮝ	mu	Ꭹ		

sayings could be useful in any way. So, Sequoyah proposed a test. He would leave the room. The Tribal Council could tell Anyokah anything they wanted, and she would write it down. Then Sequoyah would come back, look at the marks on the deerskin, and tell them what they had said. It worked again and again. "The first few times the elders called it luck," Hoose writes, "but gradually doubt gave way to excitement. Soon thousands of Cherokees wanted to learn how to read. The syllabic alphabet led to the preservation of the Cherokee language and then to the first American Indian newspaper, the Cherokee Phoenix. Before long schoolchildren were learning to read in both Cherokee and English. The letters were called talking leaves."

Source: Hoose, Phillip. *We Were There, Too!: Young People in U.S. History.* New York: Farrar Straus Giroux, 2001.

homeland could go to prison. White missionaries who said that the Cherokees should be allowed to remain on their land also received punishments such as four years at hard labor in prison.

Once again, the federal government arranged a removal treaty with a few Cherokees, who signed it behind the backs of most of the tribe. And once again the government sent the army to enforce the treaty. Seventeen thousand Cherokees were rounded up and crowded into stockades. On October 1, 1838, the first group set out on what came to be called the Trail of Tears.

Four thousand Cherokees died of hunger, thirst, sickness, or exposure in the stockades or on the brutal march westward. But in December 1838, President Martin Van Buren told Congress about "the entire removal of the Cherokee Nation of Indians to their new homes west of the Mississippi." Congress's decision to remove the Cherokees, Van Buren said, had had "the happiest effects."

CHAPTER EIGHT

WAR WITH MEXICO

"I HAVE SCARCELY SLEPT A WINK,"
Ethan Allen Hitchcock wrote in his diary on June
30, 1845. Hitchcock was a colonel in the U.S.
Army, stationed in Louisiana. His commander,
General Zachary Taylor, had just been ordered to
lead his men to the banks of the Rio Grande, a
river on the southwest side of Texas. Hitchcock
knew that this would bring trouble.

"Violence leads to violence," he wrote, "and if
this movement of ours does not lead to others and
to bloodshed, I am much mistaken." Hitchcock
was not mistaken. Taylor's march to the Rio
Grande started a bloody war—a war that gave
Americans a huge new western territory, taken
from a defeated Mexico.

Manifest Destiny

EVEN THOUGH THOMAS JEFFERSON'S
Louisiana Purchase of 1803 had doubled the size
of the United States, the country was a lot smaller
in 1845 than it is today. Its western border was
the Rocky Mountains. To the southwest was
Mexico, which had won its independence from
Spain in 1821.

Mexico was originally much larger than it is
now. It included Texas, New Mexico, Utah,
Nevada, Arizona, California, and parts of Colorado
and Wyoming. Then, with help from the United
States, Texas broke away from Mexico in 1836,
calling itself the "Lone Star Republic." In 1845, the
U.S. Congress added Texas to the United States.

By that time, many Americans believed that
their country should expand, or grow larger,
toward the west. One of these expansionists was
President James Polk. He told his secretary that
one of his main goals as president was to get
California into the United States. A newspaper
called the *Washington Union* supported Polk's idea
with these words: "The road to California will be
open to us. Who will stay [meaning halt, or stop]
the march of our western people?"

Soon afterward, in the summer of 1845, another newspaper editor, John O'Sullivan, wrote, "Our manifest destiny [is] to overspread the continent allotted by Providence for the free development of our yearly multiplying millions." O'Sullivan was saying that Americans should be free to occupy all of North America, because God meant for them to. His words "manifest destiny"—a fate or purpose that was clear to see— became a slogan for expansionists.

For a long time, Mexico and the United States had agreed that the border between them was the Nueces River, about 150 miles north of the Rio Grande. But during Texas's fight for independence from Mexico, Texans had captured the Mexican general Santa Anna and forced him to say that the border was the Rio Grande. This made Texas bigger. Afterward, President Polk promised the Texans that he would consider the Rio Grande the border, even though Mexicans still lived in the area between the two rivers.

So when Polk ordered General Taylor to move troops to the Rio Grande, he was challenging Mexico. Sending the army into territory inhabited by Mexicans was sure to cause conflict. But when

the soldiers reached the Rio Grande, they found empty villages. The local Mexicans had fled across the river to the city of Matamoros. Taylor started building a fort with cannons pointed at Matamoros.

By the spring of 1846, the army was ready to start the war that Polk wanted. All it needed was an excuse. Then one of Taylor's officers disappeared while riding along the river. He was later found with a smashed skull. Everyone figured that Mexican guerrilla fighters had crossed the river and killed him. The very next day, Mexicans attacked a patrol, killing sixteen soldiers. Taylor sent a message to Polk that the fighting had begun.

The Mexicans had fired the first shot. But they had done what the American government wanted. Colonel Ethan Allan Hitchcock knew that. Even before the attacks, he wrote in his diary:

> I have said from the first that the United States are the aggressors. . . . We have not one particle of right to be here. . . . It looks as if the government sent a small force on purpose to bring on a war, so as to have a pretext [reason] for taking California and as much of this country as it chooses. . . . My heart is not in this business . . . but, as a military man, I am bound to execute orders.

(left)
Mexican War Cartoon, 1846.

For and Against the War

PRESIDENT POLK HAD BEEN URGING Congress to declare war even before he received word of the attacks from General Taylor. As soon as Taylor's messages arrived, Polk told Congress, "Mexico has passed the boundary of the United States, has invaded our territory and shed American blood upon the American soil. . . ."

Congress declared war. Only a handful of congressmen voted against it. They were strongly opposed to slavery, and they believed that the war was an excuse to gain territory that would be made into new slave states. Joshua Giddings of Ohio called it "an aggressive, unholy, and unjust war."

Many Americans cheered the news of war. They held rallies to support it in cities across the land, and they volunteered for the army by the thousands. The poet Walt Whitman wrote proudly in a newpaper that "America knows how to crush, as well as how to expand!"

Another poet, James Russell Lowell, took a different view of the war. He wrote a poem saying that the only reason for it was "to lug new slave states in." Massachusetts writer Henry David Thoreau criticized the war. He was also jailed for refusing to pay a poll tax, but he only spent one night there. He was released because his friends paid the tax for him, without his permission.

Two years later, Thoreau wrote an essay called "Civil Disobedience." It talks about the difference between law and justice, and about how soldiers sometimes know that the orders they are following are wrong:

> Law never made men a whit more just; and, by means of their respect for it, even the well-disposed are daily made the agents of injustice. A common and natural result of undue respect for law is, that you may see a file of soldiers . . . marching in admirable order over hill and dale to the wars, against their wills, ay, against their common sense and consciences, which makes it very steep marching indeed. . . .

Many members and leaders of churches spoke out against the war. As the months passed, other voices joined in. Newspaperman Horace Greeley wrote in the *New York Tribune* that the war was unnecessary. Antislavery activist Frederick Douglass, who had once been a slave, called the war "disgraceful" and "cruel." The antislavery paper *The Liberator* went even further, wishing "the most triumphant success" to the Mexicans.

ROYAL MOUNTED MILITIA

What about ordinary people? It's impossible to know how many of them supported the war, but there is evidence that some workers were against it. Many Irish workers showed up at an antiwar meeting in New York City. They called the war a plot by slave owners. The New England Workingmen's Association also spoke out against the war.

The flood of army volunteers slowed down after the first rush of excitement. To get enough soldiers, the army was forced to pay for new recruits. It also offered land to volunteers if they served for the entire war.

Some of the men who did enlist were shocked by the bloody horror of war. After a battle outside Matamoros, for example, fifty Americans and five hundred Mexicans lay dead or wounded on the field. The screaming and groaning from both sides was terrible to hear. Other new soldiers sickened and died in miserable, unhealthy conditions, such as the crowded ships that carried them to the front. And still others deserted to the Mexican side for better pay.

(left)
Texas Rangers, 1842.

The Conquest of California

A SEPARATE WAR WENT ON IN CALIFORNIA.
Soldiers moved into California by land and sea.
One of them was a young naval officer who imagined what would happen when the United States
owned this western territory. "Population will flow
into the fertile regions of California," he wrote in
his diary.

Americans in California raided Mexican settlements that had been founded by the Spanish.
They stole horses. And they declared the territory
independent, calling it the "Bear Flag Republic."

An American naval officer gathered chiefs
from the Indian tribes in California and told them:

> The country you inhabit no longer belongs to Mexico,
> but to a mighty nation whose territory extends from
> the great ocean you have all seen or heard of [the
> Pacific], to another great ocean thousands of miles
> toward the rising sun [the Atlantic]. . . . Our armies
> are now in Mexico, and will soon conquer the whole
> country. But you have nothing to fear from us, if you
> do what is right . . . if you are faithful to your new
> rulers. . . . We shall watch over you and give you true
> liberty; but beware of sedition [treason], lawlessness,
> and all other crimes, for the army which shields can

assuredly punish, and it will reach you in your most retired hiding places.

Meanwhile, American soldiers advanced westward through New Mexico. They captured the city of Santa Fe without a battle. A few months later, though, Mexicans in the nearby city of Taos revolted against American rule. The revolt was stopped, but some of the rebels escaped to the hills. They carried out occasional attacks, killing Americans, until the U.S. Army killed 150 of them in a final battle.

In Los Angeles, too, there was a revolt. Mexicans forced the American troops to surrender in September 1846. The U.S. military did not recapture Los Angeles until December, after a bloody battle.

Victory over Mexico

BY THIS TIME GENERAL TAYLOR HAD MOVED across the Rio Grande and taken Matamoros. His army was marching southward through Mexico.

The men were becoming hard to control. Soldiers got drunk and looted Mexican villages. Cases of rape increased.

At the same time, sickness and heat were killing the soldiers. A thousand of them died on the march. At Monterrey they fought another battle with the Mexicans. So many men and horses died in agony that one U.S. officer said that the ground was slippery with foam and blood.

The U.S. Navy fired shells on the Mexican coastal city of Veracruz, killing many civilians. One shell hit a post office. Another hit a hospital. After two days and 1300 shells, the city surrendered. An American reporter wrote, "The Mexicans variously estimate their losses at from 500 to 1000 killed and wounded, but all agree that the loss among the soldiery is comparatively small and the destruction among the women and children is very great."

General Winfield Scott now moved an army of ten thousand soldiers into the heart of Mexico. A series of battles that had little point killed thousands of people on both sides. Finally, the armies of the two nations met to fight for control of Mexico City. A Mexican merchant wrote to a friend about the American conquest of the city, "In some cases whole blocks were destroyed and a great number of men, women and children killed and wounded."

In spite of their victories, the American soldiers were getting tired of marching, fighting, and risking death. Desertions were a problem. In March 1847 the army reported over a thousand deserters. More than nine thousand deserted over the course of the war.

In northern Mexico, volunteers from Virginia, Mississippi, and North Carolina rebelled against their commander. He killed one of the mutineers, but two of his lieutenants refused to help him stop the mutiny. The army later forgave the rebellious soldiers in order to keep the peace.

The glory of victory was for the president and the generals, not for the deserters, the dead, and the wounded. Many men felt anger toward those who had led them into deadly conditions and battles where so many had died. One group, the Massachusetts Volunteers, had started with 630 men. They came home with three hundred dead, mostly from disease. At a celebration dinner on their return, the men hissed at their commander.

Some volunteers who made it home ended up with little to show for their soldiering. The government had promised them land, but speculators immediately showed up to buy the land from them. Many of the men, desperate for money, sold their 160 acres for less than fifty dollars.

When Mexico surrendered, some Americans thought that the United States should take the whole country. Instead, it took just half.

In February 1848 Mexico and the United States signed the Treaty of Guadalupe Hidalgo. In the treaty, Mexico gave the entire Southwest and California to the United States. It also agreed that the border between the two nations was the Rio Grande. The United States, in turn, agreed to pay Mexico $15 million. This let people say that the nation's new territories were bought, not seized by force. One American newspaper claimed that "we take nothing by conquest. . . . Thank God."

CHAPTER NINE

SLAVERY
AND EMANCIPATION

THE UNITED STATES GOVERNMENT SUPPORTED
slavery. As the economy of the South grew, so did
the number of enslaved people. Between 1790 and
1860, the amount of cotton that the South produced rose from one thousand tons a year to 1
million tons a year. In that same period, the
number of slaves rose from half a million to 4
million. Slavery was so well established that only
something enormous—something like a full-
scale war—could end it.

Slavery in the American South

THE UNITED STATES GOVERNMENT MADE it illegal to import new slaves in 1808. Previously, many northern port cities had benefited from the slave trade. From 1808 on, slavery in the U.S. was supposed to be limited to Africans who were already enslaved and their children. But the demand for new slaves was great, so the law was often broken. In his book *From Slavery to Freedom*, historian John Hope Franklin estimates that a quarter of a million slaves were illegally imported before the Civil War began in 1861.

How can slavery be described? Maybe only people who have experienced it can say what it was like. People like John Little, a former slave, who wrote:

> They say that slaves are happy, because they laugh, and are merry. I myself and three or four others, have received two hundred lashes in the day, and had our feet in fetters; yet, at night, we would sing and dance, and make others laugh at the rattling of our chains. Happy men we must have been! We did it to keep down trouble, and to keep our hearts from being completely broken: that is as true as the gospel!

Desperation drove some slaves to revolt.

Probably the largest revolt in the United States took place near New Orleans in 1811. It involved four to five hundred slaves. The U.S. Army and militia forces attacked them and ended their revolt. In 1822 a free black man named Denmark Vesey tried to launch a revolt in South Carolina, but authorities found out about it and hanged him, along with thirty-four others. Then, in Virginia, in the summer of 1831, a slave named Nat Turner led about seventy others on a rampage from plantation to plantation. They murdered at least fifty-five men, women, and children. As their ammunition ran out, they were captured. Turner and others were hanged.

Other slaves ran away. Each year during the 1850s, about a thousand slaves escaped into the North, Canada, and Mexico. One famous escaped slave, Harriet Tubman, made nineteen dangerous trips back into slave territory, helping slaves escape on the Underground Railroad. She told them, "You'll be free or die."

Whites sometimes helped slaves, and that worried the authorities. Some feared that poor whites would encourage slave revolts—not just because they felt sorry for the slaves, but because they

hated the rich planters and wanted to see their property destroyed. Fanny Kemble, a famous actress who married a Southern planter, wrote in her journal that black slaves and white Irish workers were kept apart when they were building a canal in Georgia. The Irish were a "warm-hearted, generous people," she said, who "might actually take to sympathy with the slaves."

The Abolition Movement

SOME WHITE AMERICANS DID "TAKE TO sympathy with the slaves." They were called abolitionists because they called for the abolition, or end, of slavery. They bravely wrote newspaper articles and made speeches against slavery. They also helped many slaves escape on the Underground Railroad, a network of people who worked together to conduct runaway slaves to free territory, providing "safe houses" for them along the way. But black abolitionists were the backbone of the movement against slavery.

(left)
Underground Railroad, 1893.

The North had about 130,000 free blacks in 1830. Twenty years later there were 200,000. Many of them worked to free those who remained enslaved in the South. One of them was David Walker, son of a slave, who sold old clothes in Boston. He wrote a pamphlet called *Walker's Appeal,* urging blacks to fight for their freedom:

> Let our enemies go on with their butcheries, and at once fill up their cup. Never make an attampt to gain our freedom or natural right . . . until you can see your way clear— when that hour arrives and you move, be not afraid or dismayed. . . . God has been pleased to give us two eyes, two hands, two feet and some sense in our heads as well as [the whites]. They have no more right to hold us in slavery than we have to hold them. . . . "Every dog must have its day," the American's is coming to its end.

The *Appeal* made southern slaveholders so angry that one of them offered a reward for David Walker's murder or capture. One summer day in 1830 Walker was found dead near the doorway of his shop.

Frederick Douglass was born into slavery, learned to read and write, and escaped into the North at the age of twenty-one. He became the most famous black man of his time, speaking and writing against slavery. Douglass called "the idea of being a free man some day" a dream that "all the powers of slavery" could not destroy.

After the war with Mexico, the U.S. government brought California and other new territories into the Union as nonslave states. In return, the government had to do something for the slave states, so it passed the Fugitive Slave Act of 1850. This law made it easy for slave owners to recapture runaway slaves even after they had fled to the Northern states. It made it easy for slave owners to just pick up free blacks they claimed had run away.

Northern abolitionists, black and white, fought against the act. The year after Congress passed the law, a runaway slave named Jerry was captured and put on trial. A crowd broke into the Syracuse, New York courthouse to set him free. On July 4, 1852, Frederick Douglass gave a speech that placed the shame of slavery on the whole nation, not just the South. He said:

> Fellow Citizens: What to the American slave is your Fourth of July? I answer, a day that reveals to him more than all other days of the year, the gross injustice and cruelty to which he is the constant victim. . . .There is not

a nation of the earth guilty of practices more shocking
and bloody than are the people of these United States at
this very hour.

The government of the United States did not
strongly enforce the law that ended the slave trade,
yet it enforced runaway slave laws. The government under President Andrew Jackson worked
with the South to keep abolitionist newspapers
from being mailed in Southern states. The
nation's Supreme Court declared in 1857 that the
slave Dred Scott, even though he had lived for
some time in free territories, could not sue for his
freedom because he was property, not a person.

That government would never accept an end to
slavery through rebellion. Slavery would end only
under conditions controlled by whites, and only
when it suited the business and political needs of
the North. Abraham Lincoln was the perfect figure
to bring about the end of slavery.

Lincoln understood the needs of business.
He shared the political ambition of the new
Republican political party. Finally, he spoke the
language of doing good, and he could argue
with passion against slavery on moral grounds.
At the same time, he acted with caution in the

world of politics, and he feared that abolition would cause new problems. Although Lincoln believed that slavery was unjust, he could not see blacks as the equals of whites. The best thing to do, he thought, would be to free the slaves and send them back to Africa.

The Civil War and Slavery

THE NORTHERN ELITE, THE BANKERS AND businessmen who directed the economy of the North, wanted their kind of economy to expand. They wanted free land, free labor, and taxes that favored manufacturers. Lincoln shared their ideas. Southern planters, on the other hand, felt that Lincoln and the Republicans would make their own pleasant, prosperous way of life impossible. So when Lincoln was elected president in the fall of 1860, seven Southern states seceded, or left the Union. When Lincoln tried to take back the federal base at Fort Sumter, North Carolina, by force, four more states seceded. The South formed the Confederacy, and the Civil War was on.

Abolitionists urged Lincoln to emancipate, or free, the slaves in the South. But Lincoln made it clear that he had not gone to war to free the slaves—his goal was to bring the South back into the Union. In a letter to abolitionist and newspaperman Horace Greeley, Lincoln wrote:

> My paramount object in this struggle is to save the Union, and it is not either to save or destroy Slavery. If I could save the Union without freeing any slave, I would do it; and if I could save it by freeing all the slaves, I would do it.

But as the war grew more bitter and the North grew more desperate to win, Lincoln began to act against slavery. In September 1862 he gave the southern states four months to stop fighting, warning that he would free their slaves if they did not come over to the Union side. The fighting continued. On January 1, 1863, Lincoln issued the Emancipation Proclamation, freeing slaves in areas that were fighting against the Union. Two years later, before the war ended, Congress passed the Thirteenth Amendment to the Constitution, which ended all slavery in the United States.

These changes affected African Americans in many ways—not all of them good. Once blacks were free to enter the Union army, the war started to look more like a war for black liberation. The more whites suffered, the more they resented blacks. Angriest of all were poor whites who were drafted into the army. Rich people could buy their way out of the draft for $300. That was a huge amount of money. At that time the average skilled worker (such as a carpenter) earned about two dollars a day. Unskilled workers earned less. Draft riots in 1863 in northern cities turned whites against their black neighbors in a wave of violence and death. And the treatment of black soldiers in the army and the northern cities showed that freedom might not bring acceptance or true equality. Black soldiers were given the dirtiest and hardest work, and when they were off duty whites sometimes attacked them on the street.

The Civil War was one of the bloodiest conflicts in history up to that time. It killed 600,000 people, out of a population of 30 million. By late 1864, the South was losing. Soldiers were in short supply—but there were 4 million slaves. When some Confederate leaders spoke of enlisting slaves, one

EX-SENATOR BRUCE

Heroes of the Colored
Race Lithograph, 1881.

shocked general wrote, "If slaves will make good soldiers, our whole theory of slavery is wrong." In March 1865 Jefferson Davis, president of the Confederacy, signed a law that let blacks serve in the army of the South. But before the law had any effect, the war ended. The South had lost, and its slaves learned that they were now free.

Emancipation without Freedom

MANY YEARS AFTER THE WAR, AFRICAN Americans who had been young children in 1865 recalled the tears, songs, and hope of the slaves who heard the news of their emancipation. It was a time of great celebration, the dawn of a new day. Yet many blacks knew that their status after the war would not depend on a law that made them free. It would depend on whether they owned land or had to work for others.

Much land in the South either went back to the families of the Confederates or was bought by Northern land speculators and investors. Blacks could not afford to buy much of it. Ex-slave Thomas Hall said, "Lincoln got the praise for freeing us, but did he do it?" Hall felt that Lincoln gave the slaves freedom but did not give them the chance to support themselves. Freed slaves still had to depend on whites for work and survival.

The United States government had fought the slave states not to end slavery but to keep control of the enormous territory, resources, and market of the South. Still, the end of slavery brought new forces into politics. One force was white people concerned with racial equality. Some of them came south to teach or work for the Freedmen's Bureau that the government set up to aid the freed slaves. A second force was blacks determined to make their freedom mean something. A third force was the Republican Party. It wanted to keep control over the national government, and the votes of Southern blacks could help. Northern businessmen felt that Republican plans benefited them, so they went along for a while.

These forces created a brief period after the Civil War when blacks in the South voted, elected blacks to state legislatures and to the U.S. Senate and House of Representatives, and introduced free, racially mixed education. New laws protected them from discrimination and guaranteed them equal rights. But because blacks depended on whites for work, their votes could be bought or taken away by the threat of violence.

White violence against blacks erupted in the South almost as soon as the war ended. In May 1866, in Memphis, Tennessee, whites killed forty-six African Americans and burned more than a hundred homes, churches, and schools. The violence continued as white terrorist groups like the Ku Klux Klan organized raids, beatings, and racial murders called lynchings. The state of Kentucky alone had 116 acts of racial violence between 1867 and 1871.

As white violence rose in the 1870s, the national government grew less committed to protecting blacks. Northern politicians started to weigh the advantage of black voters' support against the advantage of a stable South controlled by whites who would accept Republican leadership. It was only a matter of time before blacks would be returned to a condition that was not far from slavery, even if they remained legally free.

In 1877 the Republican Party leaders made a deal to get their candidate, Rutherford Hayes,

elected president. In return for the necessary electoral votes, they agreed to remove Union troops
from the South. This took away the last military
protection for southern blacks. Their legal protection was crumbling, too, as the Southern states
passed laws that chipped away at equality. By the
end of the nineteenth century, the U.S. Supreme
Court approved laws that allowed segregation, or
separation of people by race. Only one Supreme
Court justice, a former slave owner named John
Harlan, argued against segregation, saying, "Our
Constitution is color-blind. . . ."

With its economy in ruins, the South needed
money. A new alliance formed between the
Northern bankers and investors and the Southern
elites. They talked about the "New South" of coal
and iron mines, business and railroads. The former slaves were swept out of the picture. By 1900,
all of the southern states had passed laws that kept
African Americans from voting and from enjoying
equal rights.

At this low point for black people in America,
blacks knew that they had been betrayed. Some
fled the South, hoping to escape violence and
poverty. Those who remained organized for self-

defense, in the face of more than a hundred lynch-ings a year. Thomas Fortune, a young black editor for the *New York Globe,* told the Senate, "The white man who shoots a negro always goes free, while the negro who steals a hog is sent to the chain-gang for ten years."

W. E. B. Du Bois, a black man who came to teach at Atlanta University, saw the betrayal of the African Americans as part of something bigger that was happening in the United States. He said that poor whites and blacks were both being exploited, or used, by politicians and big business. Because whites could vote, they didn't think they were exploited. Du Bois said, though, that the "dic-tatorship of vast capital" limited the power of their votes. He was talking about the economic system called capitalism, in which private individuals or companies, rather than the state, own the farms and factories, set prices and compete with each other in the marketplace, and accumulate wealth.

Was Du Bois right? Did the growth of American capitalism mean that whites as well as blacks were in some sense becoming slaves?

CHAPTER TEN

THE OTHER CIVIL WAR

THE WAR BETWEEN NORTH AND SOUTH was not the only conflict in the United States during the nineteenth century. There was another war going on—a struggle between classes. This struggle is often left out of textbooks. Instead, textbooks can make it seem as though the history of the time was a clash between the Republican and Democratic political parties, even though both parties represented the classes that held most of the power in the country.

The Myth of "Jacksonian Democracy"

ANDREW JACKSON, WHO WAS ELECTED president in 1828, said he spoke for "the humble members of society"—for workers and farmers. He certainly did not speak for the Indians being pushed off their lands or for enslaved African Americans. But the government needed a large base of support among white people, and the myth of "Jacksonian Democracy" was designed to win that support.

That myth led ordinary people to believe that they had a voice in government and that government looked out for their interests. It was a way of speaking for the lower and middle classes to get their support when the government needed it. Giving people a choice between two political parties, and letting them choose the slightly more democratic one, was a good way to control them. The leaders of both parties understood that they could keep control of society by making reforms that gave people some of what they wanted—but not too much.

The United States was developing with enormous speed and excitement. It was turning into an urban, or city-dwelling, nation. In 1790, fewer than a million Americans lived in cities. By 1840, the figure was 11 million. New York City alone grew from 130,000 people in 1820 to a million in 1860.

Many city-dwellers lived in extreme poverty. Working-class families in Philadelphia crowded into apartment buildings called tenements, one family to a room, with no fresh water or toilets. In New York the poor lay in the streets with the garbage. The slums had no sewers. Filthy water drained into them, causing outbreaks of deadly diseases.

The very poor could not be counted on to support the government. They were like the slaves and Indians—invisible most of the time, but frightening to the elite if they started an uprising. Other citizens, though, might support the system. Farmers who owned their land, better-paid laborers, and urban office workers were paid just enough, and flattered just enough, that in a crisis they would be loyal to the system and the upper classes that dominated it.

Big Business

BUSINESS WAS BOOMING IN NINETEENTH-century America. The opening of the West was helped by canals, railroads, and the telegraph. New equipment such as iron plows and mechanical reapers made farming more productive. But the economy was not planned or managed to meet human needs. Instead, it was driven by the quest for private profits. It cycled between booms (times of growth and prosperity) and slumps (times of depression and unemployment).

To make business more stable and to reduce competition, companies joined together. For example, many railroads merged to form one, the New York Central line. Companies also controlled competition by agreeing among themselves on the prices they would charge the public for their goods and services. In addition, they got help from the government. During just seven years in the 1850s, the state and federal governments gave away 25 million acres to railroad companies, along with millions of dollars in loans.

On the eve of the Civil War, the men who ran the country were most concerned with money and profit, not the movement against slavery.

A preacher named Theodore Parker told his congregation, "Money is this day the strongest power of the nation."

But the effort to keep politics and the economy under control did not quite work. From time to time, poor people showed their anger at the crowded cities, long hours in factories operating new industrial machines, high prices, lost jobs, disease, and miserable tenements. In 1827, as a meeting of mechanics (crafts and trades workers), one young man spoke of how hard it was to make a living, and of how laborers were at the mercy of their bosses:

> We find ourselves oppressed on every hand—we labor hard in producing all the comforts of life for the enjoyment of others, while we ourselves obtain but a scanty portion, and even that in the present state of society depends on the will of employers.

Sometimes there were sudden, unorganized uprisings against the rich. Sometimes the anger got turned against blacks, Catholics, or immigrants. And sometimes the poor organized their anger into demonstrations and strikes against the bankers, land speculators, landlords, and merchants who controlled the economy.

Workers Unite

IN 1829, THE WORKING PEOPLE OF Philadelphia held one of the first citywide meetings of labor groups in the United States. Frances Wright, a Scottish political thinker and women's rights activist, was invited to speak. Wright asked if the Revolutionary War had been fought "to crush down the sons and daughters of your country's industry." She wondered whether the new industrial machinery was lowering the value of human labor, making people servants to the machines, and crippling the minds and bodies of child laborers.

Trade unions began to form as workers banded together to bargain for better pay and working conditions. In 1835, workers in fifty different trades, such as bookbinding and cabinetmaking, organized labor unions in Philadelphia. They refused to work until their workday was limited to ten hours. Their strike succeeded.

The courts struck back at unions, calling them illegal conspiracies to hurt business. After a New York court ordered a "conspiracy" of tailors to pay a fine, twenty-seven thousand people gathered in front of City Hall to protest the court's decision. A handbill was seen in the city:

(left)
Construction crew with wood burning balloon-stack locomotive at a crossing of the Green River, 1885.

THE RICH AGAINST THE POOR!

Mechanics and working men! A deadly blow has been
struck at your liberty! . . . They have established . . .
that workingmen have no right to regulate the price of
labor, or, in other words, the rich are the only judges
of the wants of the poor man.

Later, farmers and working people across New
York State formed the Equal Rights Party to run
their own candidates for political office.

An economic crisis in 1837 caused prices of
food, fuel, and rent to soar. In New York City, a
third of the working class, or about fifty thousand
people, had no jobs. The Equal Rights Party organized a giant rally that turned into a riot when the
crowd stormed a store full of flour and wheat.

The labor movement had started off well in
Philadelphia. When religious conflict developed
between American-born Protestant workers in the
weaving trade and Irish immigrant Catholic
weavers, however, the movement fell apart.

The Irish were fleeing starvation in their own
country, where a plant disease had killed the potato
crop. These new immigrants, poor and discriminated against, had little sympathy for the plight of
black slaves in the United States. Most working-class

activists, in fact, ignored the African Americans. Ely Moore, a New York trade union leader who was elected to Congress, argued against abolition. Racism was an easy substitute for the true frustration of the working classes against the upper classes.

In 1850 the United States had a workforce of about 8.25 million people. Most of these people, free or slave, still worked in agriculture. A half million women worked outside their homes. The majority of them worked as servants. Others worked in factories (especially mills that made textiles, or cloth). About 55,000 were teachers.

Women textile workers were very active in the labor movement. Girls and women who worked in the mills of Lowell, Massachusetts, repeatedly struck for better conditions. One strike, for example, was for a workday of eleven hours rather than thirteen and a half hours. Another strike inspired an eleven-year-old protestor named Harriet Hanson to join the strikers:

> [W]hen the girls in my room stood irresolute [undecided], uncertain what to do . . . I, who began to think they would not go out, after all their talk, became impatient, and started on ahead, saying, with childish bravado, "I don't care what you do, I am going to turn out, whether anyone

else does or not," and I marched out, and was followed by the others. As I looked back at the long line that followed me, I was more proud than I have ever been since. . . .

Children started the first mill strike in Paterson, New Jersey. When the company changed their meal hour from noon to 1, the children marched off the job. Their parents cheered them on. Other working people joined the strike, which became a ten-day struggle.

Shoemakers in Lynn, Massachusetts, suffered during an economic depression in 1857. Many lost their jobs. Others had their wages cut. The shoemakers started a strike that spread to twenty-five towns and lasted for several months. Eventually, the factory owners offered higher wages to bring the workers back, but they refused to recognize the unions. Workers still had to face their employers as individuals.

During the Civil War, workers in the North had to pay high prices for food and other necessities of life, while their wages were kept low. There were strikes all over the country. In 1863, a newspaper printed a list of strikes, protests, and labor actions under the headline "Revolution in New York." The hidden anger of the poor was coming out.

(left)
Paying children for their labor in the brickyards, 1871.

White workers of the North were not enthusiastic about a war that seemed to be fought for the black slave or for the capitalist. The war, they thought, was bringing profit to a new class of millionaires. Some of their strikes ended under the threat of force by troops from the Union army.

Another source of conflict was the drafting of soldiers into the Union army. Men rich enough to pay $300 could get out of serving. The poor had no choice to but risk death on the battlefield. Draft riots broke out in New York and other cities. Poor people and workers raged against many targets: the rich, the blacks, and the Republicans. Mobs destroyed factories and the homes of wealthy people. They also burned a black orphanage and killed African Americans in the street. Troops had to be brought in to restore order.

The South had its own class conflict. Millions of Southern whites were poor farmers who did not own slaves. Some of them lived little better than slaves. Just as in the North, the poor were drafted into the army while the rich could buy their way out, and just as in the North, draft riots erupted.

Rule and Rebellion

UNDER THE NOISE OF WAR, CONGRESS
and Lincoln made a series of laws that gave business what it wanted. The Morrill Tariff made foreign goods more expensive. This let American
manufacturers raise their own prices so that consumers had to pay more for goods. The Contract
Labor Law let employers bring in foreign workers
who would work in exchange for their passage to
the United States. This gave business a source of
cheap labor and of strikebreakers—people to take
the jobs of unionized workers who went on strike.
Laws gave mill owners the right to flood other people's property, and other laws gave farmers' land to
railroad and canal companies.

State and federal laws did not even pretend to
protect working people. There were almost no
health and safety laws. The laws that did exist
were not enforced. When a mill collapsed, killing
eighty-eight workers, the court found the owners
free of blame, even though there was evidence
that they knew the building could not support the
heavy machinery inside.

After the war, soldiers returned, looking for
work. They found that women had joined the

industrial workforce during the war. Moving beyond the textile mills and tailoring jobs, women had become cigar makers and printers. Some of them had their own unions. Black workers, too, formed unions of their own.

Another economic crisis struck the country in 1873. It was one of a string of depressions that wiped out small businesses and brought hunger, cold, and death to working people while the rich remained secure—or grew richer.

The depression continued through the 1870s. Tens of thousands of people lost their jobs, even their homes. Many roamed the countryside, looking for food. Desperate people tried to get to Europe or South America. Unemployed workers held mass meetings to demand relief from the government.

In 1877, with the country in the depths of the depression, a series of railroad strikes shook the nation. Railroad workers in Martinsburg, West Virginia, went on strike to protest wage cuts and dangerous work conditions that led to deaths and injuries. They halted train traffic. Federal troops got the trains moving again, but in Baltimore citizens who supported the strikers surrounded the National Guard armory, hurling rocks at soldiers.

The soldiers answered with bullets, killing ten men and boys. A battle raged at the train depot, where the crowd smashed up an engine.

The rebellion of the railroad workers spread to Pittsburgh. After troops there killed ten people, the whole city rose in anger. Thousands looted the freight cars. Fires and fighting enveloped the city. Strikes and riots followed in Reading, Pennsylvania, and in Chicago, St. Louis, and New York. The authorities responded swiftly and violently.

When a crowd of young people shut down Chicago's railroads, lumberyards, and mills, calling workers to strike, the police attacked. "The sound of clubs falling on skulls was sickening for the first minute, until one grew used to it," said a newspaper article. "A rioter dropped at every whack, it seemed, for the ground was covered with them." At a peaceful labor meeting in New York, the speaker declared, "Whatever we poor men may not have, we have free speech, and no one can take it from us." Then the police charged, using their clubs.

The great railroad strikes of 1877 halted more than half the freight on the nation's rail lines.

When they were over, a hundred people were dead, and a thousand had gone to jail, a hundred thousand workers had gone on strike, and countless other unemployed people in the cities had been roused into action.

The railroads gave workers a few benefits. They also strengthened their own police forces. Nothing had really changed. Just as African Americans had learned that they did not have enough strength to make good the promises of emancipation, working people learned that they were not united or strong enough to defeat the combination of private wealth and government power. But their fight would continue.

CHAPTER ELEVEN

ROBBER BARONS AND REBELS

BETWEEN THE CIVIL WAR AND 1900, STEAM
and electricity replaced human muscle. The
United States built 193,000 miles of railroads.
New tools such as the telegraph, telephone, and
typewriter speeded up the work of business. Oil
and coal drove the machinery of factories and
lighted the streets and homes of cities. Inventors
and businesspeople made all this happen.

Some inventors were also businessmen.
Thomas Edison didn't just invent electrical equipment, he marketed it as well. Other businessmen
built corporations and fortunes by putting together
other people's inventions. A Chicago butcher
named Gustavus Swift combined the ice-cooled railway car with the ice-cooled warehouse to start the
country's first meat-packing plant in 1885.

Progress demanded labor. Much of the work was done by immigrants, who poured into the United States faster than ever before—5.5 million in the 1880s, 4 million in the 1890s. Many of those who came to the East Coast were from southern and eastern Europe. On the West Coast, Chinese immigrants made up one-tenth of California's population in 1880. Chinese and Jewish newcomers became the targets of racial attacks, sometimes at the hands of those who had immigrated earlier, such as the Irish.

Violence against immigrants could be murderous. In Rock Springs, Wyoming, in 1885, whites killed twenty-eight Chinese immigrants. Earlier, author Bret Harte wrote these words in memory of Wan Lee, a Chinese man killed in California:

> Dead, my revered friends, dead. Stoned to death in the streets of San Francisco, in the year of grace 1869 by a mob of halfgrown boys and Christian schoolchildren.

The greatest march of economic growth in human history took place in the United States in the late nineteenth century. The wealth it produced was like a pyramid. The supporting layers, those who built the pyramid and held it up, were the workers: blacks, whites, Chinese and

(left)
Thomas Edison with dynamo that generated the first commercial electric light, 1890s.

European immigrants, women. At the top were the new American multimillionaires.

The Rich Get Richer

SOME MULTIMILLIONAIRES STARTED IN poverty. Their "rags to riches" stories were useful for making the masses of poor workers believe that they, too, could be wealthy someday. The great majority of millionaires, however, came from upper-class or middle-class families. Those who went on to become the richest men of the era—J. P. Morgan, John D. Rockefeller, Andrew Carnegie, James Mellon, and Jay Gould—could afford to escape military service in the Civil War by paying substitutes to take their places. Mellon's father wrote to him, "There are plenty of lives less valuable [than yours]."

These men and others built huge fortunes with the help of the government and the courts. Sometimes they had to pay for that help. Thomas Edison, for example, promised New Jersey politicians

$1,000 each if they would make laws to favor his business interests.

History books often call the first transcontinental railroad a great American achievement. It was built on blood, sweat, politics, and thievery by two railway companies. The Central Pacific line started on the West Coast and went east. It spent $200,000 on bribes in Washington, D.C. to get free land and loans, and it paid its Irish and Chinese workers one or two dollars a day. The Union Pacific line started in Nebraska and went west. To avoid being investigated, it bribed congressmen by selling them shares in the company very cheaply. Its workers died by the hundreds from heat, cold, and attacks by Indians who fought the invasion of their land.

Rockefeller built a fortune in the new oil business, partly by making secret deals with railroad companies. He promised to ship his oil with them if they would give him lower rates. This arrangement saved him money, so he could sell his oil for less, which drove competing oil companies out of business. He bought them up and created a monopoly—a system in which one corporation controls all or most of an industry.

The efficient businessmen of the late nineteenth century are sometimes called robber barons. They were powerful, like the barons of medieval nobility, and much of their wealth was gained through greedy or dishonest methods. In industry after industry they created empires by keeping prices high and wages low, by crushing their competition, and by getting help from the government in the form of favorable laws and taxes. The government pretended to be neutral, but in reality it served the interests of the rich. Its purpose was to settle disputes among the upper classes peacefully, to keep the lower classes under control, and to keep the economic system stable.

The election of Grover Cleveland in 1884 showed the way things were in the United States. Many people thought that Cleveland, a Democrat, was against the power of monopolies and corporations. But Cleveland promised the captains of industry, "No harm shall come to any business interest . . . so long as I am President." After he was elected, Cleveland showed that he cared more about the rich than the poor. He refused to give $100,000 of federal money to help Texas farmers buy seed grain during a drought, even though the treasury was full of funds. That same year, Cleveland bought back government bonds held by wealthy people at more than their face value—a gift of $45 million to the rich.

Voices of Protest

A FEW POLITICIANS TRIED TO LIMIT THE power of corporations. To break up monopolies, Senator John Sherman wrote the Sherman Anti-Trust Act, which Congress voted into law in 1877. Sherman feared that without reforms, people who opposed the power of giant corporations might be drawn to dangerous new political ideas that had come out of Europe.

One idea was socialism—an economic system in which the government or the people as a whole own the means of production, such as farms, mines, and factories. These are operated for the benefit of all, not for private profit. Communism went even further, doing away with private property and with class distinctions based on wealth. In a

communist society, all goods would be owned by everyone, available to anyone according to need. A third new political idea, anarchism, held that government itself was unnecessary, even wrong.

The Sherman Anti-Trust Act was designed to reform the capitalist system just enough to prevent socialism or communism from taking hold among the workers and poor. Less than twenty years after it became law, however, the U.S. Supreme Court interpreted the act in a way that made it meaningless. At the same time, the Court was giving added protection to corporations. These decisions kept wealth at the top of the pyramid. One Supreme Court justice, David J. Brewer, said in 1893, "It is the unvarying law that the wealth of the community will be in the hands of the few. . ."

Churches, schools, business, and government tried to control people's thinking, teaching them that all was right with society. Poverty was a sign of personal failure. The rich deserved to be rich. The capitalist system was right and proper.

Not everyone accepted that view of things. Some people were ready to consider harsh criticism of the system, or to imagine other ways of living. One of

(left)
Illustration from *Harper's Weekly* depicting the Homestead Strike of 1892.

them was Henry George, a self-educated Philadelphia workingman who became a newspaperman and economist. People around the world read his 1879 book *Progress and Poverty*. George argued that a tax on land, which he called the basis of wealth, would raise enough money that the government could solve the problem of poverty. Another writer, a lawyer named Edward Bellamy, published *Looking Backward,* a novel about life in the year 2000. In Bellamy's hopeful view of the future, society was socialistic. Everyone worked and lived in cooperation, not as competing individuals.

Great movements of workers and farmers swept the land in the 1880s and 1890s. These went beyond the scattered strikes of earlier years. They were national movements that threatened the ruling elites. Revolutionary societies existed in American cities, and revolutionary talk was in the air.

In 1883, an anarchist congress took place in Pittsburgh. It drew up a statement that called for "equal rights for all without distinction to sex or race." It quoted an 1848 document called the *Communist Manifesto,* which declared, "Workmen of all lands, unite! You have nothing to lose but your chains; you have a world to win!"

The Haymarket Affair

IN 1886, THE EXISTING SYSTEM AND
the new ideas clashed. The American Federation
of Labor, a five-year-old association of labor
unions, called for nationwide strikes wherever
employers refused to shorten the workday to eight
hours. About 350,000 employees of more than
11,500 businesses went out on strike.

In Chicago alone, forty thousand people struck
(another 45,000 received a shorter workday to
keep them from striking). Outside one factory,
workers and their supporters got into a fight with
scabs—their term for the workers who stepped in
to do their jobs while they were on strike. Police
fired into the crowd, killing four strikers. After
that, August Spies, an anarchist and labor leader,
published a sheet telling workers to take up arms
against the bosses. Other anarchists spoke at a
mass meeting at Haymarket Square, to an audience of about four thousand people. It was a
peaceful meeting. Still, police arrived and ordered
the crowd to leave. Just then, a bomb exploded,
wounding sixty-six policemen. Seven of them
died. The police fired, wounding two hundred
people and killing several.

No evidence was found to show who had thrown the bomb. The authorities arrested Spies and seven other anarchists on the charge that they had urged murder. Under Illinois law, that was the same as committing murder. The evidence against the eight was their ideas and their literature, not their actions. Only one of them had been at Haymarket Square. But a jury found all eight guilty, and seven were sentenced to death. (Four were hanged, one killed himself before he could be executed, and the other three were eventually pardoned and released.)

People around the world demonstrated against the harsh sentences. In Chicago, twenty-five thousand marched in protest. Year after year, all over the country, memorial meetings for the Haymarket martyrs took place. Some people were shocked into political action by the Haymarket Affair.

The Rise and Fall of Populism

THE HAYMARKET EXECUTIONS DID NOT crush the labor movement. The year 1886 became known as "the year of the great uprising of labor." Unions formed in the sugar fields of the South, and workers went on strike. After two black strike leaders in Louisiana were arrested and then disappeared never to be seen again, gun battles broke out between strikers and militia. An African American newspaper in New Orleans reported on the violence in the town of Thibodaux:

> Lame men and blind women shot; children and hoary-headed grandsires ruthlessly swept down! The Negroes offered no resistance; they could not, as the killing was unexpected. Those of them not killed took to the woods . . . Citizens of the United States killed by a mob directed by a State judge. . . . Laboring men seeking an advance in wages, treated as if they were dogs!

A few years later, coal miners struck in Tennessee. When mine owners sent in convicts to do the work, the miners took over the mine by force. Workers at Andrew Carnegie's steel plant in Homestead, Pennsylvania, also struck. The governor sent militia to control the strike, and the plant used strikebreakers to keep producing steel. After two months, the strike collapsed.

In 1893, the country entered the biggest economic crisis it had seen. The depression lasted for years and brought a wave of strikes. A railroad workers' strike was the largest and most violent. It launched one worker, Eugene Debs, into a lifetime of activism for labor unions and socialism. Debs was arrested for supporting the strike. Two years later he wrote:

> The issue is Socialism versus Capitalism. I am for Socialism because I am for humanity. We have been cursed with the reign of gold long enough. Money constitutes no proper basis for civilization. The time has come to regenerate [renew] society—we are on the eve of a universal change.

Like laborers, farmers were suffering. The cost of things like farm machinery and railroad fees for shipping grain kept going up, but the prices for farm produce went down. Many farmers could not pay their bills, and they lost their farms.

Farmers began creating union-like organizations to help each other. They bought goods together to get lower prices, and they worked to get pro-farm laws passed. One of these associations, the Farmers

Alliance, gave birth to a new movement called pop-
ulism (political and economic beliefs and activities
"of the people"). It promoted the idea that farmers
acting together could build their own institutions—
such as affordable insurance against crop loss—and
their own political parties.

In general, populists were against monopolies
(also called trusts) and capitalism. They wanted
the government to control railway rates and banks'
interest rates, to keep them from making huge
profits. Populists did not agree, however, on race.
Some blacks and whites argued for racial unity,
feeling that all poor agricultural workers were in
the same fix and needed to stand together. Yet
racism was strong in other white populists, while
many more simply did not think that race was as
important as the economic system. Many populists were also against new immigrants. They
especially opposed immigration from eastern and
southern Europe and from Asia.

In the end, the populist movement failed to
unite blacks and whites, farmers and urban workers. A few candidates ran for political office under
the banner of the Populist or People's party, but in
city after city populists allied themselves with the

Democratic party to have a better chance of winning elections. But it was political deal-makers, not revolutionary farmers, who won most elections. Eventually, the populist movement was lost in the sea of Democratic politics.

In the 1896 election, the corporations and press threw their support behind the Republican candidate, William McKinley. It was the first campaign in which massive amounts of money were spent, and McKinley was the winner. Like many politicians, he turned to patriotism to drown out class resentment. "I am glad to know that the people in every part of this country mean to be devoted to one flag, the glorious Stars and Stripes," he said. Then McKinley showed that he thought that money was as important, as sacred, as patriotism. He added, "the people of this country mean to maintain the financial honor of this country as sacredly as they maintain the honor of the flag."

CHAPTER TWELVE

THE AMERICAN EMPIRE

"I SHOULD WELCOME ALMOST ANY WAR, for I think this country needs one." Those words were written in 1897, in a letter to a friend, by Theodore Roosevelt, who would later become president of the United States. Why would he think that the nation needed a war?

Maybe a war would take up some of the rebellious energy that people were pouring into strikes and protests. Maybe it would unite the people with the armed forces against a foreign enemy. And there was another reason—an economic one.

Before he was elected president, William McKinley had said, "We want a foreign market for our surplus goods." Senator Albert Beveridge of Indiana spelled it out in 1897. He said:

American factories are making more than the American
people can use; American soil is producing more than
they can consume. Fate has written our policy for us; the
trade of the world must and shall be ours.

These politicians and others believed that the
United States had to open up other countries to
American goods—even if those markets were not
eager to buy. If factories and farms could sell their
surplus production overseas, American companies would keep earning money, and the economy
might avoid the crises that had sparked class war
in the 1890s.

War was probably not a thought-out plan
among most of the elite ruling classes. Instead, it
grew naturally from two sources, capitalism and
nationalism. Capitalism demanded more markets.
Nationalism, the spirit of strong national pride,
made people think that the United States had a
right, or even a duty, to expand itself and to shape
the affairs of other countries.

The Taste of Empire

STRETCHING THE UNITED STATES' ARM overseas was not a new idea. The war against Mexico had already carried the United States to the Pacific Ocean. Before that, in 1823, President James Monroe had produced the Monroe Doctrine. This statement made it clear that the United States claimed an interest in the politics of the entire Western Hemisphere—North, Central, and South America. It warned the nations of Europe not to meddle with countries in the Americas.

The United States, however, didn't feel that it had to stay out of other countries' affairs. Between 1798 and 1895, the United States sent troops to other countries, or took an active role in their affairs, 103 times. In the 1850s, for example, the U.S. Navy used warships to force Japan to open its ports to American shipping.

At the end of the nineteenth century, many military men, politicians, and businessmen supported the idea of still more foreign involvement. A writer for the *Washington Post* said:

> A new consciousness seems to have come upon us—the consciousness of strength—and with it a new appetite, the

yearning to show our strength. . . . The taste of Empire is in the mouth of the people. . . .

The Spanish-American War

THE AMERICAN PEOPLE MIGHT BE MORE willing to enter into an overseas conflict if it looked like a good deed, such as helping a nation's people overthrow foreign rule. Cuba, an island close to Florida, was in that situation. For centuries Spain had held Cuba as a colony. Then, in 1895, the Cubans rebelled against Spanish rule.

Some Americans thought that the United States should help the Cubans because they were fighting for freedom, like the colonists in the Revolutionary War. The U.S. government was more interested in who would control Cuba if the Spanish were thrown out.

Race was part of the picture, because Cuba had both black and white people. The administration of President Grover Cleveland feared that a victory by the Cuban rebels might lead to "a white

(left)
Cuban fighters in the war for independence from Spain roast a pig during a break in the fighting, 1896.

and a black republic." A young British empire builder named Winston Churchill, son of an American mother, had the same thought. In 1896 he wrote a magazine article saying that even though Spanish rule in Cuba was bad, and the rebels had the support of the Cuban people, it would be better if Spain stayed in control. If the rebels won, Cuba might become "another black republic." Churchill was warning that Cuba might be like Haiti, the first country in the Americas to be run by black people.

As Americans debated about whether to join the war in Cuba, an explosion in the harbor of Havana, Cuba's capital, destroyed the U.S. battleship *Maine*. The ship had been sent to Cuba as a symbol of American interest in the region. No evidence was ever produced to show what caused the explosion, but the loss of the *Maine* moved President McKinley and the country in the direction of war. It was clear that the United States could not get Spain out of Cuba without a fight. It was also clear that the United States couldn't carve out American military and economic interests in Cuba without sending troops to the island.

In April 1898 McKinley asked Congress to

declare war. Soon American forces moved into
Cuba. The Spanish-American War had begun.

John Hay, the U.S. secretary of state, later
called it a "splendid little war." The Spanish forces
were defeated in three months. Nearly 5,500
American soldiers died. Only 379 died in battle.
The rest were killed by disease and other causes.
One cause was certainly the tainted, rotten meat
sold to the army by American meatpackers.

What about the Cuban rebels who had started
the fight with Spain? The American military pretended that they did not exist. When the Spanish
surrendered, no Cuban was allowed to discuss the
surrender, or sign the treaty. The United States
was in control. U.S. troops remained in Cuba after
the surrender. Soon, U.S. money entered the
island, as Americans started taking over railroads,
mines, and sugar plantations.

The United States told the Cuban people that
they could write their own constitution and form
their own government. It also told them that the
U.S. Army would not leave the island until Cuba's
new constitution included a new American law
called the Platt Amendment. This law gave the
United States the right to involve itself in Cuba's

affairs pretty much whenever it wanted. General Leonard Wood explained to Theodore Roosevelt in 1901, "There is, of course, little or no independence left Cuba under the Platt Amendment."

Many Americans felt that the Platt Amendment betrayed the idea of Cuban independence. Criticism went beyond the radicals (socialists and others with extreme or revolutionary views) to mainstream newspapers and civic groups. One group critical of the Platt Amendment was the Anti-Imperialism League. One of the League's founders was William James, a philosopher at Harvard University, who opposed the United States' trend toward empire building and meddling in other county's affairs. In the end, though, the Cubans had no choice but to agree to the Platt Amendment if they wanted to set up their own government.

Revolt and Racism in the Philippines

THE UNITED STATES DID NOT ANNEX CUBA, or make it part of U.S. territory. But the Spanish-American War did lead to annexation of some other territories that Spain had controlled. One was Puerto Rico, an island neighbor of Cuba. The United States had already taken over the Hawaiian Islands from its Hawaiian Queen, and the war gave it control of some other Pacific islands, too: Wake Island, Guam, and the large island cluster called the Philippines.

Americans hotly debated whether or not they should take over the Philippines. One story says that President McKinley told a visiting group of ministers how he had come to the decision to annex the Philippines. As he prayed for guidance, he became convinced that "there was nothing left for us to do but to take them all and to educate the Filipinos, and uplift and civilize and Christianize them. . . . And then I went to bed and went to sleep and slept soundly."

The Filipinos, however, did not get a message from God telling them to accept American rule. Instead, in February 1899 they rose up in revolt against the United States, just as they had revolted several times against Spain.

The taste of empire was on the lips of politicians and businessmen throughout the United States, and they agreed that the United States must keep control of its new territory. Talk of money mingled with talk of destiny and civilization. "The Philippines are ours forever," Senator Beveridge told the U.S. Senate. "And just beyond the Philippines are China's illimitable markets [markets with no limits or boundaries]. We will not retreat from either."

It took the United States three years to crush the Filipino rebellion. It was a harsh war. Americans lost many more troops than in Cuba. For the Filipinos the death rate was enormous, from battle and from disease.

McKinley said that the fighting with the rebels started when the rebels attacked American forces. Later, American soldiers testified that the United States had fired the first shot.

The famous American author Mark Twain summed up the Philippine war with disgust, saying:

> We have pacified some thousands of the islanders and buried them; destroyed their fields; burned their villages, and turned their widows and orphans out-of-doors. . . . And so, by these Providences of God—the phrase is the government's, not mine—we are a World Power.

(left)
A long line of African American soldiers who fought in the Spanish-American War, 1899.

The Anti-Imperialist League worked to educate the American public about the horrors of the Philippine war and the evils of imperialism, or empire building. It published letters from soldiers on duty in the Philippines. There were reports of soldiers killing women, children, and prisoners of war. A black soldier named William Fulbright wrote from Manila, the capital of the Philippines, "This struggle on the islands has been naught but a gigantic scheme of robbery and oppression."

Race was an issue in the Philippines, as it had been in Cuba. Some white American soldiers were racists who considered the Filipinos inferior. Black American soldiers in the Philippines had mixed feelings. Some felt pride, the desire to show that blacks were as courageous and patriotic as whites. Some wanted the chance to get ahead in life through the military. But others felt that they were fighting a brutal war against people of color—not too different from the violence against black people in the United States, where drunken white soldiers in Tampa, Florida, started a race riot by using a black child for target practice.

Back in the United States, many African Americans turned against the Philippine war because they saw it as a racial conflict, the white race fighting to conquer the brown. They were fighting injustice at home, too. A group of African Americans in Massachusetts sent a message to President McKinley, criticizing him for doing nothing to advance racial equality.

Throughout the nineteenth century, black Americans, along with women, workers, and the poor, had raised their voices against oppression. Many had found ways to resist the harshest effects of a political and economic system that ignored them. In the coming century, they would take their own steps toward change.

A YOUNG PEOPLE'S HISTORY *of the* UNITED STATES

PART TWO

CLASS STRUGGLE
to
THE WAR ON TERROR

CHAPTER THIRTEEN

CLASS STRUGGLE

ANGER WAS ON THE RISE IN AMERICA AS the twentieth century opened. The United States had just won the Spanish-American War. Emma Goldman, an anarchist and feminist of the time, later remembered how the war in Cuba and the Philippines had filled people with patriotism:

> How our hearts burned with indignation against the
> atrocious Spaniards! . . . But when the smoke was over,
> the dead buried, and the cost of the war came back to
> the people in an increase in the price of commodities
> [goods] and rent—that is, when we sobered up from
> our patriotic spree—it suddenly dawned on us that the
> cause of the Spanish American war was the price of
> sugar . . . that the lives, blood and money of the
> American people were used to protect the interests of
> the American capitalists.

Some famous American writers spoke up for socialism, with harsh words for the capitalist system. Jack London's novel *The Iron Heel*, published in 1906, offered a vision of a socialist brotherhood of man. That same year Upton Sinclair published *The Jungle*, with a character who dreams of a socialist state. *The Jungle* also brought the shocking conditions in the Chicago meatpacking industry to the nation's attention. After it was published, the government passed laws to regulate the industry.

"Muckrakers" added to the mood of dissent, or disagreement with the system. These writers raked up the mud and muck—that is, the bad conduct and unfair practices—of corporations, government, and society in general. Then they exposed it to the world in newspaper and magazine articles or in books. Ida Tarbell, for example, wrote about the Standard Oil Company's business practices. Lincoln Steffens revealed political corruption in American cities.

(left)
Emma Goldman and
Alexander Berkman,
1918.

Sweatshops and Wobblies

BUSINESSES WERE LOOKING FOR WAYS TO produce more goods and make more money. One way was to break manufacturing down into a series of simple tasks. A worker would no longer make an entire piece of furniture, for example. Instead, he or she would simply repeat only one part of the work. So the worker would do the same task over and over again—maybe drilling a hole, or squirting glue. This way, companies could hire less skilled labor. Workers became interchangeable, almost like the machines they tended, stripped of individuality and humanity.

In New York City, many immigrants went to work in garment factories called sweatshops. In sweatshops, they worked for very low wages under unhealthy working conditions. They were paid based on how many pieces of clothing they sewed, not how many hours they worked. Many others did this piecework at home.

One of New York's five hundred sweatshops was the Triangle Shirtwaist Company. Women workers there went on strike in the winter of 1909. Twenty thousand other workers joined them. One striker, Pauline Newman, later recalled the scene. "Thousands upon thousands left the factories from every side," she wrote. "It was November, the cold winter was just around the corner, we had no fur coats to keep warm, and yet there was the spirit that led us on and on. . . ."

The strike lasted for months, against police, scabs, and arrests. Yet although the workers won some of their demands, conditions in the factories did not change much. In March 1911 a fire broke out in the Triangle building. The fire raged too high in the building for the fire department's ladders to reach it. With workroom doors illegally locked by the employers, the workers, mostly young women, were trapped. Some fled the flames by throwing themselves out windows. Others burned. When it was over, 146 had died. A hundred thousand New Yorkers marched in their memorial parade.

The union movement was growing, but the biggest union, the American Federation of Labor (AFL), did not represent all workers. Its members were almost all white, male, skilled laborers. Blacks were kept out of the AFL. Women made up a fifth of the workforce in 1910, but only one in a hundred women workers was in a union. In addition, AFL officials had begun to seem no better than corporate bosses. They were protected by "goon" squads who beat up union members who criticized them.

Working people who wanted radical change needed a new kind of union. At a 1905 meeting of anarchists, socialists, and unionists in Chicago, that union was born. It was called the Industrial Workers of the World (IWW), and its goal was to organize all workers in any industry into "One Big Union," undivided by sex, race, or skills.

The IWW came to be called the Wobblies, though it's not clear why. The Wobblies were brave, and they were willing to meet force with force. When they struck against the U.S. Steel Company in Pennsylvania in 1909, state troopers came to control the strike. The IWW vowed to kill a trooper for every striker who was killed. Three troopers and four strikers died in one gun battle, but the strikers stayed out until they won.

The IWW was inspired by a new idea that was developing in Spain, Italy, and France. This was anarcho-syndicalism, the belief that workers could take power in a country, not by seizing control of the government in an armed rebellion, but by bringing the economic system to a halt. The way to stop the economic system was by a general strike, one in which all workers in all the trades and industries would join, united by a common purpose.

In the ten exciting years after its birth, the IWW became a threat to the capitalist class in the United States. The union never had more than five or ten thousand members at a time, but their ability to organize strikes and protests made a big impact on the country. IWW organizers traveled everywhere—many of them were unemployed, or moved around as migrant workers. They sang, spoke, and spread their message and their spirit.

The IWW organizers suffered beatings, imprisonment, and even murder. A criminal case involving organizer Joe Hill gained worldwide attention. Hill was a songwriter whose funny, biting, and inspiring songs made him a legend. For example, "The Preacher and the Slave" had a favorite IWW target—the church, which often seemed to ignore the very real sufferings of the poor and working classes:

Long-haired preachers come out every night,

Try to tell you what's wrong and what's right;

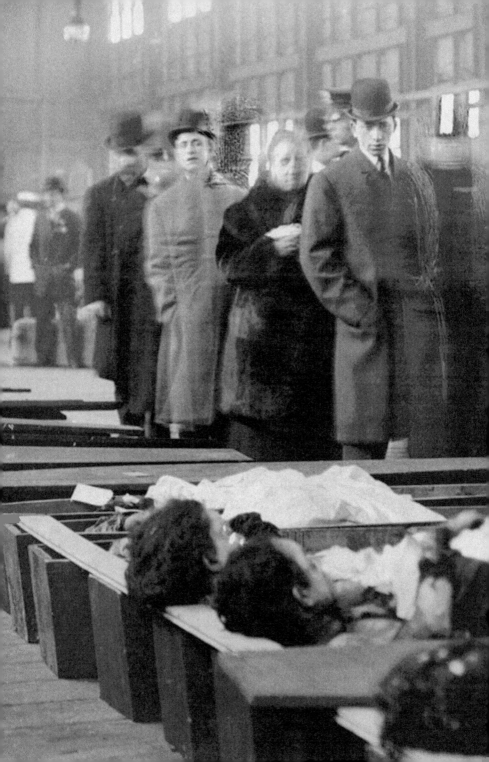

Family members arrive at the New York City morgue to identify the bodies of victims of the Triangle Shirtwaist Company Fire, 1911.

But when asked how 'bout something to eat

They will answer with voices so sweet:

—You will eat, bye and bye,

—In that glorious land above the sky;

—Work and pray, live on hay,

—You'll get pie in the sky when you die.

In 1915 Hill was accused of killing a grocer in Salt Lake City, Utah, during a robbery. There was no direct evidence that he had committed the murder, but there were enough pieces of evidence for a jury to find him guilty. Ten thousand people wrote letters to the governor of Utah, protesting the verdict, but Joe Hill was executed by a firing squad. Before he died he wrote to Bill Haywood, another IWW leader, "Don't waste any time in mourning. Organize."

Socialism, Sex, and Race

LABOR STRUGGLES WERE ON THE RISE. IN the 1890s there had been about a thousand strikes a year. By 1904 there were four thousand.

Seeing the law and the military take the side of the rich again and again, hundreds of thousands of American began to think about socialism.

Socialism had gotten its start in the United States in cities in the small circles of Jewish and German immigrants. In time, though, it spread and became thoroughly American. As many as a million people across the country read socialist newspapers.

The Socialist political party formed in 1901. Eugene Debs, who had become a socialist after being jailed during a strike, became its spokesman. To Debs, the labor union meant much more than strikes and wage increases. Its goal was "to overthrow the capitalist system of private ownership of the tools of labor . . . and achieve the freedom of the whole working class and, in fact of all mankind."

Debs ran for president five times as the Socialist candidate. At one time his party had a hundred thousand members. The strongest state Socialist organization was in Oklahoma, where more than a hundred Socialists were elected to office.

Some of the feminists active in the women's rights movement in the early twentieth century were also socialists. They debated challenging questions: If the economic system changed, would women then be full equals in society? Was it better to work toward a revolutionary change in society or to fight for rights within the existing system? Many women were less concerned with social change than with suffrage, or the right to vote. At a friendly meeting with socialist leader Eugene Debs, feminist Susan B. Anthony said, "Give us suffrage, and we'll give you socialism." Debs replied, "Give us socialism and we'll give you suffrage."

Socialists like Helen Keller did not think suffrage was enough. Blind and deaf, Keller fought for change with her spirit and her pen. In 1911 she wrote, "Our democracy is but a name. We vote? What does that mean? . . . We choose between Tweedledum and Tweedledee."

Black women faced double oppression, held down because of their race as well as their sex. An African American nurse wrote to a newspaper in 1912:

> We poor colored women wage-earners in the South are
> fighting a terrible battle. . . . On the one hand, we are
> assailed by black men, who should be our natural
> protectors; and, whether in the cook kitchen, at the

washtub, over the sewing machine, behind the baby car-
riage, or at the ironing board, we are little more than
pack horses, beasts of burden, slaves!

The early part of the twentieth century was a
low point for African Americans, with lynchings
reported every week and murderous race riots in
places like Brownsville, Texas, and Atlanta,
Georgia. The government did nothing.

Blacks began to organize. In 1905 W. E. B. Du
Bois—a respected teacher and author who was
sympathetic to the socialists—called black leaders to a meeting in Canada, near Niagara Falls.
This was the start of the "Niagara Movement."
Five years later, a race riot in Springfield, Illinois,
led to the founding of the National Association
for the Advancement of Colored People
(NAACP). Whites dominated this new group. Du
Bois was the only black officer. The NAACP
focused on education and legal action to end
racism, but Du Bois represented the Niagara
Movement's strong spirit of activism.

The Progressive Movement
and the Colorado Coal Strike

BLACKS, FEMINISTS, LABOR UNIONS, AND
socialists saw clearly that they could not count on
the national government. And yet history books
give the label "Progressive Period" to the early
years of the twentieth century. True, it was a time
of reforms—but the reforms were made unwill-
ingly. They were not meant to bring about basic
changes in society, only to quiet the uprisings of
the people.

The period got the name "Progressive"
because new laws were passed. There were laws
for inspecting meat, regulating railroads, controlling the growth of monopolies, and keeping the
nation's food and medicines safe. Labor laws set
standards for wages and hours. Safety inspection
of workplaces and payment to employees
injured on the job were introduced. The U.S.
Constitution was changed so that U.S. senators
were elected directly by vote of the people, not by
state legislatures.

Ordinary people did benefit from these changes.
Basic conditions did not change, however, for the
vast majority of tenant farmers, factory workers,

slum dwellers, miners, farm laborers, and working men and women, black and white.

The government was still dedicated to protecting a system that benefited the upper classes. Theodore Roosevelt, for example, made a reputation as a "trust buster," a politician who opposed monopolies. But two men in the service of multi-millionaire J. P. Morgan made private deals with Roosevelt to make sure that "trust-busting" wouldn't go too far. Roosevelt's advisers were industrialists and bankers, not unionists and workers.

The Progressive movement had some leaders who were honest reformers and others, like Roosevelt, who were only disguised as Progressives. In reality they were conservatives, opposed to change and concerned with preserving the balance of power and wealth. Both kinds of progressives saw their mission as fending off socialism. They felt that by improving conditions for the masses, they could prevent what one Progressive called "the menace of socialism."

The Socialist Party was on the rise. In 1910, Victor Berger became the first Socialist elected to the U.S. Congress. In 1911 there were seventy-three Socialist mayors and twelve hundred Socialists in other city and town offices. Newspapers talked about "The Rising Tide of Socialism."

The Progressives' goal was to save capitalism by repairing its worst problems. In this way, they thought, they could end the growing class war that pitted workers against the economic and political elites. But a strike of Colorado coal miners that began in September 1913 turned into one of the most bitter and violent battles in that war.

After a union organizer was murdered, eleven thousand miners went on strike. The Rockefeller family, which owned the mine, sent detectives with machine guns to raid the strikers' camps. The strikers fought to keep out strikebreakers and to keep the mines from opening. When the governor called on National Guard troops to destroy the strike, the Rockefellers paid the National Guards' wages.

Violent battles, betrayals, and massacres followed. In April 1914, the bodies of thirteen children and women were found in a pit, killed by a fire set by the National Guardsmen. The news spread across the country. Strikes, demonstrations, and protests broke out everywhere. President Woodrow Wilson finally sent in federal troops to crush the strike. Sixty-six men, women, and children had died. No soldier or mine guard was charged with a crime.

Colorado's ferocious class conflict was felt all over the land. Whatever reforms had been passed, whatever new laws were on the books, the threat of class rebellion remained—and unemployment and hard times were growing.

Could patriotism and the military spirit cover up class struggle? The nation was about to find out. In four months World War I would begin in Europe.

CHAPTER FOURTEEN

WORLD WAR I

THE NATIONS OF EUROPE WENT TO WAR IN
the late summer of 1914. The conflict that we now
call World War I would drag on for four years. Ten
million people would die on its battlefields.
Twenty million more would die of hunger and disease related to the war. And no one has ever been
able to show that the war brought any gain for
humanity that would be worth a single life.

At the time, socialists called it an "imperialist
war"—a war fought in the service of empire building, by nations that wanted to increase their power
by controlling territory or resources. The advanced
capitalist nations of Europe fought over bound-
aries, such as the region of Alsace-Lorraine,
claimed by both France and Germany. They fought
over colonies in Africa. And they fought over

(left, detail)
Eugene V. Debs
at a Labor Convention,
1910s.

"spheres of influence," areas in Eastern Europe and the Middle East that were not claimed openly as colonies but still came under the "protection" and control of some European nation.

Blood and Money

MANY NATIONS JOINED THE WAR ON ONE SIDE or the other, but the main enemies were Germany on one side and the Allies, France and Great Britain, on the other. The killing started very fast, and on a very large scale. In one early battle in France, each side had half a million casualties. Almost the entire British army from before the war was wiped out in the first three months of fighting.

The battle lines were drawn across France. For three years they barely moved. Men spent months in filthy, disease-ridden trenches. Each side would push forward, then be pushed back, then push forward again for a few yards or a few miles, while the corpses piled up. In 1916 the Germans tried to break through the lines at a place called Verdun.

The British and French counterattacked and lost six hundred thousand men.

The people of France and Britain were not told the full numbers of dead and wounded. When a German attack on the Somme River caused three hundred thousand British casualties in the last year of the war, London newspapers told readers, "Be cheerful. . . . Write encouragingly to friends at the front."

The same thing was true in Germany—the true horror of the war was kept from the people. On days when men were being blown apart in the thousands by machine guns and artillery shells, the official war reports said, "All Quiet on the Western Front." German writer Erich Maria Remarque later used that phrase as the title of his great novel about the war.

Into this pit of death and deception came the United States in 1917.

Earlier, President Woodrow Wilson had promised that the United States would keep out of the war. But the question of shipping in the North Atlantic Ocean drew the United States into the fight.

In 1915 a German submarine had torpedoed and sunk a British liner, the *Lusitania,* on its way from North America to Britain. Nearly 1,200 people,

including 124 Americans, died. The United States claimed that the *Lusitania* was carrying civilian passengers and innocent cargo, and that the German attack was a monstrous atrocity. In truth, the *Lusitania* was heavily armed. She carried thousands of cases of ammunition for the British. False cargo records hid this fact, and the British and American governments lied about the cargo.

Then, in April 1917, the Germans warned that their submarines would sink any ships that were carrying supplies to their enemies. This included the United States, which had been shipping huge amounts of war materials to Germany's enemies.

The war in Europe had been good for American business. A serious economic decline had hit the country in 1914, but things turned around when Americans began manufacturing war materials to sell to the Allies—mainly to Britain. By the time the Germans issued their warning about shipping, the United States had sold 2 billion dollars' worth of goods to the Allies. American prosperity was now tied to England's war. President Wilson said that he must stand by the right of Americans to travel on merchant ships in the war zone, and Congress declared war on Germany.

(left)
Eugene V. Debs
at a Labor Convention,
1910s.

Wilson called it a war "to end all wars" and "to make the world safe for democracy." These rousing words did not inspire Americans to enlist in the armed forces. A million men were needed, but in the first six weeks, only 73,000 volunteered. Congress authorized a draft to compel men into service. It also set up a Committee on Public Information. That committee's job was to convince Americans that the war was right.

The Radical Response

THE GOVERNMENT WANTED TO DISCOURAGE dissent and criticism of the war. It passed a law called the Espionage Act. The title makes it seem like a law against spying. But one part of the law called for up to twenty years in prison for anyone who refused to serve in the armed forces or even tried to convince others not to enlist. The act was used to imprison Americans who spoke or wrote against the war.

About nine hundred people went to prison under the Espionage Act. One of them was a Philadelphia socialist named Charles Schenck. Two months after the act became law, Schenck was sentenced to jail for printing and distributing fifteen thousand leaflets against the draft and the war. He appealed the verdict, claiming that the act violated his First Amendment rights to freedom of speech and freedom of the press. The case went to the Supreme Court.

All nine justices agreed. The Court decided against Schenck. Justice Oliver Wendell Holmes said that even the strict protection of free speech "would not protect a man in falsely shouting fire in a theatre and causing panic." This was a clever comparison. Few people would think that someone should be allowed to get away with shouting "Fire!" in a crowded theater and causing a dangerous panic. But did that example fit criticism of the war?

Socialist Eugene Debs was also involved in a case before the Supreme Court. After visiting three socialists who were in prison for opposing the draft, he made a fiery antiwar speech in the street:

> They tell us that we live in a great free republic; that our institutions are democratic; that we are a free and self-governing people. That is too much, even for a joke. . . . Wars throughout history have been waged for conquest and

plunder. . . . And that is war in a nutshell. The master class has always declared the wars; the subject class has always fought the battles. . . .

Debs was arrested for violating the Espionage Act. At his trial he declared, "I have been accused of obstructing the war. I admit it. Gentlemen, I abhor war." The judge, in turn, spoke harshly about "those who would strike the sword from the hand of his nation while she is engaged in defending herself against a foreign and brutal power." He sentenced Debs to ten years in prison. (Several years later, after the war was over, President Warren Harding released Debs from prison.)

The press worked with the government to create an atmosphere of fear for anyone who dared to criticize the war. One publication asked its readers to turn in any published material they saw that seemed seditious, or disloyal, to the country. Men joined the American Vigilante Patrol to "put an end to seditious street oratory"—basically, to prevent antiwar speechmaking. The U.S. Post Office took away the mailing privileges of newspapers and magazines that published antiwar articles. The Committee on Public Information tried to turn people into spies and informers against each other. It urged citizens to "report the man who spreads pessimistic stories. Report him to the Department of Justice."

The Department of Justice sponsored the American Protective League in six hundred towns. Its members were bankers and leading business-men. The League seized other people's mail, broke into their homes and offices, and claimed to find 3 million cases of "disloyalty." In 1918 the attorney general of the United States declared, "It is safe to say that never in its history has this country been so thoroughly policed."

Why these huge efforts? Because Americans were refusing to fight in the war. Senator Thomas Hardwick of Georgia described "general and widespread opposition on the part of many thousands . . . to the enactment of the draft law." Before the war was over, more than a third of a million men were classified as draft evaders— people who refused to be drafted, or used trick-ery or self-mutilation to avoid the draft.

The Socialist Party had been against entering the war from the start. The day after Congress declared war, the Socialists held an emergency meeting and called the declaration "a crime

WE MOURN
THE LOSS
OF OUR
COMRADES

Francisco Ferrer Association
of Jacksonville.

16877

Elizabeth Gurley Flynn
addressing crowd, 1914.

against the people of the United States." Some
well-known Socialists, including writers
Upton Sinclair and Jack London, supported
the war after the United States entered it.
Most Socialists, though, continued to oppose
the war. Some paid a heavy price for expressing
their opinions.

In Oklahoma, the Industrial Workers of the
World (IWW) planned a march on Washington
for people from across the country who objected
to the draft. Before the march, union members
were arrested. Four hunded and fifty people
accused of rebellion were put in the state peni-
tentiary. Across the country in Boston, eight
thousand Socialists and unionists at an antiwar
march were attacked by soldiers and sailors, acting on their officers' orders.

Just before the United States declared war, the
IWW newspaper had said, "Capitalists of America,
we will fight against you, not for you!" Now the war
gave the government its chance to destroy the radical union. In September 1917, Department of
Justice agents raided forty-eight IWW meeting halls
across the country, seizing letters and literature.

The following April, 101 leaders of the union

went on trial for opposing the draft and encouraging soldiers to desert. One of them told the court:

> You ask me why the IWW is not patriotic to the United States. If you were a bum without a blanket; if you had left your wife and kids when you went west for a job, and had never located them since; if your job had never kept you long enough in a place to qualify you to vote; if every person who represented law and order and the nation beat you up . . . how in hell do you expect a man to be patriotic? This war is a business man's war. . . .

All of the IWW prisoners were found guilty. Bill Haywood and other key leaders were sentenced to twenty years in prison; the rest received shorter sentences. Haywood fled to Russia, where a socialist revolution was taking place. The IWW in the United States was shattered.

After the Fighting

THE WAR ENDED IN NOVEMBER 1918. Fifty thousand American soldiers had died. But when the war was over, the Establishment—the

political and capitalist elites that ran the nation—
still feared socialism. The conflict between
Democrats and Republicans was less important
than the threat of radical change.

The government had a new tool to fight that
threat. Near the end of the war, Congress had
passed a law that let the government deport any
alien who opposed organized government or who
approved of the destruction of property. (An alien
was an immigrant who was not a U.S. citizen.
Deporting meant removing from the country.) In
1919 and 1920 the government rounded up more
than four thousand aliens, including anarchist
Emma Goldman. Eventually, they were deported
to their birth countries.

An anarchist named Andrea Salsedo was held
for two months in FBI offices in New York City.
He wasn't allowed to contact family, friends, or
lawyers. Then his crushed body was found on the
pavement. The FBI said he had committed suicide
by jumping from a window.

Two Boston anarchists, friends of Salsedo,
learned of his death and began carrying guns. They
were arrested and charged with a holdup and murder that had happened two weeks earlier. Their

names were Nicola Sacco and Bartolomeo Vanzetti.

Sacco and Vanzetti were found guilty. They
spent seven years in jail while their cases were
appealed to higher courts. All over the world, people became involved in the case. Many believed
that Sacco and Vanzetti had been found guilty just
because they were anarchists and foreigners—the
trial record and other circumstances make it look
as though this was true. In August 1927 the two
men were executed.

The Establishment had tried to silence the
voices of dissent. Reforms had been made. War
had been used to promote patriotism and crush
criticism. The courts and jails had made it clear
that certain ideas, certain kinds of resistance, were
not permitted. But still, even from the prison cells,
the message was going out: in the United States, a
society that was supposed to be without classes,
the class war was going on.

CHAPTER FIFTEEN

HARD TIMES

IT WAS FEBRUARY 1919. THE WAR HAD
ended in Europe just a few months before. The
world was in the grip of an influenza epidemic
that would claim half a million American lives and
millions more worldwide. In the United States,
the leaders of the Industrial Workers of the World
were in jail—but their dream was about to become
a reality in Seattle, Washington.

Strikes by a single union or a single kind of worker
could get results. But the IWW felt that a general
strike, with all kinds of workers walking off their jobs
together, would make a stronger statement. In
Seattle, after shipyard workers went on strike for
higher wages, more than a hundred other unions
voted to strike as well. A walkout of a hundred thousand working people brought the city to a halt.

(*left, detail*)
A caravan of strike
pickets patrol
a road south
of Tulare, 1933.

The strikers kept vital services going. Fire fighters stayed on the job, and milk stations were set up in neighborhoods to deliver milk to families. The strike lasted for five days and was peaceful. In fact, during those five days, the city had less crime than usual. But after the strike, the authorities raided Socialist Party headquarters. Thirty-nine members of the IWW went to jail as "ring-leaders of anarchy."

Why did the government react this way to the strike? Maybe the answer lies in a statement by Seattle's mayor:

> The general strike, as practiced in Seattle, is of itself the weapon of revolution, all the more dangerous because quiet. To succeed, it must suspend everything; stop the entire life stream of a community. . . . That is to say, it puts the government out of operation.

The general strike made the authorities feel powerless. It seemed to threaten the whole economic and political system of society.

Seattle's general strike was just one of many large strikes across the United States in 1919. These labor actions were part of a wave of rebellions around the world. From the Communist revolution against royal rule in Russia to a strike by railway workers in England, ordinary people were rising up, making their voices heard, and bringing about change. A writer for *The Nation* magazine said, "The common man . . . losing faith in the old leadership, has experienced a new . . . self-confidence. . . ."

The Truth about the Twenties

When the 1920s started, the wave of rebellion had died down in the United States. The IWW was destroyed. The Socialist Party was falling apart. Strikes were beaten down by force. The economy was doing just well enough for just enough people to prevent mass rebellion.

The 1920s are sometimes called the Roaring Twenties, or the Jazz Age—a time of prosperity and fun. There was some truth to that picture. Unemployment was down, and the general level of workers' wages went up. People could buy new gadgets such as automobiles, radios, and refrigerators. Millions of people were not doing badly.

But most of the wealth was in the hands of a few people at the top of society's pyramid. At the

bottom of the pyramid were the black and white tenant farmers living in poverty in the countryside, and the immigrant families in the cities who could not find work, or could not earn enough for basic needs. In New York City alone, 2 million people lived in tenement buildings that were known to be unsafe because of fire danger.

Fourteen million immigrants had come to the United States between 1900 and 1920. In 1924, Congress passed an immigration law that put an end to this flood. The new law favored the immigration of white people from English and German backgrounds. Immigration of Southern Europeans, Slavs, and Jews was severely limited, and only a hundred people a year could come from China or any African country.

Racial hatred and violence were everywhere. The Ku Klux Klan came back in the 1920s, and it spread into the North. By 1924 it had 4.5 million members.

After a long struggle, women had finally won the right to vote in national elections in 1920. Yet voting was still an upper-class and middle-class activity, and the new women voters favored the same old political parties as other voters.

(left)
A caravan of strike pickets patrol a road south of Tulare, 1933.

Labor unrest may have calmed for a time, but it had not faded away. With the Socialist Party weakened, a Communist Party formed in the United States. Communists were involved in many labor struggles, including huge textile strikes in Tennessee and the Carolinas in early 1929.

The Great Depression

DURING THE 1920S, THE AMERICAN ECONOMY seemed healthy—even booming. Prices for stocks, which are shares of ownership in corporations, rose higher than ever. Many people thought that the value of stocks would just keep going up. They invested their money by buying stocks, and they borrowed money from banks to buy still more stocks. The banks invested in stocks, too, using the money that customers had deposited.

In 1929 the boom ended with a crash. When the value of stocks started to drop, people started selling their stocks in a panic. This made the value drop even faster. Banks could not collect the loans that people had taken to buy stocks, and people could not withdraw their money from banks that had invested it and lost it. Both the stock market and the banking system spiraled swiftly downward, triggering a severe crisis in the economy. The United States had entered the Great Depression.

The economy was stunned, barely moving. More than five thousand banks closed. Thousands of businesses closed, too. Businesses that managed to stay open laid off some workers and cut the wages of other workers, again and again. By 1933 perhaps as many as 15 million people were out of work. A quarter to a third of the nation's workforce could not find jobs.

There were millions of tons of food in the country, but it was not profitable to ship it or sell it, so people went hungry. Warehouses were full of clothing and other products, but people couldn't afford to buy them. Houses stayed empty because no one had the money to buy or rent them. People who failed to pay rent were kicked out of their homes. They lived in "Hoovervilles," communities of shacks built on garbage dumps. The name comes from President Herbert Hoover, who had said just before the crash, "We in America today

CHILD WORKERS

BY THE BEGINNING OF THE SECOND DECADE OF
the twentieth century, over 2 million American children below the age of sixteen were among
America's full-time workers, many toiling twelve
or thirteen hours a day. Canneries in the gulf
towns of Mississippi employed children as young
as three years old, shucking oysters and peeling
shrimp. Small girls toiled in cotton mills in North
Carolina, spinning cotton at giant, noisy
machines. Only whites were hired for mill work,
and entire families left their farms to work in the
mills. In Pennsylvania, thousands of fourteen-
and fifteen-year-old boys were employed legally in
the mines—as miners, coal breakers, or slate
pickers—and thousands more nine- and ten-year-
olds were employed illegally, many of them suffering from chronic coughs from the coal dust.

These children weren't apprentices learning a trade, just some of the cheapest and hardest workers around.

The National Child Labor Committee was founded in 1904 to reduce and regulate childhood labor, but it wasn't until the Great Depression of the 1930s—a period of such high unemployment that adults now competed with children for the worst paying jobs—that resistance to the committee's effort, by those who were profiting from child labor, finally lessened. In 1938, President Franklin Delano Roosevelt signed the Fair Labor Standards Act, which established a minimum wage and a maximum number of daily hours for workers, and which also restricted child labor and prohibited children from working in mines or factories. In 1949, Congress amended the law to include other types of

businesses, and also restricted working hours for children under sixteen to exclude school hours.

In 1913, the National Child Labor Committee composed a "Declaration of Dependence" by and on behalf of the children of America:

Declaration of Dependence

WHEREAS, We, Children of America, are declared to have been born free and equal, and

WHEREAS, We are yet in bondage in this land of the free; are forced to toil the long day or the long night, with no control over the conditions of labor, as to health or safety or hours or wages, and with no right to the rewards of our service, therefore be it

RESOLVED, I — That childhood is endowed with certain inherent and inalienable rights, among which are freedom from toil for daily bread; the right to

play and to dream; the right to the normal sleep of the night season; the right to an education, that we may have equality of opportunity for developing all that there is in us of mind and heart.

RESOLVED, II — That we declare ourselves to be helpless and dependent; that we are and of right ought to be dependent, and that we hereby present the appeal of our helplessness that we may be protected in the enjoyment of the rights of childhood.

RESOLVED, III — That we demand the restoration of our rights by the abolition of child labor in America.

Source: Freedman, Russell. *Kids at Work: Lewis Hine and the Crusade Against Child Labor.* New York: Scholastic, 1994.

RARIG'S KID DOESN'T STARVE WHY SHOULD WE?
WHY CAN'T Y
GIVE MY DA
A JOB?

are nearer to the final triumph over poverty than ever before in the history of any land."

One of the few politicians who had spoken out for the poor during the 1920s was Fiorello La Guardia, a congressman from a district of poor immigrants in East Harlem. After the Depression started, he received a letter from a tenement dweller there:

> You know my condition is bad. I used to get pension from the government and they stopped it. It is now nearly seven months I am out of work. I hope you will try to do something for me. . . . I have four children who are in need of clothes and food. . . . My daughter who is eight is very ill and not recovering. My rent is due two months and I am afraid of being put out.

Hard times made people desperate. In *The Grapes of Wrath*, a novel about the misery of Oklahoma farmers forced off their land, author John Steinbeck called the new homeless people "dangerous." A spirit of rebellion was growing in the land.

In Detroit, five hundred men rioted when they were turned out of public housing because they couldn't afford to pay for it. In Chicago, five hundred schoolchildren, "most with haggard faces and in tattered clothes," marched through down-

(left) Children carry picket signs at a demonstration for the Workers Alliance during the Great Depression, 1937.

town to demand food from the school system. In New York City, several hundred jobless people surrounded a restaurant, demanding to be fed without charge. In Seattle, an army of the unemployed seized a public building and held it for two days.

Men who had fought in the First World War now found themselves out of work and out of money. Some held certificates from the government that were to be paid off in the future—but they needed the money now. And so war veterans began to move toward Washington, D.C., from all over the country. They came in broken-down old autos, or by stealing rides on trains, or by hitchhiking.

More than twenty thousand came. They camped across from the Capitol, in shelters made of old boxes and newspapers. President Hoover ordered the army to get rid of them. General Douglas A. MacArthur, with the help of officers such as Dwight D. Eisenhower and George S. Patton, used tanks, tear gas, and fires to break up the camp. When it was over, two veterans had been shot to death, a boy was partially blinded, two police had fractured skulls, and a thousand veterans were injured by gas.

Struggling to Survive

IN THE ELECTION OF 1932, HOOVER LOST TO the Democratic candidate, Franklin D. Roosevelt, who launched a series of reform laws that came to be called the New Deal. These reforms went far beyond earlier changes. They attempted to reorganize capitalism.

The first major law was the National Recovery Act (NRA). It took control of the economy by making government, management, and labor agree on such things as prices, wages, and competition. From the start, the NRA was controlled by big business, but it did give some benefits to working people. Two years later, though, the Supreme Court declared the NRA unconstitutional because it gave too much power to the president.

Other reforms continued. One was the Tennessee Valley Authority (TVA), which built a government-owned system of dams and power plants. The TVA provided jobs and lower electricity rates. Its critics called it "socialistic," and they were right in some ways.

The New Deal had two goals. The first was to overcome the Depression and make the economy more stable. The second was to give enough help to the lower classes to keep rebellion from turning into a real revolution.

The rebellion was real when Roosevelt took office. All across the country, people were not waiting for the government to help them. They were helping themselves.

In Detroit and Chicago, when police removed the furniture of people who had been evicted from their apartments for not paying rent, crowds gathered on the sidewalk to carry the furniture back inside. In Seattle, fishermen, fruit pickers, and woodchoppers traded with each other for supplies they needed. Often labor unions helped make these self-help arrangements.

Self-help sprouted in the coal mines of Pennsylvania. Teams of unemployed miners dug small mines on company property, hauled the coal to the cities, and sold it for less than the companies charged. When the authorities tried to halt the trade in "bootleg" coal, local juries would not convict the miners, and local jailors would not imprison them. These were simple actions, but they had revolutionary possibilities. Working people were discovering a powerful truth: that they could meet their own needs. Soon, though, a wave of large-scale labor outbursts caused the government to get involved in the labor movement.

It began with strikes by West Coast longshoremen—workers who loaded and unloaded cargo ships. They struck, tying up two thousand miles of coastline. A general strike in San Francisco followed, then another in Minneapolis, and then the biggest strike of all: 325,000 textile workers in the South.

New unions formed among workers who had never been organized. Black farmers were hit very hard by the Depression. Some were attracted to the strangers who started showing up, suggesting that they unionize. Hosea Hudson, a black man from rural Georgia who had worked the land from the age of ten, joined the Communist Party and helped organize unemployed blacks in Birmingham, Alabama. Later he recalled those years of activism:

> Block committees would meet every week, had a regular meeting. We talked about the welfare question, what was happening, we read the *Daily Worker* and the *Southern Worker* to see what was going on about unemployed relief. ... We kept it up, we was on top, so people always wanted to come cause we had something different to tell them each time.

In many strikes, the decision to act came from the rank and file—the ordinary members—not from the union leaders. Rubber workers in Akron, Ohio, came up with a new kind of strike called a sit-down. Instead of leaving the plant and marching outside, they remained inside and did not work.

The longest sit-down strike took place among auto workers in Michigan. Starting in December 1936, for forty days there was a community of two thousand strikers. "It was like war," one of them said. "The guys with me became my buddies." Committees organized recreation, classes, postal service, and sanitation. A restaurant owner across the street prepared three meals a day. Armed workers circled the plant outside, fighting off a police attack. Finally the strikers and management agreed to a six-month contract, and the strike ended.

To bring a halt to this type of labor unrest, the government set up the National Labor Relations Board (NLRB). The NLRB would recognize the legal status of unions, listen to their complaints, and settle some of their issues. At the same time, the unions themselves were trying to become more influential, even respectable. Leaders of the major associations, the American Federation of Labor

(AFL) and the Congress of Industrial Organizations (CIO), wanted to keep strikes to a minimum. They began channeling workers' rebellious energy into things like contract talks and meetings.

Some historians of the labor movement claim that workers won most during the early years of rank-and-file uprisings, before unions were recognized and well organized. While the AFL and the CIO each had more than 6 million members by 1945, their power was less than it had been before. Gains from the use of strikes kept getting whittled down. The NLRB leaned more toward the side of management than toward labor, the Supreme Court ruled that sit-down strikes were illegal, and state governments passed laws that made striking and picketing more difficult.

By the late 1930s, the worst of the Depression had passed for some people. New laws passed in 1938 limited the work week to forty hours and outlawed child labor. The Social Security Act gave retirement benefits and unemployment insurance (but not to everyone—farmers, for example, were left out). There was a new minimum wage, and the government built some housing projects. These measures didn't help everyone who needed help, but they made people feel that something was being done.

Black people gained little from the New Deal. Many worked as tenant farmers, farm laborers, domestic workers, and migrants. They did not qualify for the minimum wage or unemployment insurance. Blacks suffered job discrimination— they were the last to be hired and the first to be fired. Lynchings continued, and so did less violent forms of racial prejudice.

In the mid-1930s a young black poet named Langston Hughes gave voice to frustration and hope in a poem called "Let America Be America Again":

... I am the poor white, fooled and pushed apart,

I am the Negro bearing slavery's scars.

I am the red man driven from the land,

I am the immigrant clutching the hope I seek—

And finding only the same old stupid plan.

Of dog eat dog, of mighty crush the weak. ...

O, let America be America again—

The land that never has been yet—

The New Deal had brought an exciting flowering of the arts, such as had never happened before in American history. Federal money was used to pay thousands of writers, artists, musicians, and photographers for creative projects. Working-class audiences saw plays and heard symphonies for the first time. But by 1939, the arts programs ended. The country was more stable, and the New Deal was over.

Capitalism had not changed. The rich still controlled the nation's wealth, as well as its laws, courts, police, newspapers, churches, and colleges. Enough help had been given to make Roosevelt a hero to millions, but the system that had brought the Great Depression remained in place.

Elsewhere in the world, war was brewing. German leader Adolf Hitler was on the march in Europe. Across the Pacific, Japan was invading China. For the United States, war was not far off.

CHAPTER SIXTEEN

WORLD WAR II
AND THE COLD WAR

WORLD WAR I WAS ONLY ABOUT TWENTY YEARS
in the past when another huge war began in
Europe. Some call it the most popular war the
United States ever fought. Eighteen million
Americans served in the armed forces, and 25 million gave money from their paychecks to support
the war.

It was a war against evil—the evil of Germany's
Nazi Party, led by Adolf Hitler. After coming to
power in Germany, the Nazis began attacking Jews
and members of other minorities. Hitler's
Germany became a war machine, determined to
conquer other countries. For the United States to
step forward to defend those helpless people and
countries matched the image of the nation in
American schoolbooks, but is that what really

happened? Are there other ways to look at World War II, questions that did not get asked in the patriotic excitement of the time?

America at War

THE WAR STARTED IN 1939 AFTER GERMANY attacked Poland. Germany had already taken over Austria and Czechoslovakia. Later the Germans would invade and occupy France. Italy had already invaded the African nation of Ethiopia. Together with some smaller powers, Germany and Italy formed one side in the conflict. They were known as the Axis. Against them stood the Allies. Britain was one of the main Allied powers. Another was Russia, which now had a Communist government and had been renamed the Soviet Union.

The other side of the world was at war, too. Japan had attacked China and was moving toward Southeast Asia, which had rich resources of tin, rubber, and oil.

What did the United States do while this was happening? Hitler's attacks on the Jews did not bring the United States into the war. Neither did Germany's invasions of other countries, although President Franklin D. Roosevelt sent American aid to Britain. Neither did Japan's attack on China.

The United States entered the war after the Japanese attacked an American naval base at Pearl Harbor, Hawaii, on December 7, 1941. This strike at a link in the American Pacific empire was the reason the United States joined the fight, in Europe as well as Asia.

Once the United States had joined with England and Russia in the war, what were its goals? Was America fighting for humanitarian reasons or for power and profit? Was it fighting to end the control of some nations by others—or to make sure that the controlling nations were friends of the United States?

Noble statements about the government's goals didn't always match the things that were said privately. In August of 1941, Roosevelt and the British prime minister, Winston Churchill, announced their goals for the world after the war. They said that they respected "the right of all peoples to choose the form of government under which they will live." But two weeks earlier, a top U.S. government official had quietly promised the French government that France would regain its empire of overseas territories after the war.

Italy had bombed cities when it invaded Ethiopia. German planes had dropped bombs on cities in the Netherlands and England. These were not attacks on military targets. They were attacks on the civilian population. Roosevelt had called them "inhuman barbarism that has profoundly shocked the conscience of humanity."

But the German bombings were very small compared with British and American bombings of German cities. Raids of a thousand planes or more targeted cities. They did not even pretend to be seeking only military targets. The climax of the Allied terror bombing was an attack on the German city Dresden. More than a hundred thousand people died in a firestorm started by the bombs.

During the war, newspaper headlines were full of battles and troop movements. Behind the headlines, American diplomats and businessmen worked hard to make sure that when the war ended American economic power would be second to none in the world. At the time, the poet Archibald MacLeish was an assistant secretary of state. He wrote:

> As things are now going, the peace we will make, the peace we seem to be making, will be a peace of oil, a peace of gold, a peace of shipping, a peace, in brief . . . without moral purpose or human interest. . . .

Many people thought that the reason for the war against the Axis was to end the terrible situation of Jews in German-occupied Europe. But that wasn't a chief concern of Roosevelt. While Jews were being put in concentration camps, and Germany was getting ready to begin exterminating 6 million Jews (and millions of other minorities and dissidents) in what has come to be called the Holocaust, Roosevelt failed to take steps to save some of those doomed lives. He left it to the U.S. State Department, which did nothing.

Hitler claimed that the white German race—he called it Aryan or Nordic—was superior to others. Was the war being fought to show that his ideas of racial superiority were wrong? American blacks might not have thought so. The nation's armed forces were segregated by race. Even the blood

banks that saved thousands of lives kept blood from white people apart from blood donated by black people. A black doctor named Charles Drew had invented the blood-bank system, but when he tried to end blood segregation, he was fired.

Blacks in the United States knew the reality of racial prejudice, and sometimes racial violence, in everyday life. In 1943 an African American newspaper printed a poem about the thoughts of a black man drafted into the army:

Dear Lord, today

I go to war:

To fight, to die,

Tell me what for?

Dear Lord, I'll fight,

I do not fear,

Germans or Japs;

My fears are here.

America!

In the way it treated Japanese Americans during the war, the United States came close to the brutal, racist oppression that it was supposed to be fighting against. After the attack on Pearl Harbor, anti-Japanese feeling was strong in the government. One congressman said, "I'm for catching every

(*left*)
Japanese American citizens on their way to an internment camp flash "victory" signs, 1942.

Japanese in America, Alaska and Hawaii now and putting them in concentration camps. . . . Let's get rid of them!"

In 1942 Roosevelt gave the army the power to arrest every Japanese American on the West Coast—eleven thousand men, women, and children. Three-fourths of them had been born in the United States and were U.S. citizens. The others, born in Japan, could not become U.S. citizens because American law made that impossible.

The Japanese were taken from their homes and carried to camps in remote regions of the interior. There they were kept in prison conditions. They remained in those camps for more than three years.

The war in Europe ended in May 1945 when a beaten Germany surrendered to the Allies. By August of that year, Japan also was in desperate shape and ready to surrender. But there was one problem. The Japanese emperor was a holy figure to many of his people, and Japan wanted to keep him in place after a surrender. If the United States had agreed, Japan would have stopped the war. But the United States refused, and the fighting continued. (After the war, the United States allowed the emperor to remain anyway.)

Japan did give up—after the United States dropped atomic bombs on the cities of Hiroshima and Nagasaki in August of 1945. The bombs killed as many as 150,000 people and left countless others to die slowly of radiation poisoning. It was the first use of these deadly new weapons in war.

Why would the United States not take the small step of allowing Japan to keep its emperor if that would have ended the war without the use of atomic weapons? Was it because too much money and work had gone into the atomic bomb not to use it? Or was it because the United States wanted to end the war before the Soviet Union could enter the fight against Japan, as it planned to do? If Japan surrendered to the Soviet Union, then the Russians, not the Americans, would control postwar Japan.

Whatever the real reasons for dropping atomic bombs on Japan, at least the war was over. Or was it?

The War at Home

THE WAR YEARS WERE A PATRIOTIC TIME IN
the United States. The country seemed totally dedicated to winning the war. There was no organized
antiwar movement. Only one socialist group came
out firmly against the war. It was the Socialist
Workers Party. In 1943 eighteen of its members
went to jail under a law that made it a crime to
join any group that called for "the overthrow of
government by force and violence."

Still, many people thought the war was wrong.
About 350,000 of them avoided the draft. More
than forty thousand flatly refused to fight.

The nation's two biggest groups of labor
unions, the AFL and the CIO, had pledged not to
go out on strike during the war. Yet there were
more strikes during wartime than at any other
time in American history. In 1944 alone, more
than a million workers walked off their jobs in
mines, steel mills, and manfuacturing plants.
Many were angry that their wages stayed the same
while the companies that made weapons and
other war materials were earning huge profits.

By the end of the war, things seemed better to a
lot of people. The war had brought big corporate

(*left*)
Ethel and Julius
Rosenberg leaving
New York City
Federal Court after
arraignment, 1950.

profits, but it also had brought higher prices for farm crops, wage increases for some workers, and enough prosperity for enough people to keep them from becoming rebellious. It was an old lesson learned by governments—war solves the problem of controlling the citizens. The president of the General Electric Corporation suggested that business and the military should create "a permanent wartime economy."

That's just what happened. The public was tired of war, but its new president, Harry S. Truman, built a mood of crisis that came to be called the Cold War. In the Cold War, America's enemy was the Communist country that had been its ally in World War II, the Soviet Union.

New Wars

THE RIVALRY WITH THE SOVIET UNION WAS real. The former Russia was making an amazing comeback from the war. It was rebuilding its economy and regaining military strength. But the Truman administration presented the Soviet Union as something worse than a rival. The Soviet Union, and communism itself, were seen as immediate threats.

The U.S. government encouraged fear of communism. Any communism-related revolutionary movement in Europe or Asia was made to look as if the Soviets were taking over more of the world. When Communist-led revolutionaries gained control of the Chinese government in 1949, China became the world's most populous Communist nation—and added fuel to Americans' fear.

The growing fear of Soviet power and communism in general led to a big increase in U.S. military spending. It also led to new political partnerships between conservatives and liberals.

In politics, a conservative is someone who wants to preserve the existing order of society, government, and the economy. Conservatives tend to place a high value on security, stability, and established institutions. A liberal is someone who supports progress, often through change. If the changes are extreme, a liberal may be called a radical. Liberals tend to place a high value on individual rights, civil liberties, and direct participation in government. (The liberal position has come to be called the Left, while the conservative position is the Right.)

The United States wanted to unite conservatives and liberals, Republicans and Democrats, in support of the Cold War and the fight against communism. Events in the Asian nation of Korea helped President Truman get that support.

After World War II, Korea had been freed from Japanese control and divided into two countries. North Korea was a socialist dictatorship, part of the Soviet Union's sphere of influence. South Korea was a conservative dictatorship in the American sphere of influence. In 1950 North Korea invaded South Korea. The United Nations— which had been created during the war and was dominated by the United States—asked its member nations to help South Korea. Truman sent U.S. forces, and the United Nations army became the American army.

When American forces pushed all the way through North Korea to the Chinese border, China entered the fighting on the side of North Korea. In three years, the war killed as many as 2 million Koreans and reduced North and South Korea to

ruins. Yet when the fighting ended in 1953, the boundary between the two Koreas was where it had been before.

If the Korean War changed little in Korea, it had an effect in the United States. It caused many liberals to join with conservatives in supporting the president, the war, and the military economy. This meant trouble for radical critics who stayed outside the circle of agreement.

The Left had become a force during the Depression and the war. The Communist Party probably never had more than about a hundred thousand members, but it had influence in the labor unions, in the arts, and among Americans who had seen the failure of capitalism in the 1930s. To make capitalism more secure, to build support for an American victory over Communist foes, the nation's established powers of government and business had to weaken the Left. They did so by attacking communism. The hunt for Reds, as Communists were called, soon filled American life.

In 1947 Truman launched a program to search out "disloyal persons" in the U.S. government. In the next five years, more than 6.5 million government employees were investigated. In their book

The Fifties, historians Douglas Miller and Marion Nowack described the results:

> Not a single case of espionage was uncovered, though about 500 persons were dismissed in dubious cases of "questionable loyalty." All of this was conducted with secret evidence, secret and often paid informers, and neither judge nor jury. . . . A conservative and fearful reaction coursed the country. Americans became convinced of the need for absolute security and the preservation of the established order.

World events built support for this anti-Communist crusade. Communist parties came to power in places like Czechoslovakia and China. Revolutionary movements flared up in Asia and Africa when colonial peoples demanded independence from European powers. These events were presented to the American public as signs of a worldwide Communist plot.

Senator Joseph McCarthy of Wisconsin began his own crusade to find Communist traitors in the country's State Department and the military. He found nothing and eventually became an embarrassment to the government. Other political leaders, however, had their own ideas for crushing dissent. Liberal senators Hubert Humphrey

and Herbert Lehman suggested that suspected Communists and traitors could be held without trial in concentration camps. The camps were set up, ready for use.

The government also made lists of hundreds of organizations it considered suspicious. Anyone who joined these groups, or even seemed sympathetic to them, could be investigated. Leaders of the Communist Party were jailed.

In 1950 the government charged Julius and Ethel Rosenberg, known to be connected with the Communist Party, with giving atomic secrets to the Soviets. Although the evidence against the Rosenbergs was weak, they were executed as spies. Later investigations proved that the case was deeply flawed. But at the time, everything from movies and comic strips to history lessons and newspapers urged Americans to fight communism.

By 1960, the Establishment seemed to have succeeded in weakening the Left. The Communist-radical upsurge of the New Deal and the wartime years had been broken up. The Cold War kept the country in a permanent war economy. There were big pockets of poverty, but enough people were making enough money to keep things quiet. Everything seemed under control. And then, in the 1960s, rebellions exploded in every area of American life.

CHAPTER SEVENTEEN

BLACK REVOLT
AND CIVIL RIGHTS

THE BLACK REVOLT OF THE 1950S AND 1960S
surprised white America, but it shouldn't have.
When people are oppressed, memory is the one
thing that can't be taken away from them. For people with memories of oppression, revolt is always
just an inch below the surface.

Blacks in the United States had the memory of
slavery. Beyond that, they lived with the daily reali-
ties of lynching, insults, and segregation. As the
twentieth century went on, they found new ways
to resist.

Fighting Back

In the 1920s a black poet named Claude McKay wrote these lines:

> If we must die, let it not be like hogs
>
> Hunted and penned in an inglorious spot....
>
> Like men we'll face the murderous cowardly pack,
>
> Pressed to the wall, dying, but fighting back!

McKay's words were entered into the *Congressional Record* as an example of the dangerous new ideas of young black men. It must have seemed dangerous to the nation's leaders that blacks spoke of fighting back.

Some blacks fought the system by joining the Communist Party. The Communists had been active in the South. They had helped defend the "Scottsboro Boys," nine young black men falsely accused of rape in Alabama. Among the well-known African Americans connected to the Communist Party were the scholar W. E. B. DuBois and the actor and singer Paul Robeson.

During the 1930s the Communists organized committees to seek help for the needy. An organizer named Angelo Herndon was arrested and charged with promoting revolution. He recalled his trial:

They questioned me in great detail. Did I believe that the bosses and government ought to pay insurance to unemployed workers? That Negroes should have complete equality with white people? Did I feel that the working-class could run the mills and mines and government? That it wasn't necessary to have bosses at all? I told them I believed all of that—and more. . . .

Herndon spent five years in prison before the Supreme Court ruled that the law he had been arrested for breaking was unconstitutional. To the Establishment, men like Herndon were signs of a frightening new mood among blacks. That mood was militancy—a willingness to fight.

Toward Civil Rights

PRESIDENT HARRY TRUMAN KNEW THAT THE United States had to do something about race for two reasons. One reason was to calm the frustrated black people of the United States. The other reason had to do with America's image in the world.

Nonwhite people around the world were accusing the United States of being a racist society. America's Cold War with the Soviet Union was on, and each side wanted to gain influence around the globe. But the poor civil rights record of the United States could hold it back in world politics.

Truman created a Committee on Civil Rights in 1946. The committee recommended laws against lynching and against racial discrimination in jobs and voting. Congress took no action. However, Truman did order the armed forces to desegregate, or end racial separation. It took ten years, but the military was finally integrated, with blacks and whites no longer separated.

The nation's public schools remained segregated until courageous southern blacks took on the Supreme Court in a series of lawsuits. In 1954, in a decision called *Brown v. Board of Education,* the Court ordered the nation's public schools to stop the "separate but equal" treatment of children separated by race. The Court's big decision sent a message around the world—the U.S. government had outlawed segregation. But change came slowly. Ten years later, more than three-fourths of the school districts in the South were still segregated.

(left)
Rosa Parks speaks with an interviewer as she arrives at court, 1956.

CLAUDETTE COLVIN

AROUND 4:00 P.M. ON MARCH 2, 1955—
nine months before forty-two-year-old Rosa Parks
did it—fifteen-year-old Claudette Colvin asserted
her constitutional right to her seat on a segregated bus in Montgomery, Alabama, helping to
jump-start the Civil Rights Movement.
Confronting jeers, shoves, and insults from the
white people around her and the two policemen
who arrested her, she was charged with violating
the segregation law, disorderly conduct, and
"assaulting" the arresting officers.

Here she tells the story in her own words:

*On March 2, 1955, I got on the bus in front of Dexter
Avenue Church. I went to the middle. No white people
were on the bus at that time. It was mostly schoolchild-*

ren. I wasn't thinking about anything in particular. I think I had just finished eating a candy bar. Then the bus began to fill up. White people got on and began to stare at me. The bus motorman asked me to get up. We were getting into the square where all the buses take their routes in either direction. A colored lady got on, and she was pregnant. I was sitting next to the window. The seat next to me was the only seat unoccupied. She didn't realize what was going on. She didn't know that the bus driver had asked me to get up. She just saw the empty seat and sat next to me. A white lady was sitting across the aisle from me, and it was against the law for you to sit in the same aisle with a white person.

The bus driver looked back through the rearview mirror and again told me to get up. I didn't. I knew he

was talking to me. He said, "Hey, get up!" I didn't say anything. When I didn't get up, he didn't move the bus. He said before he'd drive on, I'd have to get up. People were saying, "Why don't you get up? Why don't you get up?" One girl said, "She knows she has to get up." Then another girl said, "She doesn't have to. Only one thing you have to do is stay black and die."

The white people were complaining. The driver stopped the bus and said, "This can't go on." Then he got up and said, "I'm going to call the cops." First a traffic patrolman came on the bus and he asked, "Are any of you gentleman enough to get up and give this pregnant lady your seat?" There were two black men in the back of the bus who were sanitation workers. They got up, and the pregnant lady went and sat in the back. That left me still sitting by the window.

I remained there, and the traffic patrolman said, "Aren't you going to get up?"

I said, "No. I do not have to get up. I paid my fare, so I do not have to get up. It's my constitutional right to sit here just as much as that lady. It's my constitutional right!"

Source: Levine, Ellen. *Freedom's Children: Young Civil Rights Activists Tell Their Own Stories.* New York: Penguin Putnam / Puffin, 1993.

For blacks, progress wasn't fast enough. In the early 1960s black people rose in rebellion all over the South. By the late 1960s there were wild uprisings in a hundred northern cities, too. What triggered this angry revolt?

A forty-three-year-old black woman named Rosa Parks sat down one day in the "white" section of a city bus. She had long been active in the NAACP, which was determined to challenge segregated seating on Montgomery buses. She was arrested.

Montgomery's blacks called a mass meeting. They boycotted the city buses, refusing to ride. Instead, they walked or organized car pools. The city was losing a lot of income from bus fares. It arrested a hundred of the boycott leaders.

White segregationists turned to violence. They exploded bombs in four black churches. They fired a shotgun through the front door of the home of Dr. Martin Luther King Jr., a minister who helped lead the boycott. But the black people of Montgomery kept up the boycott, and in November 1956 the Supreme Court made segregation on local bus lines illegal.

Martin Luther King Preaches Nonviolence

AT A MEETING DURING THE BOYCOTT, MARTIN
Luther King showed the gift of speech making that
would soon inspire millions of people to work for
racial justice. He said:

> We have known humiliation, we have known abusive
> language, we have been plunged into the abyss of
> oppression. And we decided to raise up only with the
> weapon of protest. . . . We must use the weapon of love.
> We must have compassion and understanding for
> those who hate us.

King called on African Americans to practice
nonviolence—to seek justice without doing harm
to others. This message won him followers among
whites as well as blacks. Yet some blacks thought
that King's message was too simple. Some of
those who oppressed them, they believed, would
have to be bitterly fought.

Still, in the years after the Montgomery bus
boycott, southern blacks stressed nonviolence.
One nonviolent movement started in 1960, when
four first-year students at an African American
college in North Carolina decided to sit down at a
drugstore lunch counter where only whites ate.
The store wouldn't serve them, but they did not

Reverend Martin Luther King Jr. waves to participants in the Civil Rights Movement's March on Washington, 1963.

leave. They came back, joined by others, day after day, to sit at the counter.

Sit-ins spread to other southern cities. The sit-inners experienced violence. But they inspired more than fifty thousand people—mostly blacks, some whites—to join demonstrations in a hundred cities. By the end of 1960, lunch counters were open to blacks in many places.

Freedom Riders and the Mississippi Summer

FOR A LONG TIME, IT HAD BEEN ILLEGAL TO segregate people by race during long-distance travel. But the federal government had never enforced the law in the South, where blacks and whites were still kept apart on interstate buses. In the spring of 1961, a group of black and white protestors set out to change that.

These Freedom Riders got on a bus in Washington, D.C., bound for New Orleans. They never reached New Orleans. Riders were beaten in South Carolina. A bus was set on fire in Alabama.

Segregationists attacked the Riders with fists and iron bars. The southern police did nothing. Neither did the federal government, even though FBI agents watched the violence.

Young people who had taken part in the sit-ins formed the Student Nonviolent Coordinating Committee (SNCC). They organized another group of Freedom Riders, who were attacked by a mob of whites and later arrested. By this time the Freedom Riders were in the news all over the world.

Young black children joined demonstrations across the South. In Albany, Georgia, a small town where the atmosphere of slavery lingered, blacks held marches and mass meetings. After arresting protestors, the police chief took their names. One protestor was a boy about nine years old. "What's your name?" the police chief asked. The boy looked straight at him and answered, "Freedom, Freedom." A new generation was learning how to demand its rights.

The SNCC and other civil rights groups worked in Mississippi to register blacks for voting and to organize protests against racial injustice. They called on young people from other parts of the country to help, to come south for a "Mississippi

Summer." Facing increasing violence and danger, in June of 1964 they asked President Lyndon B. Johnson and Attorney General Robert Kennedy for federal protection. They got no answer.

Soon afterward, three civil rights workers, one black and two white, were arrested in Philadelphia, Mississippi. After being let out of jail late at night, they were beaten with chains and shot to death. Later the sheriff, deputy sheriff, and others went to jail for the murders.

Black Power

THE NATIONAL GOVERNMENT HAD REFUSED, again and again, to defend blacks against violence. Still, the uproar about civil rights, and the attention it drew around the world, made Congress pass some civil rights laws, including the Civil Rights Act of 1964. These laws promised much but were ignored or poorly enforced. Then, in 1965, a stronger Voting Rights Act made a difference in southern voting. In 1952, only 20 percent of blacks who could vote had registered to do so. But by 1968, 60 percent were registered—the same percentage as white voters.

The federal government was trying to control an explosive situation without making any basic changes. It wanted to channel black anger into traditional places, such as voting booths and quiet meetings with official support.

One meeting like that had taken place in 1963, when Martin Luther King led a huge march on Washington, D.C. The crowd thrilled to King's magnificent "I Have a Dream" speech, but the speech lacked the anger that many blacks felt. John Lewis was a young SNCC leader who had been arrested and beaten many times in the fight for racial equality. Lewis wanted the meeting to express some outrage, but its leaders wouldn't let him criticize the national government.

Two months later, a black militant named Malcolm X gave his view of the March on Washington:

The Negroes were out there in the streets. They were talking about how they were going to march on Washington. . . .

It was the grass roots out there in the street. It scared the

white man to death, scared the white power structure in
Washington, D.C. to death. . . .

This is what they did with the March on Washington.
They joined it . . . became part of it, took it over. . . . It
became a picnic, a circus. Nothing but a circus, with
clowns and all. . . . It was a takeover . . . they told the
Negroes what time to hit town, where to stop, what signs
to carry, what song to sing, what speech they could make,
and what speech they couldn't make, and then told them
to get out of town by sundown.

People were still exploding bombs in black
churches, killing children. The new "civil rights"
laws weren't changing the basic conditions of life
for black people.

Nonviolence had worked in the southern civil
rights movement, partly by turning the country's opinion against the segregationist South.
But by 1965, half of all African Americans lived
in the North. There were deep problems in the
ghettos, the poor black neighborhoods, of the
nation's cities.

In the summer of 1965, the ghetto of Watts, Los
Angeles, erupted with rioting in the streets and
with looting and firebombing of stores. Thirty-
four people were killed. Most of them were black.

More outbreaks took place the next year. In 1967, the biggest urban riots in American history broke out in black ghettos across the land. Eighty-three people died of gunfire, mostly in Newark, New Jersey, and Detroit, Michigan.

Martin Luther King was still respected, but new heroes were replacing him. "Black Power" was their slogan. They distrusted "progress" that was given a little at a time by whites. They rejected the idea that whites knew what was best for blacks.

Malcolm X was Black Power's chief spokesman. He was assassinated in 1965, while giving a speech. After his death, millions read the book he wrote about his life. He was more influential in death than during his lifetime. Another spokesman was Huey Newton of the Black Panthers. This organization had guns and said that blacks should defend themselves.

King was growing concerned about problems that the civil rights laws didn't touch—problems of poverty. He also began speaking out against a war the United States was fighting in the Asian nation of Vietnam. King said, "We are spending all of this money for death and destruction, and not nearly enough money for life and constructive development."

The FBI tapped King's private phone conversations, blackmailed him, and threatened him. A U.S. Senate report of 1976 would say that the FBI "tried to destroy Dr. Martin Luther King." But destruction came when an unseen marksman shot King to death as he stood on the balcony outside his hotel room in Memphis, Tennessee.

The killing of King brought new urban violence. African Americans saw that violence and injustice against them continued. Attacks on blacks were endlessly repeated in the history of the United States, coming out of a deep well of racism in the national mind. But there was something more—now the FBI and police were targeting militant black organizers, such as the Black Panthers.

Was the government afraid that black people would turn their attention from issues such as voting to something more dangerous, such as the question of wealth and poverty? If poor whites and blacks united, large-scale class conflict could become a reality.

But if some blacks were invited into the power system, they might turn away from class conflict. So leaders of nonmilitant black groups visited the White House. White-owned banks began helping black businesses. Newspapers and televisions started showing more black faces. These changes were small, but they got a lot of publicity. They also drew some young black leaders into the mainstream.

By 1977, more than two thousand African Americans held public office in southern cities. It was a big advance—but it was still less than 3 percent of all elective offices, although blacks made up 20 percent of the total population.

More blacks could go to universities, to law and medical school. Northern cities were busing children back and forth to integrate their schools. But none of this was helping the unemployment, poverty, crime, drug addiction, and violence that were destroying the black lower class in the ghettos. At the same time, government programs to aid African Americans seemed to favor blacks over whites. When poor whites and poor blacks competed for jobs, housing, and the miserable schools that the government provided for all the poor, new racial tension grew.

No great black movement was under way in the mid-1970s. Yet a new black pride and awareness had been born, and it was still alive. What form would it take in the future?

CHAPTER EIGHTEEN

VIETNAM

"DEAR MOM AND DAD," AN AMERICAN SOLDIER wrote home from Vietnam, "Today we went on a mission and I am not very proud of myself, my friends, or my country." What kind of war would make a soldier feel that way? It was a war that made many Americans angry and ashamed of their country.

For nearly a decade, the richest and most powerful nation in the history of the world tried to defeat a revolutionary movement in a tiny, peasant country—and failed. When the United States fought a war in the southeastern Asian nation of Vietnam, it was modern military technology against organized human beings. The human beings won.

Vietnam also created the biggest antiwar movement the United States had ever seen. Thousands of people marched in the streets. Students organized protests. Artists, writers, and soldiers boldly spoke out against the war. The antiwar movement was loud and long-lasting. It helped bring the fighting to an end.

Communism and Combat

BEFORE WORLD WAR II, FRANCE CONTROLLED the Southeast Asian nation of Vietnam. When that war started, Japanese troops occupied the country. A revolutionary movement arose among the Vietnamese people, led by a Communist named Ho Chi Minh, to fight the Japanese. At the end of the war, the revolutionaries celebrated in Hanoi, a city in northern Vietnam. A million people filled the streets, rejoicing that their country was free of foreign control at last.

But the Western powers were already taking away that freedom. Before long, England and the United States saw to it that France regained control of Vietnam. Revolutionaries in the north resisted,

and in 1946 the French started bombing them. It
was the beginning of an eight-year war against the
Communist movement, called the Vietminh.
Before it was over, the United States gave a
billion dollars in military aid, along with hundreds
of thousands of weapons, to the French to use
in Vietnam.

Why did the United States help France? The
official reason was to stop the rise of communism
in Asia. Communist governments had already
come to power in China and North Korea. It was
the height of the Cold War, when communism
was seen as the greatest danger to America. But
could there have been other reasons as well?

A secret U.S. government memo from 1952
talked about Southeast Asia's resources. Its rubber, tin, and oil were important to the United
States. If a government that was hostile to the
United States came to power in Vietnam, it might
get in the way of the United States' influence and
interests. In 1954, a memo in the U.S. State
Department said, "If the French actually decided
to withdraw [from Vietnam], the U.S. would have
to consider most seriously whether to take over in
this area."

That same year, the French did withdraw from northern Vietnam. Under the peace agreement, the Vietminh agreed to remain in the north. The northern and southern parts of Vietnam were supposed to be unified after two years, and the people would be allowed to elect their own government. It seemed likely that they would choose Ho Chi Minh and the Vietminh.

The United States moved quickly to keep North and South Vietnam from being united. To bring South Vietnam under American influence, it placed the government in charge of an official named Ngo Dinh Diem. He was friendly to the United States, but the Vietnamese people disliked him.

Diem did not hold the scheduled elections. Around 1958, guerrilla attacks on his government began in South Vietnam. The guerrillas, called Viet Cong, were aided by the Communist government of North Vietnam.

The Communist movement gained strength in the south. To the Vietnamese people, it was more than a war against Diem. It was a way of reorganizing society so that ordinary villagers would have more control over their lives. Open opposition to Diem increased. Buddhist monks set themselves on fire and burned to death to protest against the South Vietnamese government.

Under the international peace agreement, the United States could send just 685 military advisers to South Vietnam. It sent thousands more, and some of them helped fight against the guerrillas. The United States had entered into a secret, illegal war.

Next, the U.S. administration decided that Diem was not helping them control South Vietnam. The Central Intelligence Agency (CIA) secretly encouraged some Vietnamese generals to overthrow him. The generals attacked Diem's seaside palace and executed him and his brother.

Three weeks later, the American president John F. Kennedy was assassinated in Texas. When his vice president, Lyndon B. Johnson, became president, he inherited the problem of Vietnam.

In August 1964, Johnson told the American public that the North Vietnamese had fired torpedos at a U.S. Navy Ship. It was a lie. The ship had been spying for the CIA in Vietnamese territorial waters, and no torpedoes were fired. But the "attack" gave the United States a reason to make war on North Vietnam. Under the U.S.

Constitution, only Congress could declare war. Instead, Congress gave the president power to take military actions in Southeast Asia without a formal declaration of war.

American warplanes began bombarding North Vietnam. They also bombed villages in South Vietnam where they thought Viet Cong were hiding. Sometimes they dropped a weapon called napalm, which is gasoline in jelly form, horribly destructive to human flesh. A *New York Times* article from September 1965 described the results:

> In another delta province there is a woman who has both arms burned off by napalm and her eyelids so badly burned that she cannot close them. When it is time for her to sleep her family puts a blanket over her head. The woman had two of her children killed in the air strike that maimed her. Few Americans appreciate what their nation is doing to South Vietnam with airpower. . . . [I]nnocent civilians are dying every day in South Vietnam.

American troops also poured into South Vietnam. By early 1968 there were more than half a million of them there. As they raided villages looking for guerrillas, the difference between an enemy and a civilian seemed to disappear.

(left) Civilians begin to evacuate homes in Cholon area of Saigon during an attack, 1968.

In March 1968 a company of American soldiers went into a village called My Lai. They
rounded up the villagers, including old people
and women carrying babies. Then they ordered
the people into a ditch and shot them. The army
tried to cover up what had happened at My Lai,
but after word got out, several of the officers
stood trial. A newspaper report of the trial
described the massacre at My Lai:

> Lieutenant Calley and a weeping rifleman named Paul
> D. Meadlo—the same soldier who had fed candy to the
> children before shooting them—pushed the prisoners
> into the ditch. . . . People were diving on top of each
> other; mothers were trying to protect their children. . . .
> Between 450 and 500 people—mostly women, children,
> and older men, were buried in mass graves.

Calley was sentenced to life in prison, but he
served just three years of house arrest. An army
officer admitted that many other tragedies like My
Lai remained hidden.

As the war went on, the United States started
bombing Laos, Vietnam's neighbor. This was to
keep the Viet Cong from operating bases there and
to destroy supply routes used by the Viet Cong. The
bombing in Laos was kept from the public. But

when the United States later bombed another Southeast Asian country, Cambodia, the news reached the public and caused an outcry of protest.

"This Madness Must Cease"

AMERICAN FIREPOWER WAS ENORMOUS, BUT it wasn't ending the resistance in Vietnam. And in the United States, the public was turning against the war. Some were horrified by its cruelty. Others simply felt that it was a failure that had killed forty thousand U.S. soldiers and wounded a quarter of a million more by early 1968.

President Johnson had stepped up a brutal war and still failed to win it. He became so unpopular that he could not appear in public without an antiwar demonstration. Protestors shouted, "LBJ, LBJ, how many kids did you kill today?"

From the start, Americans had protested against U.S. actions in Vietnam. Some of the first protests came out of the civil rights movement— maybe because black people's experience with the government made them distrust any claim that it was fighting for freedom. In 1965, young blacks in Mississippi who had just learned that a classmate was killed in Vietnam passed out a pamphlet that said: "No Mississippi Negroes should be fighting in Viet Nam for the White man's freedom, until all the Negro People are free in Mississippi."

The Student Nonviolent Coordinating Committee (SNCC), a big part of the civil rights movement, said that the United States was breaking international law in Vietnam. It called for an end to the fighting. When six SNCC members invaded an Alabama induction center (an office for entering the armed forces), they were arrested and sentenced to several years in prison.

Julian Bond, an SNCC activist, was elected to the Georgia legislature. After he spoke out against the war and the draft, the others legislators refused to let him take his seat. The Supreme Court restored Bond to his seat, saying that he had the right to free expression under the First Amendment.

In 1967, Martin Luther King Jr. spoke about the war at Riverside Church in New York:

Somehow this madness must cease. We must stop now. I speak as a child of God and brother to the suffering poor

of Vietnam. I speak for those whose land is being laid
waste, whose homes are being destroyed. . . . I speak
for the poor of America, who are paying the double
price of smashed hopes at home and death and corruption in Vietnam. . . . I speak as an American to the leaders of my own nation. The great initiative in this war is
ours. The initiative to stop it must be ours.

Catholic priests and nuns joined the antiwar
movement. Father Philip Berrigan, a priest who was
also a veteran of World War II, was one of many
people who went to jail for destroying the records at
offices of the draft board, where young men were
required to register for military service. His brother
Daniel, also a priest, was imprisoned for a similar act.

Thousands of young American men fled to
Canada or Europe. Some were avoiding the draft.
Others were soldiers, deserting. Antiwar feeling
was strong among servicepeople, both soldiers
and veterans. Some spoke out, risking punishment. A navy nurse was court-martialed for
marching in a peace demonstration while in uniform. Two black marines went to prison for talking to others against the war.

One antiwar veteran told his story in the book
Born on the Fourth of July. Ron Kovic enlisted in the

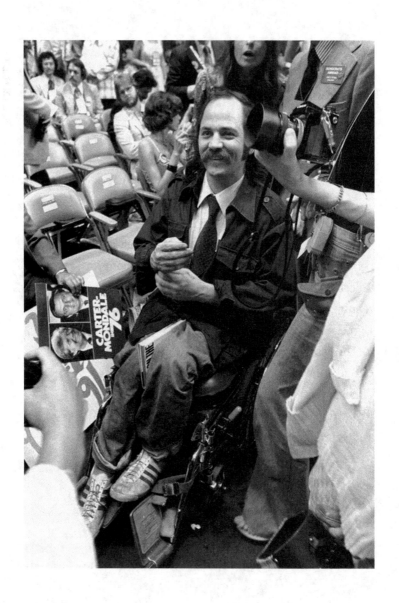

U.S. Marines when he was seventeen. He was serving in Vietnam when shellfire shattered his spine and paralyzed him from the waist down. Back in the States, in a wheelchair, Kovic demonstrated against the war. He told how he was treated after being arrested during a demonstration:

"What's your name?" the officer behind the desk says.

"Ron Kovic," I say. "Occupation, Vietnam veteran against the war."

"What?" he says sarcastically, looking down at me.

"I'm a Vietnam veteran against the war," I almost shout back.

"You should have died over there," he says. He turns to his assistant. "I'd like to take this guy and throw him off the roof."

The growth of the antiwar movement couldn't be stopped. When the bombing of North Vietnam had started in 1965, a hundred people gathered in Boston to protest it. But on October 1, 1968, a nationwide day of antiwar activity, a hundred thousand showed up in Boston and as many as 2 million people took part across the United States.

Famous voices and ordinary voices were raised against the war. Arthur Miller, a well-known playwright, was invited to the White House. He

(left)
Ron Kovic, 1976.

refused to come. Singer Eartha Kitt did accept an invitation to the White House and shocked everyone by speaking out, in front of the president's wife, against the war. A teenager who had won a prize was called to the White House to accept it. He came—and criticized the war.

Even some of those close to the government had had enough. Daniel Ellsberg, a former U.S. Marine, had helped write a top-secret history of the war for the Department of Defense. He and a friend decided to make it public. They leaked the "Pentagon Papers" to the *New York Times*, which published parts of the document.

By that time, Republican Richard Nixon had replaced Democrat Johnson as president. Nixon tried to get the Supreme Court to stop the *Times* from publishing the Pentagon Papers. He failed. The administration then put Ellsberg and his friend on trial. The trial was halted when unfair and illegal acts by Nixon's own administration—an event called the Watergate scandal—became public.

By the fall of 1973, North Vietnamese troops were established in parts of South Vietnam. The American administration could see no victory in sight. After a final, brutal wave of bombing over

the north, the United States signed a peace agreement and withdrew its forces. The South
Vietnamese government still received American
aid, but without the American military it could not
hold off an invasion from North Vietnam. In 1975
the country was united under the Communist rule
of Ho Chi Minh.

Vietnam was the first defeat to the global
American empire that had formed after World
War II. That defeat came from a revolutionary
peasant army and from an astonishing movement
of protest at home. Yet the rebellion at home was
spreading beyond the issue of war in Vietnam.

CHAPTER NINETEEN

SURPRISES

"THE TIMES THEY ARE A-CHANGIN'," sang Bob Dylan in the 1960s. Dylan wrote powerful songs of protest. In "Masters of War," he imagined the deaths of the men who organized wars and profited from them. But Dylan also sang personal songs of freedom and self-expression. His music captured the mood of the United States in the 1960s and early 1970s.

It was a time of revolt. The civil rights movement and the movement against the Vietnam War were part of a larger movement for change. People lost faith in the Establishment—the big powers like business, government, the schools, and the medical industry. They questioned what they were told. They believed that they should be free to think for themselves, and they experimented with new ways of living, teaching, working, and making art.

Unexpected new currents began to flow through American society, moving in surprising directions. Two of the biggest surprises came from women and Indians.

Women's Liberation

By 1960, more than a third of all women age sixteen and older were working outside their homes for wages. Yet only 2 percent of working mothers had nurseries for their children, and women earned a lot less than men. Society saw women as wives, mothers, housekeepers. Many men viewed women as emotional and impractical, not able to do difficult jobs.

Even in the civil rights movement, where women played an important role and stood up to danger, some women knew that men did not regard them as equals. Ella Barker, who had worked for civil rights in Harlem before going to the South to help organize protests, said:

> I knew from the beginning that as a woman, an older
> woman in a group of ministers who are accustomed to
> having women largely as supporters, there was no place
> for me to have come into a leadership role.

But women resisted. In 1964, civil rights workers were living in a Freedom House in
Mississippi. The women went on strike against
the men, who expected them to cook and make
beds while the men drove around organizing the
movement.

The times *were* a-changing. The National
Organization for Women formed in 1966. The following year, women's groups convinced President
Johnson to ban discrimination against women in
jobs related to the federal government.

By that time, women in the civil rights and antiwar movements were organizing their own meetings and taking action on women's issues. In early
1968, a women's antiwar meeting in Washington,
D.C., marched to the Arlington National Cemetery
and declared "The Burial of Traditional
Womanhood." That same year a group called
Radical Women made headlines when they
protested the Miss America contest and threw

STUDENT RIGHTS

A "SHY," "ETHEREAL," PEACEFUL FIFTEEN-YEAR-OLD
boy named John Tinker won a crucial legal battle
on behalf of civil rights during the height of the
Vietnam War, the period between 1965 and 1968,
when the country was in an uproar. John, his thir-
teen-year-old sister Mary Beth, and their fifteen-
year-old friend Chris Eckhardt were all expelled
from school after they wore armbands in school
to protest the war. "When people are getting
killed, it's important to me," John Tinker later
said. But school disrict board president Ora
Niffenegger disagreed, saying, "We must have law
and order. If we don't we have chaos."

John, Mary Beth, and Chris eventually decided
to stop wearing the armbands so that they would-

n't be thrown out of school. But they sued the Des Moines school system to protect the right to protest as a form of expression. The judge ruled against them in favor of the school's right to ban armbands.

John, Mary Beth, and Chris appealed, and when the appellate court ruling ended in a 4–4 tie, they appealed right up to the US Supreme Court. By the time the Supreme Court ruled, on February 24, 1969, John was a freshman at the University of Iowa. The Supreme Court ruled in favor of John, Mary Beth, and Chris, by a 7–2 majority. They had won their case! That ruling still protects freedom of expression today. It means that school officials can't just stop students from

expressing their thoughts and opinions because they may disagree with them.

Supreme Court Justice Abe Fortas wrote the opinion for the majority. Here are some of the things he wrote in his eleven-page opinion, short for a constitutional case:

School officials do not possess absolute authority over their students.

Students in school as well as out of school are persons under our Constitution.

[Neither] students or teachers shed their constitutional rights to freedom of speech or expression at the schoolhouse gate.

State-operated schools may not be enclaves of totalitarianism.

[Education works best when practiced with] a robust exchange of ideas which discovers truth out of a multi-

tude of tongues, [rather] than through any kind of author-
itative selection.

Source: Johnson, John W. *The Struggle for Student Rights: Tinker v. Des Moines and the 1960s.* Lawrence, Kansas: University Press of Kansas, 1997.

bras, false eyelashes, and wigs into a Freedom Trash Can.

Hoping to change the U.S. Constitution to ensure full equality of the sexes, many women worked to get an Equal Rights Amendment (ERA) passed by the states. Yet it seemed clear that even if they succeeded, the law alone would not be enough to change people's ideas about women's place in society. Shirley Chisholm, a black congresswoman, said:

The law cannot do it for us. We must do it for ourselves. Women in this country must become revolutionaries. We must refuse to accept the old, the traditional roles and stereotypes. . . . We must replace the old, negative thoughts about our feminity with positive thoughts and positive action. . . .

The women's movement of the 1960s was called Women's Liberation, or sometimes feminism. Its deepest effect might have been what was called "consciousness raising." Women read or talked about issues that affected them. This led them to rethink old roles, to reject the idea that women were inferior, and to feel a new confidence and sense of sisterhood with other women.

(*left*)
Former New York Congresswoman Bella Abzug (2nd from right) joins marchers celebrating the 60th anniversary of the passage of the 19th Amendment to the U.S. Constitution, 1980.

One of the first and most influential books of the women's movement was *The Feminine Mystique*, by a middle-class housewife named Betty Friedan. The "mystique" was society's image of women finding complete satisfaction as mothers and wives, giving up their own dreams. In trying to live up to that image, many women felt empty and lost. Friedan wrote, "The only way for a woman, as for a man, to find herself, to know herself as a person, is by creative work of her own."

Poor women had urgent concerns. Some of them wanted to eliminate hunger, suffering, and inequality right away. Johnnie Tillmon worked with other mothers on welfare to form the National Welfare Rights Organization. It wanted women to be paid for work such as housekeeping and child-rearing, saying, "No woman can be liberated, until all women get off their knees." Tillmon explained:

> Welfare's like a traffic accident. It can happen to anybody, but especially it happens to women. And that is why welfare is a women's issue. For a lot of middle-class women in this country, Women's Liberation is a matter of concern. For women on welfare it's a matter of survival.

The control of women in society was not done by the state. Instead, it happened inside the family. Men controlled women, women controlled children, and sometimes they did violence to each other when things weren't going right. But what if it all turned around?

If women liberated themselves, and men and women began to understand each other, would they find that both of them were being kept down by something outside themselves? Maybe families and relationships would become pockets of strength and rebellion against the larger system, and men and women—and children, too—would work together to change society.

An Indian Uprising

THE INDIANS WERE ONCE THE ONLY INHABITANTS of America. Then the white invaders pushed them back. The last massacre of the Indians took place in 1890 at Wounded Knee Creek in South Dakota. When it was over, between two and three hundred Indian men, women, and children were dead.

The Indian tribes had been attacked, beaten, and starved. The federal government divided them up by putting them on reservations where they lived in poverty. An 1887 law tried to turn the Indians into American-type small farmers by breaking up the reservations into individually owned plots of land. White real-estate speculators got hold of most of the land, and the reservations remained, although young Indians often left them.

For a time, it seemed that the Indians would disappear or blend away into the larger society. At the beginning of the twentieth century, only three hundred thousand of them were left. But then, like a plant that is left to die but refuses to do so, the population started to grow again. By 1960 there were eight hundred thousand Indians. Half of them lived on reservations. The other half lived in cities and towns all over the country.

As the civil rights and antiwar movements took shape in the 1960s, the Indians were also thinking about how to change their situation. They began to organize.

Indians started approaching the U.S. government on an embarrassing topic: treaties. The government had signed more than four hundred

(left)
Fear Forgets leads other Sioux in "Liberation Day" ceremonies on Alcatraz Island, 1970.

treaties with the Indians. It had broken every single one. Back when George Washington was president, the government signed a treaty with the Iroquois tribes of New York that gave certain property to the Seneca nation. But in the early 1960s, under President Kennedy, the government ignored that treaty and built a dam on this land, flooding most of the Seneca reservation.

But Indians in all parts of the country were starting to resist. In the state of Washington, an old treaty had taken land from the Indians but left them fishing rights. As the white population grew, whites wanted the fishing to themselves. After state courts closed river areas to Indians, the Indians held "fish-ins" there. They went to jail, hoping to get publicity for their protest.

Some Indians at the fish-ins were Vietnam veterans. One of them was Sid Mills. In 1968, Mills was arrested on the Nisqually River. He said, "I am a Yakima and a Cherokee Indian, and a man. For two years and four months, I've been a soldier in the United States Army. I served in combat in Vietnam—until critically wounded. . . . I hereby renounce further obligation in service or duty to the United States Army."

A dramatic event in 1969 drew more attention to the Indians' complaints than anything else had done. Alcatraz was an abandoned federal prison on an island in San Francisco Bay. It had been a hated place nicknamed "The Rock." One night seventy-eight Indians landed on Alcatraz and took it over.

Among the group's leaders were Richard Oakes, a Mohawk who directed Indian studies at San Francisco State College, and Grace Thorpe, a Sac and Fox Indian who was the daughter of Jim Thorpe, a famous football star and Olympic athlete. Their plan was to turn the island into a center for Native American environmental studies.

Other Indians came to join them. By the end of November there were more than six hundred people from fifty tribes. The government cut off telephone, electric, and water service to the island. Although many Indians had to leave, others insisted on staying. They were still there a year later, when they sent out this message:

> We are still holding the Island of Alcatraz in the true names of Freedom, Justice and Equality, because you, our brothers and sisters of this earth, have lent support to our just cause.

> We have learned that violence breeds only more violence
> and we have therefore carried on our occupation of
> Alcatraz in a peaceful manner, hoping that the govern-
> ment of these United States will also act accordingly. . .
> We are Indians of All Tribes! we hold the rock!

Six months later, federal forces invaded the island and physically removed the Indians.

Other Indian demonstrations took place—to protest strip mining on Navajo land in New Mexico, to reclaim land taken by the Forest Service in California. At the same time, Indians were doing something about the destruction of their culture. An Oklahoma Indian named Evan Haney recalled that though half the kids in his school had been Indians, "nothing in school . . . taught anything about Indian culture. There were no books on Indian history, not even in the library. . . ." Haney knew something was wrong. He found books and started learning his own culture.

As more books about Indian history came into being, teachers started to rethink the way they taught the subject. They avoided old stereotypes and looked for new sources of information for their students. Students became activists, too. An

elementary school student named Raymond
Miranda wrote to the publisher of one of his
books:

> Dear Editor,
>
> I don't like your book called *The Cruise of Christopher
> Columbus*. I didn't like it because you said some things
> about Indians that weren't true. . . . Another thing I didn't
> like was on page 69, it says that Christopher Columbus
> invited the Indians to Spain, but what really happened was
> that he stole them!

In March of 1973, the Indians of North America
made a powerful statement on the Pine Ridge
Reservation in South Dakota. Hundreds of
American Indian Movement members occupied
Wounded Knee village at the site of the 1890 massacre. The occupation was a symbol of their
demand for Indian rights and Indian land.

Within hours, federal agents, marshals, and
police surrounded the town. They began firing with
automatic weapons. The protestors inside the town
were under siege. When Indians in Michigan sent
them a small planeload of food, the authorities
arrested the pilot and a doctor who had hired the
plane. A few weeks later other planes dropped food
for the protestors. When the Indians ran to gather

it, a federal helicopter fired down on them. A stray bullet hit a man inside a church. He died.

After more gun battles and another death, the Indians and the authorities agreed to end the siege. A hundred and twenty Indians were arrested. But they had held out for seventy-one days, creating a community inside Wounded Knee and receiving messages of support from all over the world.

The 1960s and early 1970s brought many changes to American society, some large and some small but significant. People felt free to be themselves. Gays and lesbians felt less need to hide the truth about themselves, and they started organizing to fight discrimination. Men and women alike dressed less formally. Comfortable clothes such as jeans became normal for young people of both sexes. Students, parents, and teachers questioned traditional education, which had taught whole generations the values of patriotism and obeying authority while ignoring or even disrespecting women and people of color. Disabled people became a force, campaigning for legislation that would protect them from discrimination.

In those years, as part of what became known as a "cultural revolution," people became more conscious of what was happening to the environment. In 1962 Rachel Carson published *Silent Spring*, a book that shocked people into realizing that chemicals used in modern technology were poisoning the air, the water, and the earth. The book became a bestseller and sparked a movement for environmental cleanliness. In 1978, a woman named Lois Gibbs, whose children had become ill in the neighborhood of Love Canal, New York, and who saw other people suffering, became a leader in the struggle against corporations that were endangering people's lives in their pursuit of maximum profit.

Hundreds of thousands of people joined organizations like the Sierra Club, the Wilderness Society, and EarthFirst! On Earth Day in 1970, 100,000 people marched down Fifth Avenue in New York, and students at 1,500 colleges and 10,000 schools throughout the country demanded protection of the environment. Soon after, Congress passed a number of laws: the Clean Water Act, the Clean Air Act, and the Endangered Species Act. They also created the Environmental

Protection Agency. Enforcement of these acts was not a priority of the national government, and in the presidency of Ronald Reagan, funds were cut for the E.P.A. Nevertheless, the environmental movement continued its campaigns.

America had never had more movements for change in such a short time. But the Establishment had learned a lot about controlling people in its two hundred years of existence. In the mid-1970s, it went to work.

CHAPTER TWENTY

UNDER CONTROL?

"IS THE GOVERNMENT RUN BY A FEW BIG
interests looking out for themselves?"

In 1972 a research center asked Americans that
question. More than half the people who were
asked said, "Yes." Just eight years before, only
about a quarter of them had answered yes. What
had happened?

America was changing in the early 1970s. The
system was out of control. People had lost faith in
the government. A lot of them were hostile to big
business, too.

The Vietnam War created a lot of distrust and
anger. It killed fifty-eight thousand Americans,
and the people had discovered that their government had lied to them and had done terrible
deeds. Americans also lost faith in the system

because of Watergate, a political disgrace that made a U.S. president step down from office for the first time in history. Many were also deeply concerned about how the United States was acting toward other nations of the world.

Watergate

THE STORY OF WATERGATE BEGAN IN THE White House. Richard M. Nixon, a Republican, was president. To help him win a second term in the White House when voters went to the polls in November, his supporters formed the Committee to Re-Elect the President (CREEP).

Five burglars were caught in Washington, D.C., in June 1972. They were breaking into an office in the Watergate apartment that happened to be the headquarters of the Democratic Party's national committee. Police discovered that the burglars had equipment for taking photographs and wiretapping telephones. One of them was James McCord Jr., an officer of CREEP. Another burglar

(left)
Newspaper headlines being read by tourists in front of the White House, 1974.

335

carried an address book. It contained the name E. Howard Hunt and gave Hunt's address as the White House. Hunt, it turned out, worked for Nixon's lawyer.

The burglars weren't just linked to important officials in Nixon's campaign committee and his administration. They also had ties to the country's Central Intelligence Agency. News of the arrests and the burglars' high-level connections got out to the public before anyone could stop it.

Everyone was asking: Did the president have anything to do with the burglary? Did he know about it? Five days after the arrests, Nixon told reporters that "the White House has had no involvement whatever in this particular incident."

But over the next year, a different picture became clear. One after the other, people in the Nixon administration began to talk, sometimes to protect themselves from facing charges. They gave information in court, in meetings of the Senate committee that investigated the Watergate case, and to reporters. They revealed misdeeds by John Mitchell—the attorney general, who is supposed to be the U.S. government's senior lawyer. Also guilty were two of Nixon's top assistants, Robert Haldeman and John Ehrlichman. Nixon himself was deeply involved.

The Watergate burglary wasn't the Nixon administration's only crime. A long list of facts came to light. Here are just some of them:

- Attorney General Mitchell had controlled a secret fund of hundreds of thousands of dollars to use against the Democratic Party. Ways to hurt the Democrats included forging letters, stealing campaign files, and leaking false news stories to the press.

- Gulf Oil Corporation and other big American businesses had given millions of dollars in illegal contributions to Nixon's campaign.

- In September 1971, after the *New York Times* started printing the Pentagon Papers, which told of U.S. actions in Vietnam, the administration targeted Daniel Ellsberg, who had given the Pentagon Papers to the *Times*. Hunt and another Nixon supporter had burglarized the office of Ellsberg's psychiatrist, looking for information to use against Ellsberg.

- Henry Kissinger, Nixon's secretary of state, had broken the law by having the telephone calls of journalists and government officials recorded. Material from this spying was kept in a safe in the White House.

• Nixon had taken an illegal tax deduction of more than half a million dollars.

The list went on and on. Then, while the administration's wrongs were coming to light, the vice president, Spiro Agnew, got into trouble. Agnew was accused of taking bribes in return for political favors. He resigned from his post as vice president in October 1973. Nixon chose a Republican congressman named Gerald Ford to replace him.

But soon Nixon fell from power, too. The House of Representatives was ready to vote on whether or not to impeach, that is, to officially charge him for official misconduct. If that had happened, Nixon would then face a trial in the U.S. Senate. If the Senate convicted Nixon, he would be removed from office. Nixon knew that the House would vote for impeachment and that the Senate would convict him.

Nixon did not wait to be impeached by the House of Representatives. He resigned voluntarily on August 8, 1974. "Our long national nightmare is over," said Gerald Ford, who took Nixon's place as president.

How did the Watergate scandal and the president's resignation affect the government? One businessman said, "What we will have is the same play with different players." A political adviser named Theodore Sorensen said something similar: "All the rotten apples should be thrown out. But save the barrel."

The barrel—the system—was saved. Big business and powerful corporations still had great influence in Washington under President Ford. Whether Nixon or Ford or any Republican or Democrat was president, the system would work pretty much the same way. The power of corporations on the White House is a fact of the American political system, and that didn't change after Watergate. The companies that had made illegal contributions to Nixon's campaigns got very light punishment—tiny fines, much smaller than the millions they had given.

America Overseas

MANY SECRETS CAME TO LIGHT DURING the Watergate investigation. One of them involved Cambodia, a Southeast Asian country next to Vietnam. In 1969–1970, the United States had dropped thousands of bombs on Cambodia. The bombing of Cambodia was part of the Vietnam War, but it was concealed from the American public and even from Congress. When it was revealed, it fed people's doubts about the government's foreign policy.

Foreign policy is how a country's government acts toward other nations. For a long time, U.S. foreign policy was focused on fighting in Vietnam. But that war became unpopular with the American people, and after it ended, some government and business leaders feared that the public might not support other military actions overseas.

Henry Kissinger worried about that very thing. Kissinger continued to serve as U.S. secretary of state under President Ford. In April 1975 he was supposed to give a speech at the University of Michigan. Many students were unhappy about this because of Kissinger's role in the Vietnam War. They protested so strongly that he decided not to come. It was a low time for the administration. How could the government improve its image?

"The U.S. must carry out some act somewhere in the world which shows its determination to continue to be a world power," Kissinger said. The next month, the United States seized a chance to make that statement of power.

An American cargo ship called the *Mayaguez* was sailing near Tang Island. The island is part of Cambodia, where a revolutionary government had just taken power. Cambodians stopped the ship and took its crew to the mainland. The crew later said that they were treated with courtesy.

President Ford sent a message to Cambodia to release the ship and crew. After thirty-six hours, U.S. planes started bombing Cambodian ships—even the boat that was carrying the American sailors. Soon Cambodia released the Americans, but Ford had already ordered an attack on Tang Island, even though he knew the soldiers weren't there.

Forty-one Americans were killed in the attack on Tang Island. Why the rush to bomb? And why did Ford order the Cambodian mainland bombed, even after the *Mayaguez* and the crew were recovered?

Why? To show the world that the giant America, defeated by tiny Vietnam, was still powerful. But many journalists and television reporters called the *Mayaguez* operation "successful" and "efficient." The Establishment, it seemed, stood behind the idea that America should shown its authority everywhere in the world. This was true of both liberals and conservatives, Democrats and Republicans.

Congress acted in the *Mayaguez* affair just as it had acted in the early years of the Vietnam War—like a flock of sheep. In 1973, disgusted with Vietnam, Congress had passed a law called the War Powers Act. This law said that the president must consult with Congress before taking military action. But in the *Mayaguez* affair, Ford ignored the law. His assistants called eighteen members of Congress to tell them about the military action. Only a few protested.

Watergate had made both the Central Intelligence Agency and the Federal Bureau of Investigation (FBI) look bad. Those agencies had broken the laws they were sworn to uphold, and they had helped Nixon with illegal acts. When Congress set up committees to study the CIA and

(left)
Part of a Cambodian task force attempting to clear Route 7 east of Skoun watches as American air support bombs Communist positions nearby, 1970.

the FBI after Watergate, it found even more dirty secrets.

The CIA had been plotted to assassinate the leaders of foreign nations, such as Cuba's Fidel Castro. It had smuggled a livestock disease into Cuba that destroyed half a million pigs belonging to people on the island. The CIA had also worked to upset the government of Chile. That government was headed by Salvador Allende, a Marxist. He had been freely elected by the people of Chile—but the United States disagreed with his politics.

As for the FBI, it had spent years trying to break up and destroy left-wing and radical groups. It sent forged letters, it opened mail illegally, and it performed more than ninety burglaries in just six years alone. The FBI even seems to have taken part in the murder of Fred Hampton, an African American activist in the Black Panthers.

All of this information reached the public in thick, hard-to-read reports. Television reporters did not say much about it, and the newspapers did not give full coverage. The Senate even let the CIA review its report *about* the CIA, in case the report had information that the CIA did not want people to read! So that while the investigations made it look as if an honest society was fixing its problems, the mass media and the government did nothing to encourage an open, public discussion of those problems.

Nixon stepping down as president . . . Congress looking into bad deeds by the CIA and the FBI . . . these things were supposed to win back the confidence of the American people in their government. Did they work?

A poll in 1975 found that people's confidence in the military, in buisiness, and in government had plunged since 1966. Only 13 percent of people said that they had confidence in the president and Congress.

Maybe people's lack of satisfaction had something to do with the economy. Unemployment was rising. People were losing their jobs and running out of unemployment benefits. More and more Americans were feeling worse about the future.

In the year 1976, with a presidential election on the way, the Establishment worried about the public's faith in the system. That year was also the bicentennial, or two-hundredth anniversary, of the Declaration of Independence. A great celebration was planned. Organizers might have thought that it would bring back American patriotism and end the mood of protest that had developed since the 1960s.

But there didn't seem to be much enthusiasm for the Bicentennial. In Boston, a 200th anniversary of the Boston Tea Party was planned. But a huge crowd turned out at an unofficial "counter-celebration," where people dumped boxes into Boston Harbor. Marked "Gulf Oil" and "Exxon," those boxes were symbols of corporate power in America. The mood of protest had not gone away.

CHAPTER TWENTY-ONE

POLITICS AS USUAL

TEN MILLION CHILDREN WHO LIVED IN THE
United States in 1979 might not have been able to
go to the doctor or get medicine when they were
sick. That's because they had no known source of
regular health care. Eighteen million kids under
the age of seventeen had never been to a dentist.

Marian Wright Edelman pointed out these
facts. She was the head of the Children's Defense
Fund, working to make life better for America's
children, especially those who lived in poverty. She
wanted people to know about the holes in the
safety net that was supposed to protect kids,
because the U.S. Congress had just taken $88 mil-
lion away from a children's health program.

The United States was in the grip of serious
problems. The Vietnam War and the Watergate

scandal had made many people distrust the government. A lot of them also worried about money: Would they have enough to support them and their families in the future? Would they slide into poverty? The environment was another concern, as people became aware of dangers such as air and water pollution.

Only bold changes in the social and economic structure could solve these problems. But none of the politicians from the two major parties, Republican or Democrat, suggested big changes. Instead, both parties stayed true to what historian Richard Hofstadter has called "the American political tradition."

Two big parts of that tradition are capitalism and nationalism. The economic system of capitalism encourages the growth of great fortunes alongside desperate poverty. Nationalism, the belief that the interests of the United States must always come first around the world, encourages war and preparations for war. Toward the end of the twentieth century, government power swung back and forth between Democrats and Republicans, but neither party offered a new vision of how things could be.

A Little Bit to the Left

JIMMY CARTER, A DEMOCRAT, WAS PRESIDENT from 1977 to 1980. He moved America toward the left, toward liberalism—but only a little. In spite of some gestures toward black people and the poor, and talk about human rights in the rest of the world, the Carter presidency stayed within the limits of traditional American politics.

Carter named Andrew Young, a black man who had worked in the civil-rights movement, as the U.S. ambassador to the United Nations. In the black nations of Africa, Young built up goodwill for the United States. The Carter administration also urged the white-ruled nation of South Africa to end apartheid, a system of laws that kept blacks from gaining economic or political equality.

The black fight against apartheid had plunged South Africa into disorder. If that disorder turned into all-out civil war, American interests could be threatened. Radar systems in South Africa helped track the planes and satellites of many nations, and the country was a source of important raw materials, especially diamonds, which are used in industry as well as in jewelry. If the United States took a stand against apartheid because it was

morally wrong, America also had practical reasons for wanting a stable, peaceful South Africa.

During the Vietnam War, Carter had presented himself as a friend of the antiwar movement. But Carter had not opposed President Nixon's bombing attacks, and when the war ended, he refused to give aid to help Vietnam rebuild itself. As president, Carter continued U.S. support for oppressive governments in Iran, Nicaragua, the Philippines, and Indonesia. These governments allowed the use of harsh and undemocratic methods—such as torture and mass murder—against political dissidents. Still, they received American aid, including military aid.

If Carter's job was to restore public faith in the system, his greatest failure was that he did not solve people's economic problems. While the military budget remained enormous, the government saved money in other ways. The Department of Agriculture, for example, said that it would save $25 million a year by no longer giving free second helpings of milk to needy schoolchildren.

The price of food and other necessary goods was rising faster than people's wages. Many people didn't even earn wages. Among young people,

(left)
Jimmy Carter, the thirty-ninth president of the United States, 1976.

especially young black people, 20 to 30 percent could not find jobs.

Wealth and Poverty in America

IN 1980, CARTER LOST THE PRESIDENTIAL election to Republican Ronald Reagan. The faint liberalism of the Carter years was gone. After two terms as president, Reagan would be followed by another Republican, George Bush.

The Reagan and Bush administrations followed similar policies. These included cutting benefits to poor people, lowering taxes for the rich, and raising the military budget. The two administrations also filled the federal court system with conservative judges who would interpret the law in ways that favored right-wing, Establishment interests. For example, the Reagan-Bush Supreme Court brought back the death penalty. It also said that poor people could be forced to pay for public education.

During Reagan's first four years as president,

the U.S. military was given more than a trillion dollars. Reagan tried to pay for this by cutting benefits to the poor. The human costs of these cuts went deep. More than a million children lost free school lunches, even though some of those kids depended on school lunches for more than half of their daily nutrition. Aid to Families with Dependent Children (AFDC), a welfare program that provided money for single mothers, came under attack, too. Soon a quarter of the nation's children—twelve million kids—were living in poverty.

One mother wrote to her local newspaper:

I am on Aid to Families with Dependent Children, and both my children are in school. . . .

It appears we have employment offices that can't employ, governments that can't govern and an economic system that can't produce jobs for people ready to work. . . .

Last week I sold my bed to pay for the insurance on my car, which, in the absence of mass transportation, I need to go job hunting. I sleep on a piece of rubber foam somebody gave me.

So this is the great American Dream my parents came to this country for: Work hard, get a good education, follow the rules, and you will be rich. I don't want to be rich. I just

want to be able to feed my children and live with some
semblance of dignity. . . .

With strong ties to wealthy corporations, both
the Democratic and Republican political parties
criticized welfare programs. But how did the general public feel about helping those less fortunate?

A poll in early 1992 showed that when questioned about "welfare," 44 percent of people said
that too much money was being spent on it. But
when questioned about "assistance to the poor,"
only 13 percent thought too much was being
spent, and 64 percent thought not enough was
being spent. Americans, it seemed, still felt generous to those in need, but "welfare" had become a
political term, so people's answers depended upon
how the question was worded.

During the Reagan years, the gap between rich
and poor in the United States grew dramatically.
In 1980, the top officers of corporations made
forty times as much in salary as the average factory worker. By 1989 they were making ninety-
three times as much.

On the lower levels of society, everyone was
doing worse than they had been. Blacks,
Hispanics, women, and the young suffered espe-

POLITICS AS USUAL

cially severe economic hurts. At the end of the 1980s, at least a third of African American families fell below the official poverty level. Unemployment among blacks was much higher than among whites, and life expectancy was lower. The victories of the civil rights movement had made it possible for some African Americans to move ahead, but left others far behind.

Desert Storm

THE MOST DRAMATIC TURN IN INTERNATIONAL affairs since the end of World War II happened early in the presidency of George Bush. In 1989, protests against dictatorship broke out in the Soviet Union and the Eastern European nations controlled by the Soviet Union.

Almost overnight, it seemed, the old Communist governments fell apart. New non-Communist ones came into being. The wall that had divided democratic West Germany from Communist East Germany was torn down in front of wildly cheering citizens. Most remarkable of all, these things happened without civil war, in response to overwhelming demand from the people.

The sudden collapse of the Soviet Union left U.S. political leaders unprepared. Several trillion dollars had been taken from American taxpayers to pay for a huge military buildup all over the world to defend the United States from the "Soviet threat." Now the threat was gone. It was a chance for the United States to create a new foreign policy. Hundreds of billions of dollars could be freed from the military budget to pay for constructive, healthful projects.

But that didn't happen. There was a kind of panic, as leaders wondered what they could do to keep up the military establishment that had cost so many dollars over so many years. As if to prove that the gigantic military force was still needed, the Bush administration started two wars in four years.

The first war was in Panama, in Central America, where General Manuel Noriega ruled as dictator. For years the United States had overlooked Noriega's corrupt and brutal ways because he went along with the U.S. Central Intelligence Agency in many ways. But once Noriega was openly known as a drug trafficker, his usefulness was over.

The United States invaded Panama in December 1989, saying that it wanted Noriega to stand trial for drug crimes. American troops quickly captured Noriega, who went to trial and then to prison in the United States. But the U.S. bombing of Panamanian neighborhoods killed hundreds, perhaps thousands, of civilians and left fourteen thousand homeless.

If Panama was a "small" war, Bush's second war was massive. In August 1990, the Middle Eastern nation of Iraq invaded its smaller neighbor, oil-rich Kuwait. On October 30, the Bush administration made a secret decision to make war on Iraq.

The American people were told that the war was being fought to free Kuwait from the Iraqis and to keep Iraq from developing a nuclear bomb. In reality, the two main reasons for going to war were to give the United States a greater voice in the control of Middle East oil and to boost Bush's chances of reelection by showing that he could win a war on foreign soil.

For months, the government and the major media lectured the public about the danger from

Saddam Hussein, the brutal dictator of Iraq. Even so, less than half the American public favored the idea of war. That did not prevent the administration from sending half a million men to the Persian Gulf, next to Iraq.

In January 1991, Congress gave Bush the authority to make war. Air attacks on Iraqi forces began. Bush called the war Desert Storm. News about the fighting was tightly controlled by the military and the government. The big story of the war was "smart bombs," weapons guided by lasers. These bombs were supposedly so accurate that military targets could be pinpointed, saving civilian lives.

The public was deceived about how "smart" these bombs really were. Thousands of Iraqi civilians, including women and children, died in the bombings, especially after the U.S. Air Force went back to using ordinary bombs. One Egyptian witness described the attack on a hotel south of the Iraqi capital of Baghdad this way: "They hit the hotel, full of families, and then they came back to hit it again."

The war lasted barely six weeks. Afterward, it was clear that the bombings of Iraq had caused

(left)
U.S. troops stationed in Saudi Arabia during the Gulf War, 1991.

starvation, disease, and the deaths of thousands of children. And although the U.S. government had painted Saddam Hussein as a grave danger in the months leading up to the war, at the end of the war he remained in power. The United States had wanted to weaken him, but not get rid of him, it seemed. Hussein had been useful in the past, keeping the neighboring nation of Iran from becoming too powerful in the region, and he might be useful again.

President Bush and the major media cheered the U.S. victory in Desert Storm. They claimed that the lingering ghost of Vietnam and the bitter failure to win the war there were finally laid to rest. The United States had showed the rest of the world what it could do.

But June Jordan, a black poet in California, had a different view. She compared the joy of victory in war to the effect of a deadly drug, saying, "I suggest to you it's a hit the same way that crack is, and it doesn't last long."

CHAPTER TWENTY-TWO

RESISTANCE

A YOUNG ACTIVIST NAMED KEITH MCHENRY
was arrested time and time again in the early
1990s. So were hundreds of other people. What
was their crime? Giving free food to poor people—
without a license to distribute food.

McHenry and others like him were part of a
program called Food Not Bombs. Their acts of
courage and defiance helped keep alive a spirit of
resistance at a time when the power of corporate
wealth and government authority seemed overwhelming.

In the 1960s, the surge of protest against race
segregation and against war had become a powerful national force. The resistance of the late 1970s,
the 1980s, and the early 1990s was different.
Activists struggled uphill against uncaring politi-

cal leaders. They tried hard to reach their fellow Americans, even though many people saw little hope in either voting or protest.

Politicians mostly ignored this resistance. The major media didn't mention it very often. But thousands of local groups were busy around the country. Activists in these groups worked for the environment, women's rights, housing for the homeless, and an end to military spending.

No More Nukes!

THE MOVEMENT AGAINST NUCLEAR WEAPONS started in the late 1970s, when Jimmy Carter was president. It was small but determined. Christian activists who had protested the Vietnam War were the pioneers of the movement. They were arrested for nonviolent but dramatic acts at the White House and the Pentagon, the nation's military headquarters. They trespassed on forbidden areas and poured their own blood on symbols of the war machine.

More people joined the antinuclear movement in the 1980s as a protest against President Ronald Reagan's huge military budget. Women took a leading role. Shortly after Reagan was elected, two thousand women gathered in Washington, D.C. They marched on the Pentagon and surrounded it. A hundred and forty of them were arrested for blocking the entrance.

A few doctors started teaching the public about the medical harm that nuclear war would bring. They formed Physicians for Social Responsibility. The group's leader, Dr. Helen Caldicott, became one of the movement's most powerful spokespeople.

Scientists who had worked on the atomic bomb added their voices to the antinuclear movement. Just before he died of cancer, one scientist urged people to organize "a mass movement for peace such as there has not been before."

A mass meeting such as there had not been before took place in New York City's Central Park on June 12, 1982. Close to a million people gathered to call for an end to the arms race, which had the United States and the Soviet Union racing to build up stockpiles of deadly weapons. It was the largest political demonstration in American history.

Social Issues

THE ARMS RACE WASN'T THE ONLY THING THAT sparked protest. People reacted angrily to Reagan's cuts in social services. In 1981, people who lived in East Boston took to the streets to protest the loss of government money to pay for teachers, police, and firefighters in their community. For fifty-five days they blocked major streets during rush hour. The *Boston Globe* reported that the protestors were "mostly middle-aged, middle- or working-class people who said they had never protested anything before." Said Boston's chief of police, "Maybe these people are starting to take lessons from the protests of the sixties and seventies."

Many people saw a link between the nation's military policy and its failing system of social welfare. Money was being spent on guns instead of on children. In 1983 Marian Wright Edelman of the Children's Defense Fund made a speech to a graduating class of students. She said:

> You are graduating into a nation and world teetering on the brink of moral and economic bankruptcy. Since 1980, our President and Congress have been . . . bringing good news to the rich at the expense of the poor. . . . Children are the major victims.

(left)
Marion Wright Edelman, president of the Children's Defense Fund, 1985.

In the South, there was no great movement like the civil rights movement of the 1960s. Still, hundreds of local groups organized poor people, black and white. In North Carolina, a woman named Linda Stout, whose father had been killed by industrial poisons, started the Piedmont Peace Project. Its members were hundreds of textile workers, maids, and farmers. Many of them were low-income women of color who found a voice through the group.

Latinos (Americans of Mexican or Latin American descent) also raised their voices against injustice. Back in the 1960s, Mexican American farmworkers led by César Chávez had taken action against unfair and oppressive working conditions. They went on strike and organized a national boycott, urging customers not to buy California grapes until the workers received better treatment.

Latinos' struggles against poverty and discrimination continued in the 1970s and 1980s. Copper miners in Arizona, mostly Latinos, went on strike after the company that owned the mines cut their wages, benefits, and safety protection. The striking miners were attacked by state troopers, tear gas, and helicopters, but they held out for three years. Finally a combination of government and corporate power defeated them and ended the strike.

But there were victories, too. Latino farmworkers, janitors, and factory workers gained pay raises and better working conditions through labor strikes. In New Mexico, Latinos fought real-estate developers to keep the land they had lived on for decades—and won. By this time 12 percent of Americans were Latino, the same percentage as for African Americans. The Latino population would keep growing, and it would begin to make its mark on American music, art, language, and culture.

War and Antiwar

THE VIETNAM WAR HAD ENDED IN 1975. Sometimes, though, it came back into public attention in the 1980s and 1990s. This could happen when someone announced a change in thinking about the war.

One person whose ideas turned completely

around was Charles Hutto, a soldier who had been part of the massacre at the Vietnamese village of My Lai, where U.S. troops shot hundreds of women and children. Looking back, Hutto told a reporter:

> I was nineteen years old, and I'd always been told to do what the grown-ups told me to do. . . . But now I'll tell my sons, if the government calls, to go, to serve their country, but to use their own judgment at times . . . to forget about authority . . . to use their own conscience. I wish some-body had told me that before I went to Vietnam. I didn't know. Now I don't even think there should be a thing called war . . . cause it messes up a person's mind.

Many Americans felt that Vietnam had been a terrible tragedy, a war that should not have been fought. After that hard lesson, people would not automatically support a new war just because the Establishment wanted to fight it. That's why President George Bush launched the air war against Iraq in 1991 with overwhelming force. He wanted the war to be over before a national anti-war movement could form.

But resistance and protest started in the months leading up to the war. Six hundred students marched through Missoula, Montana, shouting

(left)
Protest against
the Gulf War, 1991.

antiwar slogans. In Boston, a group called Veterans for Peace joined the annual Veterans Day parade. Onlookers applauded when they walked past carrying signs that read "No More Vietnams."

As Bush moved toward war, Vietnam veteran Ron Kovic, author of *Born on the Fourth of July*, made a speech that was broadcast on two hundred television stations. Kovic urged citizens to "stand up and speak out" against war. He said, "How many more Americans coming home in wheelchairs—like me—will it take before we learn?"

On the night the war began, five thousand protestors gathered in San Francisco and formed a human chain around the Federal Building. Police broke the chain by swinging clubs at the protestors' hands. On the other side of the country, in Boston, a seven-year-old girl made her voice heard, too. She wrote a letter:

Dear President Bush. I don't like the way you are behaving. If you would make up your mind there won't be a war we won't have to have peace vigils. If you were in a war you wouldn't want to get hurt. What I'm saying is: I don't want any fighting to happen.

Once the fighting started, and patriotic messages filled the media, the majority of Americans said they supported the war. Still, some people courageously spoke out against it.

In the 1960s, Julian Bond had been kicked out of the seat he had been elected to fill in the Georgia Legislature for daring to criticize the Vietnam War. In that same room, Representative Cynthia McKinnon made a speech attacking the bombing of Iraq. Many of her fellow lawmakers walked out, refusing to listen, but she held her ground.

Patricia Biggs was a student at East Central Oklahoma State University. She and another young woman sat quietly on top of the school's entrance gate with signs that read, "Teach Peace . . . Not War." Biggs explained:

> I don't think we should be over there [in Iraq]. I don't think it's about justice and liberty, I think it's about economics. The big oil corporations have a lot to do with what is going on over there. . . . We are risking people's lives for money.

Nine days after the war started, more than 150,000 people marched through the streets of Washington, D.C., and listened to antiwar speeches. A woman from Oakland, California, held up the folded American flag that had been given to her when her husband was killed in

Vietnam. She told the crowd, "I learned the hard way that there is no glory in a folded flag."

The Iraq War lasted just six weeks. Right after it ended, patriotic fever was high. In one poll, only 17 percent of people said that the war had not been worth its huge cost. But four months later, 30 percent felt the war had not been worth it. The war had not won Bush the lasting support of the people. He ran for reelection in 1992, after the war spirit had faded away, and lost.

Remembering Columbus

THE YEAR 1992 WAS THE QUINCENTENNIAL, or five-hundredth anniversary, of Christopher Columbus' arrival in the Americas. Columbus and his fellow conquerors had wiped out the Native American peoples of Hispaniola. Later, the United States government had destroyed Indian tribes as it marched across North America. As the quincentennial approached, the surviving Indians were determined to have their say.

In 1990 Indians from all over the Americas met in Ecuador, South America, to organize against the celebrations that were being planned to honor Columbus' conquest. Two years later, during the quincentennial, other Americans joined them in speaking out against Columbus.

For the first time in all the years that the United States had celebrated Columbus Day, there were nationwide protests against honoring a man who had kidnapped, enslaved, and murdered the Native people who had greeted him with gifts and friendship. All over the country, people held counter-Columbus events.

The Columbus controversy sparked a burst of activity in universities and schools. Traditional or mainstream thinkers saw American history as the progress of European culture into a wilderness. They were upset by the movement to look at history in new ways, to tell the stories of the Indians Columbus had murdered, the blacks who had been denied freedom, and the women who had had to fight for equality. But they could not stop the tide of new thinking.

Socially conscious teachers created books and workshops for other teachers. They encouraged educators to tell their students the truths about Columbus that were left out of traditional textbooks. One student, a girl named Rebecca, had this to say about the traditional teachings:

> Of course, the writers of the books probably think it's harmless enough—what does it matter who discovered America, really. . . . But the thought that I have been lied to all my life about this, and who knows what else, really makes me angry.

Rebecca was not the only angry American. As the United States entered the 1990s, the political system was in the control of the very rich. Corporations owned the major media. The country was divided into extreme wealth and extreme poverty, separated by a middle class that felt troubled and insecure. Yet a culture of protest and resistance survived. Some people refused to give up the vision of a more equal, more human society. If there was hope for the future of America, it lay with them.

CHAPTER TWENTY-THREE

THE END OF THE TWENTIETH CENTURY

EACH YEAR SOMEONE WINS THE NOBEL PEACE
Prize for seeking a peaceful solution to one of the
world's problems. In 1996 the prize went to two
men who were working to find a fair way to end a
war in East Timor, an Asian country that was
fighting for independence from Indonesia.

Before receiving the prize, one of those men,
Jose Ramos-Horta, spoke at a church in Brooklyn,
New York. He recalled a visit to America almost
twenty years earlier:

> In the summer of 1977, I was here in New York when I
> received a message telling me that one of my sisters,
> Maria, twenty-one years old, had been killed in an aircraft
> bombing. The aircraft, named Bronco, was supplied by
> the United States. . . . Within months, a report about a
> brother, Guy, seventeen years old, killed along with many

other people in his village by Bell helicopters supplied by the United States. Same year, another brother, Nunu, captured and executed with an [American-made] M-16.

Why were American weapons killing people in East Timor, a country on the far side of the world, when the United States was not at war there? Because the United States gave military aid to Indonesia. Toward the end of the twentieth century, the United States became the world's leading provider of weapons to other nations. At the same time, it continued to build up its own military machine.

Military spending took money away from social programs. Dwight Eisenhower, who was president in the middle of the twentieth century, had known that. In one of his best moments, Eisenhower said, "Every gun that is made, every warship launched, every rocket fired, [means] a theft from those who are hungry and are not fed, those who are cold and are not clothed."

During the 1990s, under the eight-year presidency of Bill Clinton, the United States continued to be a place where some people were hungry and cold. It remained a nation where one-fourth of all children lived in poverty and homeless people huddled in the streets of every major city. The country's leaders did not look for bold solutions to the problems of health care, education, child care, unemployment, housing, and the environment.

Moving Toward the Middle

CLINTON WAS A SMART, YOUNG DEMOCRAT in 1992, when Americans elected him to his first term as president. He promised to bring change to the country, and his presidency began with that hope. Upon his reelection in 1996, Clinton declared, "We need a new government for a new century."

But during eight years in office, Clinton failed to live up to his promise of change. Instead, he delivered more of what the country had gotten from the presidents before him.

Like other politicians, Clinton seemed to be more interested in getting votes than in bringing about social change. To win votes, he decided to move the Democratic Party closer to the center—

in other words, to make the party less liberal and more conservative, so that it would not be too different from the Republican Party. To do this, he had to do just enough for the blacks, women, and working people who had traditionally been Democrats to keep their support. At the same time, he tried to win over white conservative voters by coming out in favor of welfare cuts and a strong military.

Even before he was elected, Clinton was eager to show that he took a tough position on matters of "law and order." As governor of Arkansas, he flew back to his home state for the execution of a mentally retarded man on death row.

Soon after he became president, Clinton approved an attack by the Federal Bureau of Investigation (FBI) on a group of religious extremists who had sealed themselves up, with weapons, inside a group of buildings in Waco, Texas. Instead of waiting to see if the crisis could be solved through talking, the FBI attacked with rifle fire, tanks, and tear gas, killing at least eighty-six men, women, and children.

In 1996, Republicans and Democrats in Congress voted in favor of a new law called a

"Crime Bill." Clinton supported the bill, which made more crimes punishable by death. It also set aside $8 billion of federal money to build new prisons. Throughout his presidency Clinton chose federal judges whose liberalism was of the mild, middling kind. Often their decisions were just like those of more conservative judges.

Clinton was no different from other people in power, whether Democrats or Republicans. To keep themselves in power, they turned the public's anger toward groups that could not defend themselves. The target could be criminals, immigrants, people on welfare, or certain governments hostile to the United States, such as Iraq or Communist Cuba. By urging people to focus on these sources of possible danger, political leaders drew attention away from the failures of the American system.

Choices

THE UNITED STATES WAS THE RICHEST COUNTRY in the world. With 5 percent of the world's population, it used or ate or bought 30 percent of everything that was produced worldwide. But only a tiny fraction of Americans benefited from the country's great wealth.

Starting in the late 1970s, the richest 1 percent of people in the country saw their wealth grow enormously. Changes in the tax laws meant that by 1995, that richest 1 percent had gained more than a trillion dollars. It owned 40 percent of the country's wealth. Between 1982 and 1995, the wealth of the four hundred richest families in the country had jumped from $92 billion to $480 billion. In the same time period, the cost of living rose faster than the average wage of ordinary working people. People earning an average wage could buy about 15 percent *less* in 1995 than in 1982.

If you looked just at the richest part of the American population, you could say the economy was healthy. Meanwhile, 40 million people had no health insurance. Babies and young children in the United States died of sickness and malnutrition at a higher rate than in any other industrial country. Jobs weren't always the answer. In 1998, a third of all working people in the country didn't earn enough to lift them above the government's official poverty level. Many people who worked in factories, stores, or restaurants couldn't afford housing, health care, or even enough food.

Two sources of money were available to pay for social programs to attack poverty, joblessness, and other national problems.

The first source was the military budget. One expert on military spending suggested that gradually lowering the country's military budget to $60 million a year would fit the country's needs, now that the Soviet Union had collapsed and the Cold War had ended.

A big drop in the military budget would have meant closing U.S. military bases around the world. It would have meant that the nation would turn its back on war. The basic human desire of people to live in peace with one another would guide its foreign policy. That was a choice that didn't get made. The military budget kept rising. By the end of Clinton's presidency, military spending was about $300 billion a year.

The second source of money for social programs was the wealth of the superrich. A "wealth tax" could have added $100 billion a year to the nation's treasury. Clinton did raise the tax rate on the superrich and on corporations, but only slightly. It was a pitifully small step compared with the nation's needs.

Together, cuts in the military budget and higher taxes on the superrich could have given the government as much as $500 billion each year to pay for dramatic changes. This money could have paid for health care for everyone and for programs to create jobs for all. Instead of giving out contracts for companies to build bombers and nuclear submarines, the government could have given contracts to nonprofit agencies to hire people to build homes, clean up rivers, and construct public transportation systems.

Instead, things continued as before. Cities kept falling into disrepair. Farmers were forced off their land by debts. Young people without jobs or hope turned to drugs and crime. The response of the government was to build more jails and lock up more people. By the end of the Clinton years, the United States had more than 2 million people in prison—a higher percentage of the population than any other country in the world, except maybe Communist China.

Visions of Change

CLINTON CLAIMED THAT HIS DECISIONS WERE based on the opinion of the American people. But opinion surveys in the 1980s and 1990s showed that Americans favored health care for everyone. They also were in favor of guaranteed jobs, government help for the poor and homeless, military budget cuts, and taxes on the rich. Neither the Republicans nor the Democrats were willing to take these bold steps.

What if the American people acted on the feelings they showed in those surveys? What if citizens organized to demand what the Declaration of Independence promised: a government that protected the equal rights of all to life, liberty, and the pursuit of happiness? This would call for an economic system that distributed wealth in a thoughtful and humane way. It would mean a culture where young people were not taught to seek success as a mask for greed.

Throughout the Clinton years, many Americans did protest government policy. They demanded a more fair and peaceful society. They did not get much attention in the media, though. Even a gathering of half a million children and

adults, of all colors, who came to the nation's capital to "Stand for the Children" was mostly ignored by television and newspapers. Still, activists for peace, women's rights, and racial equality continued their struggle—and won some victories.

The labor movement was alive, too. A protest at Harvard University in Massachusetts showed how different groups could work together to reach a goal.

Many of Harvard's janitors and other campus workers did not earn enough to support themselves and their families. Some had to work two jobs, as much as eighty hours a week. So students organized to demand that the workers be paid a "living wage."

The students staged rallies to win support for their cause. Local city council members and union leaders took part. Two young movie stars, Matt Damon and Ben Affleck, also showed up to speak in favor of a living wage. Damon had attended Harvard before going to Hollywood. Affleck told how his father had worked at a poorly paid service job at Harvard.

When university administrators refused to talk with the campus workers, students took over an administration building and stayed in it day and

(left)
The police confront the anti-WTO demonstrators, 1999.

night for several weeks, supported by hundreds of people outside and by donations from all over the country. Finally the university agreed to raise workers' pay and give them health benefits. Soon students and workers were organizing living wage movements at other schools.

In 1999 a great gathering of demonstrators met in Seattle, Washington. They wanted to show the people of America and the world how the power of giant multinational corporations controls the lives of ordinary people.

The World Trade Organization (WTO) was meeting in Seattle. Representatives of the world's richest and most powerful companies and countries were there to make plans to maintain their wealth and power. Their goal was to bring the principles of capitalism to work everywhere, through free-trade agreements between nations.

Protestors claimed that free-trade agreements would let corporations roam the globe looking for cheap labor and places where they could operate without strict environmental laws. The issues of free trade are complicated, but protestors asked a simple question: Should the health and freedom of ordinary people all over the world be sacrificed so that corporations can make a profit?

Tens of thousands of demonstrators showed up to march, make speeches, and carry signs. They were labor unionists, women's rights activists, farmers, environmentalists, consumers, religious groups, and more. The media focused on the small number of demonstrators who broke windows and created trouble, but the overwhelming majority of demonstrators were nonviolent.

Hundreds were jailed, but the protests continued. News of them traveled all over the world. The WTO talks collapsed, showing that organized citizens can challenge the most powerful corporations of the world. Mike Brannan, writing for a union newspaper, captured the protestors' mood:

> The kind of solidarity that all of us dream of was in the air as people sang, chanted, played music, and stood up to the cops and the WTO. The people owned the streets that day and it was as much a lesson for us as it was for corporate America.

Protestors started showing up wherever meetings of the rich and powerful took place. Large international organizations such as the World Bank and the International Monetary Fund could not ignore the movement. They started talking about concern for the environment and for working conditions. Would this lead to real change? It was too soon to tell, but at least the voices of protest had been heard.

CHAPTER TWENTY-FOUR

THE
"WAR ON TERRORISM"

"I DON'T THINK THEY CARE ABOUT PEOPLE LIKE us," the woman said. She was a cashier at a filling station. Her husband was a construction worker. She added, "Maybe if they lived in a two-bedroom trailer, it would be different."

Who was she talking about? "They" were the two candidates for president in 2000. The Republican candidate was George W. Bush, son of the man who had been president before Bill Clinton. The Democratic candidate was Al Gore, who had been vice president for eight years.

That cashier wasn't the only person who thought that neither of the two candidates really cared about her and people like her. Many others felt the same way. An African American woman who managed a McDonald's, earning barely more than the minimum wage, said, "I don't even pay attention to those two, and all my friends say the same. My life won't change."

Almost half the voters in the country would not even go to the polls on Election Day 2000. Many saw no real difference in the candidates. They had no way to know that the candidate who became president would soon have to deal with a national crisis—a terrorist attack on the United States that would start a new cycle of war.

A Close Election

BUSH, THE REPUBLICAN CANDIDATE, WAS known for his close ties to the oil industry. Both candidates, though, had support from big business. Bush and Gore had other things in common, too.

Both candidates favored a large military and the continued use of land mines (even though other nations in the world had banned these deadly devices, which can kill or injure civilians many years after combat ends). Both supported the death penalty and the growth of prisons. Neither of them had a plan for free national health care, or for a big increase in low-cost housing, or for a dramatic change in environmental controls.

There was a third candidate. His name was Ralph Nader, and he was nationally known as a critic of the way large corporations control the American economy. Nader's plan for the nation focused on health care, education, and the environment. But Nader was shut out of the debates between presidential candidates that were broadcast on national television. Without the support of big business, he had to raise money from the small contributions of people who believed in his program.

When Election Day came, it turned out to be the strangest election in American history. Gore received hundreds of thousands more votes than Bush. Under the Constitution, though, presidents aren't elected by the direct vote of the people, sometimes called the popular vote. Instead, each state has a certain number of electors. The electors' votes determine who becomes president.

Twice in American history, in 1876 and 1888, a president had been elected who *wasn't* chosen by the majority of voters. That's because the electors' votes don't always match the popular vote. For example, if 45 percent of the voters in a state voted for candidate A, and 55 percent voted for candidate B, the electoral votes might not be divided between the two candidates. Candidate B might get all the electoral votes.

That's how things work in the state of Florida—and that's what caused a raging argument about the presidential election of 2000. Across the nation, the electoral vote between Gore and Bush was extremely close. It was so close that Florida's electoral votes would decide the election.

But it was not clear whether Gore or Bush had received more votes in Florida. It seemed that many votes had not been counted, especially in districts where a lot of black voters lived. Also, ballots were disqualified on technical grounds, and marks made on ballots by voting machines were not clear.

In short, Florida's popular vote was in doubt. Florida's electoral vote hung in the balance, and so did the presidency. But Bush, the Republican candidate, had an advantage. His brother was governor of Florida, and Florida's secretary of state, Katherine Harris, was also a Republican. Her job gave her the power to certify, or officially declare, who had more votes. She rushed through a recount of some of the ballots and announced that Bush had won the Florida vote. This made Bush the new president.

Democrats appealed to the Florida Supreme Court. The court, which was dominated by Democrats, ordered Harris not to certify a winner until the recount of the popular vote was complete. Harris set a deadline for recounting, and although thousands of votes were still disputed, she declared Bush the winner by 537 votes.

Gore prepared to challenge her decision. He wanted the recount to continue, as the Florida Supreme Court had ordered. To keep this from happening, the Republican Party took the case to the nation's highest court, the U.S. Supreme Court.

Four Supreme Court justices felt that the Florida recount should continue. They argued that the Court did not have the right to interfere with the way the Florida Supreme Court had interpreted its state's electoral law. But the five conservative judges on the court overruled the Florida Supreme Court and halted the recount. In the end, the U.S. Supreme Court's ruling let

Harris's certification stand. Bush got Florida's electoral votes.

John Paul Stevens was one of the liberal justices who had voted not to interfere with the Florida Supreme Court. With some bitterness, he summed up the results of the Court's decision:

> Although we may never know with complete certainty the identity of the winner of this year's presidential decision, the identity of the loser is perfectly clear. It is the nation's confidence in the judge as an impartial guardian of the rule of law.

The Terrorist Attack and the Response

NINE MONTHS AFTER BUSH TOOK OFFICE, on September 11, 2001, a terrible event pushed all other issues into the background. Hijackers on three planes flew the huge jets, loaded with fuel, into the twin towers of the World Trade Center in New York City, and into the Pentagon in Washington, D.C.

(right)
The World Trade Center south tower bursts into flames, New York City, September 11, 2001.

Americans all over the country watched, horrified, as the towers collapsed in an inferno of

concrete and metal. Thousands of people who worked in the towers were buried in the wreckage. So were hundreds of firefighters and police officers who had gone to their rescue.

Nineteen men from the Middle East, most from Saudi Arabia, had made this attack against huge symbols of American wealth and power. They were willing to die to strike a deadly blow against the superpower that they saw as their enemy.

President Bush immediately declared a "war on terrorism." Congress rushed to give the president the power to take military action without the formal declaration of war that the U.S. Constitution requires. Only one member of Congress disagreed—Barbara Lee, an African American representative from California.

The administration believed that the attack was ordered by Osama bin Laden, a Saudi Arabian who supported a militant form of Islam, the Muslim religion. He was thought to be hiding somewhere in the Asian nation of Afghanistan, so Bush ordered the bombing of Afghanistan.

The president set out to capture or kill Osama bin Laden and to destroy his militant Islamic organization, called Al-Qaeda. But after five months of bombing, Osama bin Laden remained free. Bush had to admit to Congress that "tens of thousands of trained terrorists are still at large" in "dozens of countries."

Bush and his advisers should have known that terrorism could not be defeated by force. Evidence from many countries and time periods shows that when countries respond to terrorist acts with military force, the result is more terrorism.

The bombing of Afghanistan was devastating to the country, which had already suffered a 1979 invasion by the Soviet Union, followed by a civil war. Although the Pentagon claimed that the United States was bombing only military targets, human rights groups and the press reported at least a thousand civilians killed. But the mainstream press and major television networks did not show Americans the full extent of the human suffering in Afghanistan. Instead, the media encouraged a mood of revenge.

Congress passed a law called the Patriot Act. It gave the Department of Justice the power to hold noncitizens on nothing more than suspicion, without charging them with a crime, and without the protections guaranteed in the Constitution.

And although President Bush cautioned Americans not to take out their anger on Arab Americans, the government rounded up people for questioning. Most were Muslims. A thousand or more were held without charges.

In the wartime atmosphere, it became hard for citizens to criticize the government's actions. A retired telephone worker was at his health club when he made a remark critical of President Bush. Later he was questioned by the Federal Bureau of Investigation (FBI). A young woman found two FBI agents at her door. They said they had gotten reports of posters on her wall, criticizing the president.

Still, some people spoke out against the war. At peace rallies all over the country, they carried signs with slogans such as "Our Grief Is Not a Cry for Revenge" and "Justice, Not War."

Family members of people who had died in the September 11 attacks wrote to the president. They urged him not to match violence with violence, not to bomb the people of Afghanistan. Amber Amundsen's husband, an Army Specialist, had been killed in the attack on the Pentagon. She wrote:

(left)
Demonstrators holding signs gather at an anti-war rally in Washington, 2001.

I have heard angry rhetoric [speech] by some Americans, including many of our nation's leaders, who advise a heavy dose of revenge and punishment. To those leaders, I would like to make clear that my family and I take no comfort in your words of rage. If you choose to respond to this incomprehensible brutality by perpetuating [continuing] violence against other innocent human beings, you may not do so in the name of my husband.

Some families of September 11 victims traveled to Afghanistan to meet Afghan families who had lost loved ones in the American bombing. One of the Americans was Rita Lasar, whose brother had died in the attack. Lasar said that she would devote the rest of her life to working for peace.

Critics of the bombing felt that terrorism was rooted in deep complaints against the United States. The way to stop terrorism was to respond to these complaints.

Some of the Islamic world's complaints were easy to identify. The United States had stationed troops in Saudi Arabia, where Islam's holiest shrines are located. For ten years the United States had kept Iraq from trading with other countries—a move that was supposed to be political, but one that had caused the deaths of hundreds of thousands of children by keeping food and medicine out of the country, according to the United Nations. The United States also supported the nation of Israel in its occupation of land claimed by Palestinian Muslims.

To change its position on these matters, the United States would have to withdraw military forces around the world. It would have to give up political and economic power over other countries. In short, America would have to stop being a superpower. This was something that the military-industrial interests of both political parties could not accept.

Three years before September 11, 2001, a former U.S. Air Force officer named Robert Bowman had written about terrorist attacks on American embassies in Africa. He described the roots of terrorism:

> We are not hated because we practice democracy, value freedom, or uphold human rights. We are hated because our government denies these things to people in Third World countries whose resources are coveted [desired] by our multinational corporations. That hatred we have sown has come back to haunt us in the form of terrorism. . . . Instead of sending our sons and daughters around the

world to kill Arabs so we can have the oil under their sand,
we should send them to rebuild their infrastructure, supply clean water, and feed starving children. . . .

In short, we should do good instead of evil. Who would try
to stop us? Who would hate us? Who would want to bomb
us? That is the truth the American people need to hear.

Voices such as Bowman's were mostly shut out
of the American media after the September 11
attacks. But there was a chance that their powerful
message might spread among the American people, once they saw that meeting violence with violence did not solve the problem of terrorism.

CHAPTER TWENTY-FIVE

WAR IN IRAQ, CONFLICT AT HOME

THE UNITED STATES MADE "WAR ON TERROR" its mission after the September 11, 2001, terrorist attacks on New York City and Washington, D.C. Soon that mission would lead American troops into war in the Middle Eastern nation of Iraq. As voices at home spoke out against the war, the administration of President George W. Bush faced other troubles. A deadly hurricane made people around the world question the U.S. government's commitment to social justice, and debates about immigration made people ask what it means to be an American. In an election in 2006, voters in the United States showed that they were ready for change.

Afghanistan after the U.S. Invasion

WHEN UNITED STATES FORCES BOMBED AND invaded Afghanistan, they failed to capture Osama bin Laden or to destroy the Al-Qaeda organization. Yet the military operation killed thousands of Afghan civilians and forced hundreds of thousands from their homes.

U.S. leaders justified this terrible toll on the grounds that the invasion had removed the Taliban from power.

The Taliban was a fundamentalist Islamic group that had been ruling Afghanistan with an iron hand. Among other things, the Taliban insisted on strict interpretations of Islam that denied rights to women. The defeat of the Taliban brought a group called the Northern Alliance into power. Its record was far from spotless. In the mid-1990s, the Northern Alliance had committed many acts of violence against the people of Kabul and other Afghan cities.

In his 2002 State of the Union Address, Bush claimed that getting rid of the Taliban meant that "women are free" in Afghanistan. This was a false claim, according to an organization of Afghan women. And two years after the U.S. invasion, the

New York Times gave a discouraging account of things in Afghanistan. Women were not free, bandits roamed the land, warlords controlled huge areas, and the Taliban was making a comeback.

Sixteen months into the war, a Scotsman who took medical aid to Afghan villages was distressed at what he saw. He wrote, "The country is on its knees. . . . It is one of the most heavily land-mined countries in the world . . . 25 percent of all children are dead by the age of five." Sadly he concluded, "Surely, at the start of our 21st century, we should have evolved beyond the point where we reduce a country and a people to dust, for the flimsiest of excuses." But as of August 2006, air strikes were still killing Afghan civilians, and the *New York Times* reported widespread "corruption, violence and poverty."

The attack on Afghanistan had not brought democracy or security, and it had not weakened terrorism. If anything, the violence unleashed by the United States had angered people in the Middle East and created more terrorists.

Weapons of Mass Destruction?

WITH AFGHANISTAN STILL IN TURMOIL, the Bush administration began to set the stage for a war against Iraq. Richard Clarke, adviser to the president on terrorism, later said that immediately after the September 11 attacks the White House looked for reasons to attack Iraq—even though no evidence linked Iraq to the attacks.

Bush and the government officials close to him wanted the American public to think that Iraq and its dictator, Saddam Hussein, threatened the United States and the world. They accused Iraq of concealing "weapons of mass destruction," including plans to build a nuclear bomb.

A United Nations team made hundreds of inspections all over Iraq. It found no weapons of mass destruction, or any evidence that Iraq was working on a nuclear weapon. U.S. vice president Richard Cheney, though, insisted the weapons were real. Condoleezza Rice, the secretary of state, spoke menacingly of "a mushroom cloud," like the cloud caused by the atomic bombing of Hiroshima, Japan. The government also pointed to Hussein's cruel and illegal acts, such as the use of chemical poisons to massacre five thousand

Iraqis from the Kurdish ethnic minority. But
Hussein had killed those Kurds in 1988, and at
the time the United States had not objected loudly.
Back then, Iraq and the United States had been on
the same side against Iran, another nation in the
Middle East.

What was the real reason for building up the
idea of war against Iraq in 2002? Maybe the reason lay underground. Iraq had the world's second
largest oil reserves, after Saudi Arabia. Ever since
the end of World War II in 1945, the United States
had been determined to control the oil of the
Middle East. Oil shaped U.S. decisions about the
Middle East during both Democratic and
Republican presidencies. The administration of
President Jimmy Carter, a liberal Democrat, had
produced the "Carter Doctrine." Under this doctrine, the United States claimed the right to
defend its interest in Middle Eastern oil "by any
means necessary, including military force."

In September 2002, the Bush administration
said that it would take military action on Iraq on
its own, without the support of other countries.
This violated the charter of the United Nations,
which allows military action only in self-defense,

and only when approved by the U.N. Security
Council. Nevertheless, the United States prepared
to make war on Iraq. Protests took place all over
the world. On February 15, 2003, ten to fifteen
million people across the globe demonstrated
against the coming war at the same time.

The Iraq War Begins

DESPITE THE PROTESTS, THE UNITED STATES
government launched a massive attack on Iraq
on March 20, 2003. "Operation Iraqi Freedom,"
as it was called, dropped thousands of bombs on
Iraq and sent more than a hundred thousand soldiers into the country. Hundreds of U.S. soldiers
were killed. Thousands of Iraqis died, many of
them civilians.

After three weeks, U.S. forces occupied Iraq's capital, Baghdad. After six weeks, major military opera-
tions were declared over. President Bush stood
triumphantly on a U.S. aircraft carrier, in front of a
huge banner that said, "Mission Accomplished."

But the mission to control Iraq wasn't accomplished. Violence grew as Iraqi insurgents
attacked the U.S. army. The capture of Saddam
Hussein in December 2003 did nothing to stop
the attacks.

Iraqis grew more and more resentful of the
U.S. occupation of their country. American troops
rounded up Iraqis suspected of being insurgents.
Thousands of Iraqis were held prisoner. When
photos appeared showing U.S. troops torturing
Iraqi prisoners, there was evidence that this
behavior had the approval of the U.S. secretary of
defense. All of these things fed the fire of Iraqi
hostility toward the United States. Polls showed
that a vast majority of the Iraqis wanted U.S.
troops out of Iraq.

The Bush administration refused to consider
withdrawing from Iraq. Meanwhile, U.S.
casualties were mounting. By the middle of
2006, more than 2,500 Americans had died.
Thousands more were wounded, often quite
severely. The administration went to great
lengths to keep the American public from
seeing the coffins, and to keep the armless
and legless veterans out of sight.

As bad as American casualties were, Iraqi casualties were much greater. By mid-2006, hundreds of thousands of Iraqis had died. The country was a shambles. People lacked clean water and electricity and lived amid violence and chaos.

At the beginning of the war, a large majority of the American people had accepted the Bush administration's argument that Saddam Hussein had "weapons of mass destruction," and that the invasion of Iraq was part of the "war on terror." The major media did not question this, and the Democratic Party largely supported the war.

But as the war went on, the situation became clearer. Operation Iraqi Freedom had brought neither democracy, nor freedom, nor security to Iraq. The U.S. government had deceived the American people about "weapons of mass destruction" that did not exist. It had claimed that the attacks of September 11, 2001, were linked to Iraq, when there was no evidence to show this. It had supported torture and imprisonment without trial for thousands of people in Iraq and in the United States.

The administration was also using the war as an excuse for violating Americans' constitutional rights. Under the Patriot Act, the United States could pick up people in Afghanistan and other places and accuse them of terrorism. Instead of treating them as prisoners of war, who have rights under international law, the government created a new label for them: "unlawful enemy combatants." They were locked up in Guantánamo Bay, a U.S. military installation in Cuba. Rumors of torture came out of this prison, and some prisoners committed suicide.

In the fall of 2006, the U.S. Congress passed a bill that allowed the Central Intelligence Agency (CIA) to continue the harsh interrogation of suspected terrorists in secret prisons around the world. The bill also did away with the right of habeas corpus for an "unlawful enemy combatant," even a U.S. citizen. The loss of this right, which is guaranteed in the U.S. Constitution's Bill of Rights, meant that prisoners would not be brought before a court to challenge their arrest.

The Anti-War Movement

PROTESTS AGAINST THE WAR IN IRAQ TOOK place all over the United States. They were smaller than the huge anti-war demonstrations of the Vietnam era, but they showed that the Bush administration's policies were losing support.

Cindy Sheehan, whose son Casey died in Iraq, spoke out powerfully against the war. When she camped near Bush's ranch in Crawford, Texas, she drew support from all over the country. In a speech to a Veterans for Peace gathering in Dallas, Sheehan addressed President Bush: "You tell me the truth. You tell me that my son died for oil."

As the war in Iraq continued, young people who had joined the military began to reconsider. Diedra Cobb of Illinois declared herself a conscientious objector, someone whose moral beliefs prevent her from fighting. Cobb wrote, "I joined the Army thinking that I was, quite possibly, upholding some of the mightiest of ideals for the greatest, most powerful country on this earth. . . . There had to be some good that would come out of the carnage, in the end. But this is where I made my mistake, because in war there is no end."

(left)
Anti-war activist Cindy Sheehan speaks to the news media at the White House, 2005.

Between the beginning of the war and the end of 2004, according to CBS news, 5,500 soldiers deserted. Many went to Canada. One of them was a former staff sergeant in the Marine Corps. He told a hearing in Toronto that he and his fellow marines shot and killed more than thirty unarmed men, women, and children, including a young Iraqi who got out of his car with his arms in the air.

An English newspaper, *The Independent,* reported on U.S. deserters. It said, "Sergeant Kevin Benderman cannot shake the images from his head. There are bombed villages and desperate people. There are dogs eating corpses thrown into a mass grave. And most unremitting of all, there is the image of a young Iraqi girl, no more than eight or nine, one arm severely burnt and blistered, and the sound of her screams."

It was getting harder to get young Americans to join the armed forces, so the military stepped up its recruiting efforts. Recruiters targeted teenagers. They visited high schools, approaching students at football games and in school cafeterias. Anti-war groups took up the challenge. They visited schools to tell young people the other side of the story.

By 2006, polls showed that a majority of Americans were against the war and lacked confidence in President Bush. Some journalists began to speak out boldly, even in media that earlier had supported the administration or remained quiet. On Memorial Day, May 30, Andy Rooney told viewers of the television show *60 Minutes* that he was a veteran of World War II. Then he said, "We use the phrase 'gave their lives,' but they didn't give their lives. Their lives were taken from them. . . . I wish we could dedicate Memorial Day, not to the memory of those who have died at war, but to the idea of saving the lives of the young people who are going to die in the future if we don't find some new way— some new religion maybe—that takes war out of our lives."

Salt Lake City, Utah, is generally considered a conservative place, one that would support the administration's war in Iraq. But thousands of people cheered Mayor "Rocky" Anderson when he called President Bush a "dishonest, war-mongering, human-rights violating president." Bush's time in office, declared Anderson, would "rank as the worst presidency our nation has ever had to endure."

Two Storms

THE BUSH ADMINISTRATION TRIED HARD TO keep the country in a fiercely nationalistic mood—a mood of "us versus them" that would whip up support for the Iraq war and other administration policies. One result of this strong nationalist feeling was a wave of resentment against millions of immigrants, especially Mexicans, who had come to the United States without legal status. These immigrants were seen as taking jobs from people in the United States, even though various studies showed that they did not hurt the economy, but helped it.

Congress approved plans to build a 750–mile fence along the southern borders of California and Arizona. It was supposed to keep out Mexicans who were trying to escape the poverty in their home country. The U.S. government did not seem to see the irony in the idea of a fence to keep poor Mexicans from coming *into* territory that the United States had seized from Mexico in the 1840s.

In the spring of 2005, Congress discussed laws to punish people who were in the United States illegally. Huge demonstrations took place around the country, especially in California and the

(*left*)
Protesters holding a massive American flag during the immigration rally in downtown Dallas, 2006.

Southwest, as hundreds of thousands of people demanded equal rights for immigrants. The protestors included both immigrants and Americans who supported them. One of their slogans was "No Human Being Is Illegal."

The Bush administration faced growing disapproval of the war in Iraq and criticism of its immigration policy at home. Then a natural disaster struck. In August 2005, Hurricane Katrina hit the Gulf Coast states of Mississippi and Louisiana. The levees that protected the city of New Orleans from the Mississippi River gave way. Together, the storm and flood destroyed much of the city, killed or injured thousands of people, and left hundreds of thousands homeless.

Americans and the world were shocked when the federal government was slow and inefficient in helping survivors in the stricken city. "People around the world cannot believe what they're seeing," said an article in the *Washington Post*. "From Argentina to Zimbabwe, front-page photos of the dead and desperate in New Orleans, almost all of them poor and black, have sickened them, and shaken assumptions about American might. How can this be happening, they ask, in a nation whose wealth and power seem almost supernatural in so many struggling corners of the world. . . International reaction has shifted in many cases from shock, sympathy and generosity to a growing criticism of the Bush administration's response to the catastrophe of Hurricane Katrina."

The Katrina experience also reminded people that while millions in Africa, in Asia, and even in the Untied States were dying of malnutrition and sickness, and while natural disasters were taking huge tolls of life all over the world, the United States government was pouring its enormous wealth into war and the building of empire.

In November of 2006, Americans went to the polls to elect members of the House of Representatives and the Senate. The voters had many issues on their minds. One of the most important must have been the disastrous war in Iraq, and the way it was draining the nation's wealth.

When the votes were counted, the Democratic Party had taken control from the Republicans in both the House of Representatives and the Senate by a narrow margin. This didn't mean that Americans were filled with enthusiasm for the Democrats, but it did mean that they were saying "no" to the administration of George W. Bush, the Republican president. The voters had taken the power of government away from the president's party, and they had given politicians a chance to lead the country in a new direction. It was a rare democratic moment in the recent history of the nation.

CHAPTER TWENTY-SIX

"RISE LIKE LIONS"

I AM OFTEN ASKED HOW I CAME TO WRITE this book. One reason is that after twenty years of teaching history and political science, I wanted to write a different kind of history book—one that was different from the ones I had had in school, and the ones given to students across the country.

By that time, I knew that there is no such thing as a pure fact. Behind every fact that a teacher or writer presents to the world is a judgment. The judgment says, "This fact is important, and other facts, which I am leaving out, are not important." I thought that some of the things that had been left out of most history books were important.

The beginning of the Declaration of Independence says that "We the people" wrote the document. But the authors of the Declaration were really fifty-five privileged white men. They belonged to a class that wanted a strong central government to protect their interests. Right down to this day, government has been used to serve the needs of the wealthy and powerful. This fact is hidden by language that suggests that all of us—rich and poor and middle class—want the same thing.

Race is another issue. I did not realize, when I first started to study history, how badly twisted the teaching and writing of history had become by ignoring nonwhite people. Yes, the Indians were there, and then they were gone. Black people were visible when they were slaves, then they were freed, and they became invisible. It was a white man's history. Massacres of Indians and of black people got little attention, if they were mentioned at all.

Other themes and issues were also overlooked in the standard, mainstream telling of history. The suffering of the poor did not get much attention. Wars were plentiful, but histories did not tell us much about the men and women and children on all sides who were killed or crippled when leaders made the decision to go to war. The struggles for justice by Latino people in California and the Southwest were often ignored. So were the claims of gay and lesbian people for their rights, and the change in the national culture that they brought about.

The title of this book is not quite accurate. A "people's history" promises more than any one person can deliver, and it is the hardest kind of history to recapture. I call it that anyway because, with all its limits, it is a history that is disrespectful of governments and respectful of people's movements of resistance.

Most history books suggest that in times of crisis we must look to someone to save us. In the Revolutionary crisis, the Founding Fathers saved us. In the Civil War, Lincoln saved us. In the Depression, Franklin D. Roosevelt saved us. Our role is just to go to voting booths every four years. But from time to time, Americans reject the idea of a savior. They feel their own strength, and they rebel.

So far, their rebellions have been contained. The Establishment—the club of business leaders, generals, and politicians—has always managed to keep up the pretense of national unity, with a government that claims to represent all the people. But the Establishment would like Americans to forget the times when people who seemed helpless were able to resist, and people who seemed content demanded change. Blacks, women, Indians, young people, working people—all have found ways to make their voices heard, and to bring about change.

Most histories say little about revolt. They place the emphasis on the acts of leaders, not the actions of ordinary citizens. But history that keeps alive the memory of people's resistance suggests new kinds of power.

Imagine the American people united for the first time in a movement for fundamental change. Imagine society's power taken away from the giant corporations, the military, and the politicians who answer to corporate and military interests.

We would need to rebuild the economy for efficiency and justice. We would start on our neighborhoods, cities, and workplaces. Work would be found for everyone. Society would benefit from the enormous energy, skill, and talent that is now unused. The basics—food, housing, health care, education, transportation—would be available to all.

The great problem would be to bring about all this change through cooperation, not through systems of reward and punishment. Social movements of the past give hints of how people might behave if they were working together to build a new society. Decisions would be made by small groups of people, working as equals. Perhaps a new, diverse, nonviolent culture would develop over time. The values of cooperation and freedom would shape people's relationships with one another and the raising of their children.

All of this takes us far from history, into the realm of imagination. But it is not totally removed from history. There are glimpses of such possibilities in the past—in the labor movement, for example, or the Freedom Rides, or the cultural changes of the 1960s and 1970s.

Two forces are now rushing toward the future. One wears a splendid uniform. It is the "official" past, with all its violence, war, prejudices against those who are different, hoarding of the good earth's wealth by the few, and political power in the hands of liars and murderers.

The other force is ragged but inspired. It is the "people's" past, with its history of resistance, civil disobedience against the military machine, protests against racism, multiculturalism, and growing anger against endless wars.

Which of these forces will win the future? It is a race we can all choose to join, or just to watch. But we should know that our choice will help determine the outcome.

Women garment workers in New York City, at the start of the twentieth century, gained inspiration for their own movement of resistance from the words of the poet Shelley:

> Rise like lions after slumber
>
> In unvanquishable number!
>
> Shake your chains to earth, like dew
>
> Which in sleep had fallen on you—
>
> Ye are many, they are few!

Glossary

Abolitionism Movement to abolish, or end, something, such as slavery

Anarchism A belief that governments are by nature oppressive, and that people should live free from the authority of the state, the church, and corporate power, and share the wealth of the earth

Annex To take control of a territory and add it to a country

Capitalism Economic system in which income-producing property (such as farms and factories) is owned by individuals or corporations and competititon in a free marketplace determines how goods and services will be distributed and priced

Communism The idea that capitalism has outlived its usefulness, that it must be replaced by a system in which the economy is collectively managed, and its wealth distributed according to people's needs

Conservative Tending to support established institutions and traditional values and to be wary of social change

Democracy Government that is ruled by the people, who usually elect representatives to form the government

Depression A period of low economic activity and high unemployment

Elite A group that is powerful within a society, often because of having money, or herditary authority, or noble status

Emigrant Someone who leaves his or her home country to live in a different country

Federalist Supporter of a strong central, or federal, authority; supporter of national interests over states' rights

Feminism The belief that women are equal to men and
deserve equal rights

Immigrant Someone who comes into a country to live there

Imperialism Empire building

Indenture A contract that binds a person to work for someone else for a certain length of time

Left-wing Liberal or radical

Liberal Tending to support strong civil liberties and to be
open to social change

Massacre Killing a number of people, usually in a brutal or
violent way

Militia Citizens who are armed and can act as soldiers in an
emergency

Monopoly An economic situation in which an entire industry
is controlled by a single corporation, or just a few of them

Nationalism Strong loyalty to one's country or ethnic group,
with the feeling that that country or group is more important than others, or has higher standing, and that its interests should always be supported

Racism The belief that racial differences make some people
better or worse than others; also, treating people differently because of race

Radical Extremely critical of the existing social system

Ratification The process by which something is voted on,
accepted, and made into law

Right-wing Politically **conservative**

Socialism A society of equality, in which not profit but usefulness determines what is produced

Speculator Someone who buys large amounts of land, not to
use it but to resell it at a profit

Strike An action by people in a **union** who refuse to work
until their demands are met

Suffrage The right to vote

Terrorism Acts of violence, possibly against civilians, carried
out for political reasons by people who do not formally
represent a state or its armed forces

Union Association of workers who bargain for wages and benefits together instead of one by one

Index

"smart bombs"
  kill civilians in Iraq, 359
Smith, John, 16
social class struggle, 214–217, 233,
  294. *See also* class struggle
Social Security Act, 254
socialism, 175, 177, 182, 203,
  211–212, 215–216, **429**
  fear of, 232
  seen as "menace," 215
Socialist Party, 211, 215, 227, 230,
  240
  falling apart, 237
  headquarters raided in Seattle,
    236
Socialist Workers Party, 267
soldiers, 73, 78
  attack antiwar marchers, 230
  black, 194, 196
  break strikes, 216
  break up veterans' demonstra-
    tion, 248–249
  declare themselves conscien-
    tious objectors, 413
  desert, 129, 133
    Iraq War, 414
    Vietnam War, 307
  die from eating spoiled meat,
    191
  dig trenches in Saudi Arabia,
    359
  go unpaid, 74, 82
  kill strikers, 167
  kill women, children, and
    POWs, 196
  loot and rape, 132
  march against their con-
    sciences, 127
  mutiny, 75, 133
  write home from Vietnam, 297
songwriters, 207, 210
Sorensen, Theodore, 339
South, The
  desegregation of schools, 279
  public opinion of segregation,
    292
  rebellion of blacks, 284
  secession of states, 143–144

sit-ins, 285, 287
theft of Indian lands, 107,
  112–116
South Africa, 349, 351
Soviet Union, 268–270, 355
  arms race, 363
  collapse, 356
Spain, 2, 7–8, 10, 15
  colonies, 26, 107, 109, 189–191,
    193
Spanish-American War, 189–192,
  201
Speckled Snake, 115
Spies, August, 179–180
spy ships, 301
Stamp Act of 1765, 61
  protests against, 56, 61
Stand for the Children, 383, 385
Standard Oil Company, 203
Stanton, Elizabeth Cady, 101
state troopers
  as strikebreakers, 206
steelworkers, 181–182
Steffens, Lincoln, 203
Stevens, John Paul, 394
stock market crash, 1929, 240
strikes, 96–97, 98–99, 157, 163,
  181–182, 235–236, 238,
  251–252, **430**
  coal miners, 216
  communist involvement, 240
  copper miners, 366–367
  for 11-hour workday, 161
  for 10-hour workday, 159
  for 8-hour workday, 179
  factory workers, 98–99, 161,
    163
  garment workers, 204–205
  Homestead Strike of 1892, 176,
    181–182
  Latinos and, 366–367
  railroad workers, 166–168, 182
  statistics, 210
  steelworkers, 206
  strikebreaking, 181–182, 216
  during World War II, 267
  See also general strikes; sit-
    down strikes

HOWARD ZINN (1922–2010) influenced several generations of Americans with his ideas on politics and history, most importantly his belief that we can't be neutral on a moving train—that history has no bystanders, only participants. After serving as a bombardier in World War II, Zinn became a lifelong antiwar activist. His experiences in the civil rights and antiwar movements taught him that change happens not because of what our elected leaders decide, but when mass movements force our leaders to act responsibly and justly. Howard Zinn's three most important books are *A People's History of the United States* (including the Spanish-language edition, *La otra historia de los Estados Unidos*), *Voices of a People's History of the United States*, by Howard Zinn and Anthony Arnove, and *The Zinn Reader*, for which Zinn chose the shorter writings from across the span of his career as a teacher, activist, and historian.

REBECCA STEFOFF is the author of many books for children and young adults. In addition to writing on a number of topics in American history, including a biography of the Shawnee chieftain Tecumseh and a ten-volume series of historical atlases, she has adapted Ronald Takaki's award-winning history of Asian Americans, *Strangers from a Different Shore*, into a series for young readers. Stefoff received her B.A. from Indiana University and her M.A. from the University of Pennsylvania. Currently she lives in Portland, Oregon.

To Be Like Jesus

TO BE
LIKE JESUS

Inspiration From the
GOSPEL *of* LUKE

SISTER ANN SHIELDS, S.G.L.

PUBLISHED BY ST. ANTHONY MESSENGER PRESS
CINCINNATI, OHIO

Unless otherwise noted, Scripture passages have been taken from the *Revised Standard Version*, Catholic edition. Copyright 1946, 1952, 1971 by the Division of Christian Education of the National Council of Churches of Christ in the USA. Used by permission. All rights reserved.
Note: The editors of this volume have made minor changes in capitalization to some of the Scripture quotations herein. Please consult the original source for proper capitalization.

Cover design by Candle Light Studio
Cover images copyright Photodisc and Shutterstock/Szefei
Book design by Mark Sullivan

Library of Congress Cataloging-in-Publication Data

Shields, Ann, 1939-
To be like Jesus : inspiration from the Gospel of Luke / Ann Shields.
p. cm.
Includes bibliographical references (p.   ) and index.
ISBN 978-0-86716-951-5 (pbk. : alk. paper) 1. Bible. N.T. Luke—Meditations. 2. Catholic Church—Prayers and devotions. I. Title.
BS2595.54.S55 2010
242'.5—dc22

2009049750

ISBN 978-0-86716-951-5

Copyright ©2010, Sr. Ann E. Shields and the Servants of God's Love.
All rights reserved.

Published by Servant Books, an imprint of St. Anthony Messenger Press.
28 W. Liberty St.
Cincinnati, OH 45202
www.ServantBooks.org

Printed in the United States of America.

Printed on acid-free paper.

10 11 12 13 14   5 4 3 2 1

CONTENTS

An Open Letter to Readers

As I begin this series of reflections on the Gospel of Luke, there are a number of things I would like to share as preparation for your prayer and study.

Firstly, please do not sit down and read this little book from cover to cover in one or two sittings. You could; it is not large. The main purpose of this book is not to give you information, though I do hope you gain some. The main purpose is to allow not only your mind but your heart and your spirit to be open to God's voice speaking to you through His Word. I want you to *pray* and *reflect* and *make application* for a good period of time on *each* Gospel passage of the Sundays in Ordinary Time, Cycle C, most of which are taken from the Gospel of Luke. I pray that these reflections will help you toward a real encounter with the living God and His plan for your life.

So I ask that you read *one reflection a week* in preparation for Sunday Mass, taking portions of your daily prayer time during the week to read that Gospel over and over, ponder it, and apply it to your life. Then ask God for the grace to live what you have learned. Go slowly! Good things take time.

Pope Benedict teaches, "'[S]piritual reading' of Sacred Scripture ...consists in [poring] over a biblical text for some time, reading it and rereading it, as it were, 'ruminating' on it as the Fathers say and squeezing from it, so to speak, all its 'juice,' so that it may nourish meditation and contemplation and, like water, succeed in irrigating life itself."[1]

Have you ever watched a cow chew its cud? I have. When Pope Benedict asks us to *ruminate* on the Word, that's what he is talking about. Ponder, chew, reflect on the meaning over and over and over, then put yourself in some of the Gospel scenes, and ask yourself honestly what you might have said or done if you had been present. You'll see some things that will surprise you, some things that will challenge you about yourself. Always remember: This is the *living Word*. God's Spirit is present in the Word; there is power to change flowing from God's Word. Ask for it!

Archbishop of Denver Charles Chaput spoke about this power of the Word in an address to the National Catholic Bible Conference on June 26, 2009:

> Time and again, in the history of the Chosen People and God's Church, renewal has come about by the recovery of God's Word. God's Word has the power to change hearts and history. And by recalling such periods of renewal in salvation history, we can learn important lessons for our own day.
>
> In the Old Testament, the most dramatic example of renewal through God's Word is the story of Josiah, which is found toward the end of 2 Kings and 2 Chronicles [see 2 Kings 22—23; 2 Chronicles 34—35].... The story of Josiah is a story of the renewal of God's people through the recovery of God's Word....
>
> Renewal happened because Josiah recovered God's Word

and made it available to everyone.... We need to remember the lesson of Josiah's witness; that is, that we need to hear God's Word, not just one day a week but every day, until it soaks deeply into our souls. This is what Josiah did....

Another key lesson to draw from Josiah is the need for hope in the midst of darkness. The culture of Josiah's day had capitulated to the worst forms of paganism. His personal pursuit of holiness flew in the face of his own family's wickedness. The Temple of Jerusalem itself had been converted into a pagan shrine, and all of this profanity had gone on for more than a generation. The God of Israel was abandoned so completely that the book of the Torah was lost.

...Josiah refused to despair in the face of the overwhelming task.... [S]ince Josiah imbibed God's Word so deeply into his heart, the memory of him retains the flavor of God's sweet Word. Our lives too must be infused with the sweet fragrance of God's Word and the bright hope that it brings us in the midst of our own dark times![2]

Finally, let me make a few points relative to the Gospel of the apostle Luke.

1. Luke was a gentile, and he wrote his Gospel sometime between AD 80 and 90.

2. His main theme is the overarching universal message of salvation. Christ has come for all people and all nations.

3. Luke's Gospel is the only one to give us the parables of the Prodigal Son and the Good Samaritan. He is the only author to tell us of Gabriel's announcement to Mary. Luke alone records Jesus as a boy, when he was lost to Mary and Joseph in the

temple. Only Luke's Gospel records the Magnificat, the Benedictus prayed by Zechariah, the Gloria sung by the angels at the birth of Christ, and the Song of Simeon—all of which are daily prayers of the whole Church.

4. Luke's treatment of the blessed Mother in this Gospel is unparalleled.[3]

Remember these points as you read. It will help you appreciate how the Holy Spirit inspired Saint Luke. May you be very blessed in your relationship with Christ as you allow Saint Luke to guide you into a deeper and richer understanding of Christ and His teaching. And may the grace of God give you a hunger and thirst for the truth, the Truth which is really a person—Jesus Christ.

Do not let your own weaknesses, faults, and sins deter you. Repent and get up again and again. You honor the Lord by such fidelity, and there is no limit to His patience and His forgiveness. May God bless and lead you day by day. May the Christ of the Gospels capture your heart and your mind in such a way that you will never be the same. For this intention you have my prayer.

Sr. Ann Shields, SGL

CHAPTER 1

Listen to Him!

As the people were in expectation, and all men questioned in their hearts concerning John, whether perhaps he were the Christ, John answered them all, "I baptize you with water; but he who is mightier than I is coming, the thong of whose sandals I am not worthy to untie; he will baptize you with the Holy Spirit and with fire."

. . .

Now when all the people were baptized, and when Jesus also had been baptized and was praying, the heaven was opened, and the Holy Spirit descended upon him in bodily form, as a dove, and a voice came from heaven, "You are my beloved Son; with you I am well pleased."

Luke 3:15–16, 21–22

This is one of those familiar passages that we hear every year—more than once if we attend daily Mass. The tendency is to listen to the first few words, say to ourselves, "Oh, I know that," and then indulge in some distraction until the Gospel is completed. Let me recommend that you get yourself in the habit of praying this prayer or something like it before Mass begins: "Lord, help me, by the grace of your Spirit, to really listen to your Word today, that I might receive the wisdom and life-giving power it contains."

We see in this passage that the people have been touched by John's teaching, and many have responded to his call of repentance and conversion. They even have begun to wonder if John is the promised Messiah.

It is easy, when we do something good—perform a generous act, for example, or give advice that is gratefully accepted—to think of ourselves as "pretty good." We give ourselves a pat on the back and take whatever compliments we receive. Often we do not acknowledge the source that enables us to be of help. And that can get us into trouble.

All of us should take a long look at John the Baptist. He is *genuinely* humble. When he realizes what people are saying about him, when he sees the admiration and devotedness of his disciples, he immediately announces the truth. He attributes nothing to himself! "I baptize with water," he says—that is, "I am giving you the opportunity to repent of your sins"—*but* "there is one greater than I who is coming. I am not fit to perform the action of the lowest slave."

John acknowledges the truth of who he is and the truth of who God is. He knows that he is the messenger, that no matter how popular he is, he cannot save *anyone*. He can lead people to Jesus, but only Jesus can save.

Note too the humility of Jesus in presenting Himself for baptism, identifying with the sins of men, not setting Himself apart: He "emptied himself, taking the form of a servant, being born in the likeness of men" (Philippians 2:7).

Do I walk in the truth of who I am and who God is? How strong is pride in me, to want to be acknowledged and thanked for everything I do? How willing am I to have as my first priority that Jesus be seen and known and loved by what I think and say and do?

Note too the presence of the Trinity in this passage. As Jesus is baptized, the Holy Spirit reveals Himself in the form of a dove, and the Father speaks: "This is my beloved Son." Are you able to "hear" in your spirit that God the Father calls *you* his beloved son or daughter? When you were baptized you were brought into the family of God. This is not just a poetic or dramatic figure of speech. God graced you through the sacrament to enter into a personal, eternal relationship. Do you know, genuinely *know*, God as your Father? Ask the Holy Spirit to help you: He will reveal the truth to you.

We need to give God time in silence each day, learning to know Him through the Scriptures so we can distinguish His voice from all the voices and noises and distractions that the world offers. The Holy Spirit genuinely wants to lead us and guide us into the fullness of truth—into the fullness of a relationship with Him. All good things take time. Are you giving Him that time?

Let God, through His Spirit, plant the seed of His Word in your heart. Then give it the water and the nourishment it needs.

FURTHER REFLECTION

Your words were found, and I ate them,
  and your words became to me a joy
  and the delight of my heart.

Jeremiah 15:16

CHAPTER 2

Do Whatever He Tells You

On the third day there was a marriage at Cana in Galilee, and the mother of Jesus was there; Jesus also was invited to the marriage, with his disciples. When the wine failed, the mother of Jesus said to him, "They have no wine." And Jesus said to her, "O woman, what have you to do with me? My hour has not yet come." His mother said to the servants, "Do whatever he tells you." Now six stone water jars were standing there, for the Jewish rites of purification, each holding twenty or thirty gallons. Jesus said to them, "Fill the jars with water." And they filled them up to the brim. He said to them, "Now draw some out, and take it to the steward of the feast." So they took it. When the steward of the feast tasted the water now become wine, and did not know where it came from (though the servants who had drawn the water knew), the steward of the feast called the bridegroom and said to him, "Every man serves the good wine first; and when men have drunk freely, then the poor wine; but you have kept the good wine until now." This, the first of his signs, Jesus did at Cana in Galilee, and manifested his glory; and his disciples believed in him.

John 2:1–11

In Year C of the Liturgical Cycle of Ordinary Time, the Gospel is usually that of Luke, but here is an exception. I have included it in this book because of what it teaches about our relationship to the Blessed Mother.

Again, it is a familiar passage, so don't get distracted and pass over certain crucial words. In fact, before you go further, read this passage out loud so you have two senses involved, hearing and seeing. That will help you take in and retain more of what this Gospel passage is showing.

Jesus performs His first miracle at a neighborhood wedding. Jesus, His mother, and His disciples are all invited. What a blessing it is to be able to gather with family and friends and genuinely rejoice in the gift of love between man and woman. Jesus did; His mother did. Make sure to include the Lord and His mother in your celebrations. They love to be invited!

So here the people are celebrating, and suddenly it becomes apparent that the new bride and groom are in for a very embarrassing moment that will spoil the festivities. They have run out of wine. Mary recognizes the problem. What does she do first? She goes to her Son. I don't think it is overly pious, when we are in a similar situation and no apparent solution is obvious, to turn to Mary and ask her to talk to her Son. Why not?

Mary looks at Jesus and says, "They have no wine." She doesn't ask Him to do anything; she just informs Him of the problem. Can you see the look that passes between them? And look at Jesus' response: How does *your concern* affect me? Jesus makes it clear that this is not the time for the beginning of his public ministry.

But Mary is undeterred. Because of love, of genuine charity toward this couple, she boldly tells the servers, "Do whatever he tells you." She has such confidence in her Son that she can ask Him to move up the timetable of His public revelation to help a poor embarrassed couple.

And He does! Not only does He change the water—gallons upon gallons of it—into wine, but He makes it the best wine! He not only answers Mary's request; He supplies the very best and in superabundance!

So remember that Jesus loves to be present in the festive, joyful moments of our lives. And remember to go to His mother in all your needs. She desires to help because God has given her that role, and Jesus listens to her requests even when His timetable seems to be different. Go to her especially when you are confused or in impossible or embarrassing situations. God is concerned about every aspect of our lives, not just the "religious" ones.

And when you know that God is asking something of you that you find difficult or seemingly impossible, ask His mother to pray for you, that you may "do whatever He tells you."

FURTHER REFLECTION

It is written,

"Man shall not live by bread alone,

but by every word that proceeds from the mouth of God."

Matthew 4:4

CHAPTER 3

How Deep Is Your Faith?

Inasmuch as many have undertaken to compile a narrative of the things which have been accomplished among us, just as they were delivered to us by those who from the beginning were eyewitnesses and ministers of the word, it seemed good to me also, having followed all things closely for some time past, to write an orderly account for you, most excellent Theophilus, that you may know the truth concerning the things of which you have been informed....

And Jesus returned in the power of the Spirit into Galilee, and a report concerning him went out through all the surrounding country. And he taught in their synagogues, being glorified by all.

And he came to Nazareth, where he had been brought up; and he went to the synagogue, as was his custom, on the sabbath day. And he stood up to read; and there was given to him the book of the prophet Isaiah. He opened the book and found the place where it was written,

"The Spirit of the Lord is upon me,
because he has anointed me to preach good news to the poor.
He has sent me to proclaim release to the captives
and recovering of sight to the blind,
to set at liberty those who are oppressed,
to proclaim the acceptable year of the Lord."

And he closed the book, and gave it back to the attendant, and sat down; and the eyes of all in the synagogue were fixed on him. And he began to say to them, "Today this Scripture has been fulfilled in your hearing."

Luke 1:1–4; 4:14–21

First, a few facts to position this excerpt from the Gospel of Luke:

Luke is probably a second-generation Christian, so his Gospel is heavily dependent on eyewitness accounts. He writes as an historian, careful to quote reliable sources as opposed to opinions; he is very careful to transmit apostolic tradition. His main goal, after ascertaining the historical facts, is to use those facts to build up the faith of the Christian community.[1]

Theophilus is a well-known personage of the time, distinguished by position or service, who may have supported Luke in his efforts—that is, a benefactor or a seeker of truth being evangelized by Luke through his account. No other mention of this person is given in historical documents, except for a similar dedication in Luke's Acts of the Apostles (see Acts 1:1).

Now let's take a look at the verse "And Jesus returned...." From where did He return? The preceding verses tell us that He is returning from the desert, where He fought great temptations successfully through the powerful use of Scripture. Whenever you are trying to understand a particular section of Scripture, always look at what incident or teaching preceded it. This gives you context, which is a tremendous help in understanding God's teaching, direction, and goals.

Jesus is becoming known. The people honor Him and are eager to hear Him. Then He comes into His hometown, visits the synagogue, and is given the passage from Isaiah to read. Jesus is in front of all those who knew Him as a boy and as a very young man. He would have always seemed very much like them. Now He stands up, proclaims that the Spirit of God is on Him and that He is anointed to preach good news to the poor and release to the captives. The blind will see, and the prisoner will be set free from his burdens.

Jesus announces "the acceptable year"—that is, the jubilee year, a year celebrated every fifty years in Israel's history, when all debts are cancelled and all property and slaves are returned to their original owners. The prophet Isaiah, whom Jesus quotes, projected this jubilee year into the future, when the Messiah would come to set the people free from idols and from sin. Jesus announces, "Today this Scripture is fulfilled in your hearing." In other words, the Messiah has come!

In the next meditation we will see the reactions of the people to this announcement. But for now, put yourself in that synagogue. Knowing yourself, knowing your own level of faith in Christ, what would you have done if you had heard Jesus say, "Today this Scripture is fulfilled"?

Only the Messiah could say that. Would you have been shocked? Would you have walked out shaking your head, sure that Jesus, Mary's son, was crazy? Would you have been angry, confused, bewildered? What would you have done if you were in the synagogue that day?

How deep is your faith in Christ? When your faith is challenged, how do you respond? Do you go directly to Jesus for help? Do you trust Him? If you are doubtful do you ask Him questions, or do you walk away?

These are questions to ask in the Lord's presence. It is very important to know whether your faith is shallow or weak, weak but growing, or not as stable as you want it to be. How do you strengthen your faith? What can you do to "water" your faith, to help it grow?

Jot down your current responses to these questions in a little notebook, where you can refer to them. We will come back to the question of faith later.

If you think your faith is weak or if you have never answered those kinds of questions before, pray to the Holy Spirit. In baptism and confirmation you were given many graces: Faith is a huge one, but you have to activate it and use it, or it grows weak for lack of exercise. Say daily, "Lord, increase my faith." Explore your personal convictions about Christ and His gospel. Ask the Lord to lead you to the fullness of truth—the truth of who He is, the truth of His teaching, the truth of who you are, and the destiny for which God created you. You will never regret the time spent on these questions.

FURTHER REFLECTION

You are my hiding place and my shield;

I hope in your word.

Psalm 119:114

CHAPTER 4

Know the Truth

And he began to say to them, "Today this Scripture has been fulfilled in your hearing." And all spoke well of him, and wondered at the gracious words which proceeded out of his mouth; and they said, "Is not this Joseph's son?" And he said to them, "Doubtless you will quote to me this proverb, 'Physician, heal yourself; what we have heard you did at Capernaum, do here also in your own country.'" And he said, "Truly, I say to you, no prophet is acceptable in his own country. But in truth, I tell you, there were many widows in Israel in the days of Elijah, when the heaven was shut up three years and six months, when there came a great famine over all the land; and Elijah was sent to none of them but only to Zarephath, in the land of Sidon, to a woman who was a widow. And there were many lepers in Israel in the time of the prophet Elisha; and none of them was cleansed, but only Naaman the Syrian." When they heard this, all in the synagogue were filled with wrath. And they rose up and put him out of the city, and led him to the brow of the hill on which their city was built, that they might throw him down headlong. But passing through the midst of them he went away.

Luke 4:21–30

Have you ever been in a situation in which the whole tone, the whole emotional environment, has changed very quickly? You can find yourself a bit off balance. What is going on? There was peace, and now a certain hostility invades. You look around for friends who might give you a clue as to why the atmosphere has changed. What has happened?

Let's take a look at the concluding verses from the last meditation: People were listening attentively to Jesus' reading of Isaiah, and even in today's passage it says that they all spoke well of Him. But there is a hint of change in their attitude: "Is not this Joseph's son?" In other words, "How can this guy we know be talking like this?"

Jesus now introduces the Old Testament prophets who lived during very difficult times. God was angry with the Israelites for their unfaithfulness and instead blessed the gentiles, the pagans of that time, a widow and a leper. The crowd listening to Jesus gets very angry. Why? They believe that the Messiah is coming to liberate *them*. They, not the pagans, are the chosen people. Their belief system is threatened; they cannot even entertain the idea that they might be wrong.

And what do we do when our deeply held beliefs are challenged? Perhaps we ask questions; perhaps we try to understand what the other person is saying. Or maybe we just attack those who challenge us.

And so it is with the crowd to whom Jesus speaks. They are furious with Him because He questions their beliefs. They even attack physically, pushing Him to the top of the hill, prepared to throw Him down to His death. This son of Joseph, the carpenter, is saying that the Messiah is coming for *all*, even the pagans, who will put their faith in God. In the minds of this crowd that is blasphemy, so they literally try to kill Him. But Scripture says, "He passed through their midst and went away."

We are living in an age when we need to clearly know what we believe and how to defend it with clarity *and* charity! If we react in anger to others' attacks on our faith or on the person of Jesus Christ, we only raise the walls of defense and push people away. Hitting people over the head with the words of truth will not convert them. God is love, and He desires that we become good disciples. This means:

• We need to read Scripture, the *Catechism of the Catholic Church*, and good books that can immerse us in the truth!

• Remember that the truth is a *person*—Jesus. Our goal is not just to get good information but to draw closer and closer to Him. Then when we speak, by the power of His Spirit, we can convey the love God has for those who are confused.

• All of us working in the political arena, the pro-life movement, parish renewal, evangelism, and so on have to *die to* ourselves, especially when we feel like wringing someone's neck. When we get frustrated with people who will not listen, we have to consider what Jesus would do—*pray*! Ask Jesus for His heart of compassion even in the face of sin and stubbornness. Only He can change the hearts and minds of those we are trying to reach. Let Him be the Savior. We are the servants, the disciples.

• Jesus' disciples are to be like Him. Yes, read and study, so you are prepared to answer your accusers with the truth, but even more, be immersed in the Spirit of the One who is all truth and all mercy. Again, this happens in prayer. God can work in you if you surrender to His plan, His timing.

• Make sure that Jesus Christ is at the center of your life, your relationships, your home, your work, and your recreation. Then offer yourself to be used to bring to others the only truth that can set people free!

FURTHER REFLECTION

Jesus then said to the Jews who had believed in him, "If you continue in my word, you are truly my disciples, and you will know the truth, and the truth will make you free."

John 8:31

CHAPTER 5

They Left Everything

While the people pressed upon him to hear the word of God, he was standing by the lake of Gennesaret. And he saw two boats by the lake; but the fishermen had gone out of them and were washing their nets. Getting into one of the boats, which was Simon's, he asked him to put out a little from the land. And he sat down and taught the people from the boat. And when he had ceased speaking, he said to Simon, "Put out into the deep and let down your nets for a catch." And Simon answered, "Master, we toiled all night and took nothing! But at your word I will let down the nets." And when they had done this, they enclosed a great shoal of fish; and as their nets were breaking, they beckoned to their partners in the other boat to come and help them. And they came and filled both the boats, so that they began to sink. But when Simon Peter saw it, he fell down at Jesus' knees, saying, "Depart from me, for I am a sinful man, O Lord." For he was astonished, and all that were with him, at the catch of fish which they had taken; and so also were James and John, sons of Zebedee, who were partners with Simon. And Jesus said to Simon, "Do not be afraid; henceforth you will be catching men." And when they had brought their boats to land, they left everything and followed him.

Luke 5:1–11

There are a number of lessons to be learned from this passage. Let's take a look at a few of them:

These are professional fishermen: They know their job; they know this lake, where best to find the fish and at what time of day. On this scene comes Jesus. He is what? A carpenter. The disciples know this, and so, from a human point of view, why would they listen to His advice about fishing?

Can't you imagine them thinking, "He is not familiar with this lake; He doesn't have the experience we do." You could understand, couldn't you, if the disciples said, "Jesus, that's a bad idea, and we don't want to waste the time going out again. We've been out all night. The fish aren't biting. We'll try another day." We learn from experience, and these fishermen had lots of experience.

You and I can look back on our lives and see how much wisdom we have gained from experience. We have a certain confidence as a result. That is a blessing from God, and we should always thank Him for the insight, the wisdom, that comes from our daily living.

Nevertheless, with all the know-how Simon has gained from experience, look at what he says to Jesus: "We have worked hard all night and caught nothing, *but at Your word*, because You have asked it, even though it makes no sense to me, I will take the boats back out." Simon heeds the word from Jesus to "let down the nets," and the result is the biggest catch they have ever had.

That is faith, brothers and sisters. It took faith in Jesus, not wisdom or expertise, to bring in a huge catch. Peter is stunned, and he begins to realize who Jesus is. He perceives in a veiled way divinity, and his response is to fall down before Jesus in humility.

Have you ever found yourself in this position? God, either directly or through others, is asking you to do something that makes no sense from a human perspective. Maybe it's a new job or a new project at work, maybe it is offering yourself for some new ministry in the parish, maybe it is taking on a new leadership role. It's exciting to be offered a position or directly invited. But you may think that you have no experience in this area, and you quickly eliminate yourself from consideration.

It may be that God is offering you an opportunity to see Him work *through you*, and what He asks of you is faith. Sometimes—not always but sometimes—God takes us outside of our comfort zone, outside the scope of our acquired wisdom, and asks us to trust Him because He has a plan to use us for the building of His kingdom. This teaches us to depend more on Him because we have not walked, so to speak, this path before. We *have* to depend on Him.

Have you had such an experience in your life? How did you handle it? Did your faith grow?

If you haven't had an experience like this, imagine it. How might you respond? How strong is your faith in a God who wants to care for you in every circumstance?

Ask the Lord to increase your faith in God, who knows your every need and desires to provide for you—sometimes even beyond your understanding or expectation. He needs disciples who trust their Lord and who are willing to take the risk of being labeled foolish, all for the glory of God.

FURTHER REFLECTION

Let your compassion come to me, that I may live;

for your law is my delight.

Psalm 119:77

CHAPTER 6

Blessed Are You

And he came down with them and stood on a level place, with a great crowd of his disciples and a great multitude of people from all Judea and Jerusalem and the seacoast of Tyre and Sidon, who came to hear him and to be healed of their diseases....

And he lifted up his eyes on his disciples and said:

"Blessed are you poor, for yours is the kingdom of God.

"Blessed are you that hunger now, for you shall be satisfied.

"Blessed are you that weep now, for you shall laugh.

"Blessed are you when men hate you, and when they exclude you and revile you, and cast out your name as evil, on account of the Son of man! Rejoice in that day, and leap for joy, for behold, your reward is great in heaven; for so their fathers did to the prophets.

"But woe to you that are rich, for you have received your consolation.

"Woe to you that are full now, for you shall hunger.

"Woe to you that laugh now, for you shall mourn and weep.

"Woe to you, when all men speak well of you, for so their fathers did to the false prophets."

Luke 6:17, 20–26

Does this passage make you uncomfortable? Jesus calls the poor blessed; he calls those who mourn blessed; he calls the hated and despised and excluded blessed! Such statements are the very opposite of what the world has taught us to value: prestige, position, power.

We know this, and yet how influenced are we by the power of the media and the Internet, the film and music industries? How affected are we by what the world offers as goals and priorities? Do we envy the successes and possessions and influence of friends and coworkers?

Most people, even those who read this passage often in prayer, are more affected than they would wish to be by the world's attractions. Many just shrug their shoulders and say, "I don't get it." Brothers and sisters, we *need* to get it. These are Jesus' words!

Jesus is telling us quite plainly that we need to take on his priorities and values. We need a conversion or a deeper conversion. Conversion means a turning away from something to begin a new direction—toward another kind of goal from that which we were pursuing. Every Christian needs to turn *away* from what the world says is most important for our happiness and to turn *toward* what the gospel says is most important.

Besides prayer and asking for grace, we need to allow God's Word to lead us. When I begin to embrace the values that come from the mind and heart of my heavenly Father, who desires my good above all else, then my conversion begins.

> Blessed are you when you find no satisfaction in the material wealth of the world but only in the riches of a relationship with Christ.

Blessed are you who hunger for justice and mercy, for generosity and compassion, for love flowing from the heart of God; you will have your fill.

Blessed are you who weep over the pain suffered by so many in the world and offer your prayer and service to alleviate as much of it as you can.

Blessed are you who are willing to serve and stand for and defend the defenseless, the poor, the outcasts of the world, because you love Jesus—because you know that every man, woman, and child is created in His image and is loved by Him, no matter how much their sin may have distorted His image.

Blessed are you who love Jesus and will do whatever is in your power to serve Him in the "distressing disguise of the poor."

Are these the values and motives that shape you as a Christian in the middle of a very secularized society? If they are, then blessed are you, for one day you will laugh and rejoice and inherit the kingdom of God forever. Whether you are materially rich or materially poor is of little consequence. What is of great consequence is whether you have found the treasure hidden in the field, the pearl of great price, and are willing to give up all things for union with Christ.

If these are not the values you live by, are you willing to ask Jesus to give you the grace of conversion? He will turn you upside down and inside out, and I guarantee, you will never be happier.

Let me tell you about a young man whom I have known since he was a small boy. A few years ago he graduated with a business degree from a very well-known university. He decided to volunteer for the Peace Corps for two years, using his newly acquired business skills to help people in Benin start businesses of their own. Once he was there, though, he saw the desperate need for a home for children in distress. So while helping people acquire the knowledge and skills to open new and needed small businesses, my young friend also went about raising money and seeking supplies and people to build the children's home and get it staffed—quite an undertaking!

I e-mailed my friend and asked him what he would say about this Gospel passage in light of his experience. Here is his answer:

> Early on in my service, I suddenly realized that it was not so much about the work I was doing but rather about the person I was serving. It's very easy to go into a volunteer situation such as the one I was in with grand schemes to improve the community's way of life, change things for the better, and so on. However, in my experience, that is not enough and is often just a recipe for frustration. When we are serving and we are doing it for Christ, we need to be able to see His face in those we are serving, and if we don't even acknowledge those we are serving, how would this be possible? So the work, the project, is not leading anywhere if I don't put the person first.
>
> I guess another way of putting it is that the call to love can't be answered by loving a project, or your work, or even a community from a general perspective. It needs to be answered by loving a person. It's this realization that has made my service much more fulfilling. It brings its own set of challenges and frustrations, but it certainly leads to more peace and joy.

May this realization be ours in all the service we render.

FURTHER REFLECTION

How can a young man keep his way pure?

By guarding it according to your word.

Psalm 119:9

CHAPTER 7

Love Your Enemies

But I say to you that hear, Love your enemies, do good to those who hate you, bless those who curse you, pray for those who abuse you. To him who strikes you on the cheek, offer the other also; and from him who takes away your cloak do not withhold your coat as well. Give to every one who begs from you; and of him who takes away your goods do not ask them again. And as you wish that men would do to you, do so to them.

If you love those who love you, what credit is that to you? For even sinners love those who love them. And if you do good to those who do good to you, what credit is that to you? For even sinners do the same. And if you lend to those from whom you hope to receive, what credit is that to you? Even sinners lend to sinners, to receive as much again. But love your enemies, and do good, and lend, expecting nothing in return; and your reward will be great, and you will be sons of the Most High; for he is kind to the ungrateful and the selfish. Be merciful, even as your Father is merciful.

Judge not, and you will not be judged; condemn not, and you will not be condemned; forgive, and you will be forgiven; give, and it will be given to you; good measure, pressed down, shaken together, running over, will be put into your lap. For the measure you give will be the measure you get back.

Luke 6:27–38

There have been countless sermons preached on this passage of Scripture, and each of us has probably heard a number of them. But so often nothing changes in our personal lives: We continue to gossip, to nurse our grievances and our grudges, to harden our hearts in lack of forgiveness, to justify our unwillingness to let go of some real or perceived injustice.

The only way to break through lifelong patterns of unforgiveness is to take time—daily for a while—and reflect on all God has forgiven you. Your sin contributed to His crucifixion: Your sin and mine helped to nail Him to that cross. The debt of all our sin—large and small—for which we repent is cancelled! How often do we thank Him for the freedom He has won for us?

You have a Father who so loves you that He not only forgives when you ask for it but He *forgets*! Yes, "as far as the east is from the west, so far does he remove our transgressions from us" (Psalm 103:12). See also Isaiah 43:25: "I, I am He who blots out your transgressions for my own sake, and I will not remember your sins." This is how God loves. This is how God forgives.

Ponder that for your own life, and no longer carry like a heavy burden the past mistakes and sins for which you have asked forgiveness. God has not only given forgiveness but also forgotten the sin. Even if you repeatedly fall in the same area, each time you ask forgiveness, the sin is forgiven and forgotten! This is how *God* loves. And He tells us in effect, "Now go and do likewise. Love one another as I have loved you!"

We can "be merciful, even as [our] Father is merciful" only when we know how deeply we are loved—and that takes time before the Lord and reading the truth of His love in the Scriptures. Let the truth, the living water, seep into your mind and soul. Let the truth water the parched and dry land of your heart.

It may take months; deserts are not turned into fertile fields overnight. Besides, God *wants* time with you, in order to build a personal relationship with you. Remember, He loves you. If you were the only person on the face of the earth, you are so infinitely precious that He would have died for you alone!

Once you begin to walk in growing confidence of His love, *then* you can begin to love others as God would wish. As God has forgiven you, you can, in turn, forgive. And then today's Scripture passage is no longer an impossible ideal but a courageous call to union with Christ in His love for His people.

Just tell the Lord, "Help me to know the love You have for me and the forgiveness You have so generously given me. Then help me to love others as You have loved me. Come, Holy Spirit, teach me, lead me. Give me Your courage, Your wisdom, Your peace. With these I will be wealthy beyond price."[1]

FURTHER REFLECTION

Your word is a lamp to my feet
and a light to my path.

Psalm 119:105

CHAPTER 8

Judge Rightly

One of the Pharisees asked him to eat with him, and he went into the Pharisee's house, and sat at table. And behold, a woman of the city, who was a sinner, when she learned that he was sitting at table in the Pharisee's house, brought an alabaster flask of ointment, and standing behind him at his feet, weeping, she began to wet his feet with her tears and wiped them with the hair of her head, and kissed his feet, and anointed them with the ointment. Now when the Pharisee who had invited him saw it, he said to himself, "If this man were a prophet, he would have known who and what sort of woman this is who is touching him, for she is a sinner." And Jesus answering said to him, "Simon, I have something to say to you." And he answered, "What is it, Teacher?" "A certain creditor had two debtors; one owed five hundred denarii, and the other fifty. When they could not pay, he forgave them both. Now which of them will love him more?" Simon answered, "The one, I suppose, to whom he forgave more." And he said to him, "You have judged rightly." Then turning toward the woman he said to Simon, "Do you see this woman? I entered your house, you gave me no water for my feet, but she has wet my feet with her tears and wiped them with her hair. You gave me no kiss, but from the time I came in she has not ceased to kiss my feet. You did not anoint my head with oil, but she has anointed my feet with ointment. Therefore, I tell you, her sins, which are many, are forgiven, for she loved much; but he who is forgiven little, loves little." And he said to her, "Your sins are forgiven." Then those who were at table with him began to say among themselves, "Who is this who even forgives sins?" And he said to the woman, "Your faith has saved you; go in peace."

Luke 7:36–50

This is one of those Gospel passages where the meaning should be very clear to everyone at the first reading. The Pharisee is sure he can earn God's favor by being obedient to every part of the Law—all 613 precepts of it. As long as he is fulfilling these detailed rules, then he can, in a certain way, be sure that he has "bought" God's approval.

This is legalism, and it is particularly a sin of otherwise good people. They are always at Mass on Sunday, maybe even at daily Mass. They go to confession frequently; they participate in many devotional exercises privately and in church. They may even serve faithfully in parish and diocesan activities. *But* if they are doing such things *primarily* to win God's approval and that of others, their worship and service are empty in God's sight.

If we fall into this sort of legalism, one other error falls close on its heels, that of being judgmental. If we stand on the "lofty heights" and look down on others who don't do all we do, we have compounded our sin. This produces blindness and deafness to true Christian living, in us and in others. The Pharisee has made this very serious error: He judges someone a terrible sinner who in fact is approved by God. (You do not want to find yourself opposing God!)

What *are* we called to do?

First of all, we are to live God's commandments because we love Him, and we want to be like Him and live with Him forever! We can never gain God's approval by trying to *earn* His love. The commandments are there so that we can set our course right, to follow the path He has marked out for us, as a way of *thanking* Him for saving us through the death of His Son. The highest compliment we can pay God is to tell Him we are eternally grateful for what He has done in creating and saving us and that we want to become like Him by following the path He has marked out for us. That is true humility, and His help will be with us every moment.

The second lesson we learn from this Gospel passage is that we can never judge the state of someone's soul. Sometimes we are in a position of authority, from which it is necessary to make judgments about people's actions but *never* about the state of their souls! Only God knows the heart—really!

The Pharisee judged the sinful woman's eternal destiny. He had no understanding of her encounter with God and the work of grace in her soul. He judged her soul based on comparing her to his external actions! But Jesus knew her level of repentance, her gratitude, and her decisions to change. He saw her humility in the way she ministered to Him even in the midst of condemnation and scorn and rejection from the "righteous."

God taught me a lesson about judging others in a very clear way. I was speaking at a large conference. All morning, wherever I walked, a man would follow me. His constant interruptions when I was speaking with others irritated me. And every time I was alone, he seemed to appear. My frustration was mounting, though I tried to be kind.

An administrator of the conference saw my dilemma and, as I left the stage at lunchtime, came to escort me out of the arena. As I came down the steps from the stage, this man came through the crowd and touched my hand.

"Sister, the Lord wants to tell you something," he said, and he proceeded to give me truth that could only have come from the heart of God. I was stunned! He smiled and said, "I have a head injury from an accident, and I know I annoyed you, but I felt I had to give you this message that I think is from God."

I came down to the foot of the steps and put my arm around him. Crying, I asked for his forgiveness and thanked him for his perseverance. He smiled, even laughed a little, and assured me that he forgave me.

This experience taught me to be very careful in my judgments of people who are disabled, annoying, or disruptive. We do not know whom God has chosen to speak to us, the human instruments that God uses to bring us out of sin and into the light of His love.

Never make judgments about the state of another's soul, and be very slow about any other kinds of judgments—even when you have the authority and need to make them. Always talk to God first.

FURTHER REFLECTION

> For my thoughts are not your thoughts,
>
> neither are your ways my ways, say the LORD.
>
> For as the heavens are higher than the earth,
>
> so are my ways higher than your ways
>
> and my thoughts than your thoughts.

Isaiah 55:8–9

CHAPTER 9

Who Do You Say I Am?

Now it happened that as he was praying alone the disciples were with him; and he asked them, "Who do people say that I am?" And they answered, "John the Baptist; but others say, Elijah; and others, that one of the old prophets has risen." And he said to them, "But who do you say that I am?" And Peter answered, "The Christ of God." But he charged and commanded them to tell this to no one, saying, "The Son of man must suffer many things, and be rejected by the elders and chief priests and scribes, and be killed, and on the third day, be raised."

And he said to all, "If any man would come after me, let him deny himself and take up his cross and follow me. For whoever would save his life will lose it; whoever loses his life for my sake, he will save it."

Luke 9:18–24

In a previous book I wrote, *Deeper Conversion*, I commented on a similar passage in Matthew about the necessity, and often the courage needed, to clearly declare that Jesus Christ is Lord of your life.[1] When Jesus asks that question of his disciples, "Who do you say that I am?" He is asking that same question of each of us. In prayer we need to declare—and often—who He is for us.

This is a way of professing our faith in Him! It is a way of clearing out the temptations to put ourselves or our careers or ministries or other people on the thrones of our lives. There is room for only *one* on the throne of the Christian life, and that is Jesus, our Lord, our Savior, our King, our God. Professing that truth out loud and often during your daily time of prayer brings great grace and clarity as you go through your day, with all the demands and interactions with people and decisions that need to be made.

But in this reflection I want to focus on another part of that conversation that Jesus was having with his disciples: "If any man would come after me, let him deny himself and take up his cross and follow me." What does that mean for each of us in the twenty-first century?

First of all, it means exactly what it did in the first century. If you want to be a true Christian, not one in name only but a disciple Jesus would recognize, then you need to focus on those words: *Let him deny himself.*

When I was a little girl, I was, like most of us, introduced to Lent and its practices: I should give up things because Jesus gave up His life for me and because I wanted to be more like Jesus. Candy and ice cream were my usual two sacrifices. As I got older I learned that I should do something with the money I would have spent on that candy and ice cream. And so I learned about children, hungry and sick, in other parts of the world, and I saved up my nickels and dimes for the missions—all well and good. However, St. Paul wrote, "When I was a child, I spoke like a child, I thought like a child, I reasoned like a child; when I became a man, I gave up childish ways" (1 Corinthians 13:11).

Jesus tells us that if we want to be his follower, then we need to deny *self!* Denying ourselves things can be a very necessary part of the process, but as we mature we need to come to the point of giving over our whole lives—that is, our bodies, our minds and hearts, our hopes and dreams, our talents and gifts and treasure—to Him who alone can enable us to fulfill the purpose for which we were created.

Every Christian has to learn that lesson, and it is not easy. To die to self is real death. It at times can be violent (internally) because we are disordered: We see only from our little perspective, and we want to protect at all costs (says the flesh) whatever gives us happiness. It is only when we lose our life that we can honestly say, "Jesus, I want You to be Lord of my life. I entrust myself to You with all my hopes and fears. Lead me, guide me, direct me according to Your plan for my life. I want to fulfill the purpose for which You created me. Help me to yield, for in You is true freedom. In You is the *fullness* of life!"

And I can promise that if you live according to this prayer of surrender, you will know genuine joy—not as the world gives but as God gives. As my father used to say, "You can take that to the bank."

FURTHER REFLECTION

I rise before dawn and cry for help;

I hope in your words.

Psalm 119:147

CHAPTER 10

Follow Me

When the days drew near for him to be received up, he set his face to go to Jerusalem. And he sent messengers ahead of him, who went and entered a village of the Samaritans, to make ready for him; but the people would not receive him, because his face was set toward Jerusalem. And when his disciples James and John saw it, they said, "Lord, do you want us to bid fire come down from heaven and consume them?" But he turned and rebuked them. And they went on to another village.

As they were going along the road, a man said to him, "I will follow you wherever you go." And Jesus said to him, "Foxes have holes, and birds of the air have nests; but the Son of man has nowhere to lay his head." To another he said, "Follow me." But he said, "Lord, let me first go and bury my father." But he said to him, "Leave the dead to bury their own; but as for you, go and proclaim the kingdom of God." Another said, "I will follow you, Lord; but let me first say farewell to those at my home." Jesus said to him, "No one who puts his hand to the plow and looks back is fit for the kingdom of God."

Luke 9:51–62

Let me begin by giving you some historical context. It will help you understand this passage and the importance of the message. *The Navarre Bible* commentary states:

> The Samaritans were hostile toward the Jews. The enmity derived from the fact that the Samaritans were descendants of marriages of Jews with gentiles who repopulated the region of Samaria at the time of the Assyrian captivity (8th Century BC). There were also religious differences: the Samaritans had mixed the religion of Moses with various superstitious practices and did not accept the temple of Jerusalem as the only place where sacrifices could properly be offered. They built their own temple on Mount Gerazim in opposition to Jerusalem (cf John 4:20); this was why, when they realized that Jesus was headed for the holy City, they refused him hospitality.[1]

Jesus' public ministry and life on this earth as man is drawing to a close. He has his face set to carry out the Father's will in Jerusalem. He knows it will end in the victory over sin and death, but He knows a very heavy trial awaits Him in the cosmic battle of good and evil.

Jesus has made preparations for this long journey, including the sending of a few disciples ahead to find hospitality. And what do they find? Jesus is the Lord of all life, yet those without faith refuse Him the simple but essential needs of the body. They are bound and blinded by centuries of prejudice.

Unredeemed human nature can cause major blocks to God's action from one generation to the next. Is there a way that long-standing prejudice of some sort—perhaps in your extended family—has blinded you to God's actions through certain people? Are you in danger of rejecting God because of the blindness and deafness that prejudice can cause?

You can break the cycle of prejudice by renouncing the lies or fears that bred it in the first place and giving them no more room in your life. All God needs is a docile (teachable) spirit on your part.

James and John, furious at the discourtesy extended to Jesus and secondarily to them, do what men (and women) have often done when they are deeply offended and think they have righteousness (justice) on their side. They plan to retaliate. Let's attack, they say. We sometimes want to hurt those who have hurt us— by arms, by words, or worse, by praying a curse upon them. We want to cast fire.

But look carefully: What does Jesus do? "He turned and rebuked them." I have no idea what He said to James and John, but I can imagine His saying, "Don't you yet understand, you who are my closest companions? Don't you see how I love and forgive? Can't you imitate me?"

Jesus didn't argue; he didn't fight. He just left those Samaritans and went on to another town, where He hoped He could find lodging. And the Samaritans were far poorer as a result, though they did not know that.

Jesus is very near us when we are hurt or ridiculed, when we are excluded, shut out. Of course such things make us angry, but how do we express that anger?

Know that God is near. Stop before you make some retort; maybe slip away from the scene of the action. Decide honestly, with God's grace, that it won't do any good to say something right then.

Pray, "Lord, show me what to do here." Ask God to show you the right time and place to address the problem. Maybe you should ask for an apology or for a meeting when the principal people have calmed down. This is making a response rather than just a reaction. A considered response always stands the chance of reconciliation, whereas reacting will only exacerbate the problem.

I am not saying that taking these steps will immediately resolve the issue, but it will put you in a position to be used by God to foster reconciliation. You cannot make someone reconcile, but you are God's servant when you try to set the right tone and foster the conditions for forgiveness. Trust God that, even if the result you hope for doesn't immediately happen, you have done the right thing. Stay in that posture, and God will use you! Sometimes He mercifully lets us see the fruits of our labors to foster reconciliation. Sometimes, like Jesus, we have to wait.

The other major lesson in this passage has to do with the people Jesus goes on to meet. To the first, the one who says, "I will follow you wherever you go," Jesus says, "You really don't know what you are saying. I have no home, no resting place; I am on mission to preach and teach and minister. Even the foxes and the birds have more provided for them than I do. Knowing this, do you still want to follow me?"

To the second person Jesus says, "Follow me." What an incredible privilege to have the Son of God call someone to serve with Him. But the person is surprised and does what we often do when we haven't had time to prepare. "Sure, sure, I will do it, but first…" And then there is a string of excuses to delay responding to God's invitation.

Now, you might say, "But, Sister, he is asking to bury his father. Surely that trumps everything." Of course Jesus wants us to care for our parents and provide for them—that is part of the fourth commandment. It is a primary way of serving God, if done in the right spirit. What Jesus is emphasizing here though, in a hyperbolic way, is that nothing, not even family needs, should supersede God's call. He is looking for the right spirit, the right attitude, the willingness to give up things that are high on our priority list. Let us nourish that spirit in our hearts.

FURTHER REFLECTION

Let my cry come before you, O LORD;

give me understanding according to your word!

Psalm 119:169

CHAPTER 11

Your Names Are Written in Heaven

After this the Lord appointed seventy others, and sent them on ahead of him, two by two, into every town and place where he himself was about to come. And he said to them, "The harvest is plentiful, but the laborers are few; pray therefore the Lord of the harvest to send out laborers into his harvest. Go your way; behold, I send you out as lambs in the midst of wolves. Carry no purse, no bag, no sandals; and salute no one on the road. Whatever house you enter, first say, 'Peace be to this house!' and if a son of peace is there, your peace shall rest upon him; but if not, it shall return to you. And remain in the same house, eating and drinking what they provide, for the laborer deserves his wages; do not go from house to house. Whenever you enter a town and they receive you, eat what is set before you; heal the sick in it and say to them, 'The kingdom of God has come near to you.' But whenever you enter a town and they do not receive you, go into its streets and say, 'Even the dust of your town that clings to our feet, we wipe off against you; nevertheless know this, that the kingdom of God has come near.' I tell you, it shall be more tolerable on that day for Sodom than for that town...."

The seventy returned with joy, saying, "Lord, even the demons are subject to us in your name!" And he said to them,

"I saw Satan fall like lightning from heaven. Behold, I have given you authority to tread upon serpents and scorpions, and over all the power of the enemy; and nothing shall hurt you. Nevertheless do not rejoice in this, that the spirits are subject to you; but rejoice that your names are written in heaven."

Luke 10:1–12, 17–20

I want to make several points in regard to this passage.

Note how it begins with the words *after this*. After what? Look back to the passage we read for last Sunday. Jesus was giving substantial teaching to those who wished to follow him more closely. He spoke to them of the cost. Then, says this week's Gospel, the Lord appointed seventy people to carry the message of salvation. My point: Always look at the context; it helps you understand the passage better and see its importance.

"As lambs in the midst of wolves…." Serving God will be hard, Jesus is saying. You will feel very vulnerable at times and overwhelmed by the work.

"Carry no purse." This doesn't mean being foolish about what you need. But look first to the Lord for His direction, and no matter what you carry, put your trust in Him, not in things. When a group of people receive you and hence Christ, accept what they offer to sustain you, and then bring to them the healing, the mercy, the peace of Christ. Keep your message clear and simple.

If people don't receive you, they are rejecting Christ. It will go easier for the people of Sodom, even though their sins were grievous, than for the people who reject the gospel message. Christ did not come to those people of the Old Testament, but for these people the kingdom of God *is* among them—Christ Himself—and they refuse to hear and see. Therefore their punishment will be greater.

The second part of the passage narrates the disciples' return from their first missionary journey. They are excited: God really did use them. They preached exactly what Christ told them to, and the truth of their message was blessed by signs and wonders. Can you hear them? "Jesus, I was scared, but I did what You said, and I told them the story that You once told us, and they listened! They actually listened and believed! Then I prayed for their sick like You taught us, and people were healed. Jesus, it happened!"

Can you imagine Jesus' joy as the disciples shared their stories and new insights? He must have laughed and listened and rejoiced and prayed with them. What tremendous fellowship!

But then—and this is an important point for us all—Jesus says to them, "Don't let your rejoicing stop here. Move on—in faith. Rejoice that you are on the path to eternal life, and you are leading others to follow that same path. Rejoice that your names are written in heaven."

In other words, always keep your mind on the ultimate goal for yourselves and for others! The healing, the deliverance from the power of Satan—don't let these wonderful things become a destination, an end point. The goal of these blessings is to help us fix our minds and hearts on the eternal life to come.

In our daily lives we need to be conscious that we are going to live forever. We want that eternal life to be with the Father, the

Son, and the Holy Spirit. This is the one goal, the one prize, for the Christian: union with God. Don't allow anything, no matter how good, how exciting in this world, sidetrack you from that.

FURTHER REFLECTION

It is good for me that I was afflicted,
   that I might learn your statutes.
The law of your mouth is better to me
   than thousands of gold and silver pieces.

Psalm 119:71–72

CHAPTER 12

Go and Do Likewise

And behold, a lawyer stood up to put him to the test, saying, "Teacher, what shall I do to inherit eternal life?" He said to him, "What is written in the law? What do you read there?" And he answered, "You shall love the Lord your God with all your heart, and with all your soul, and with all your strength, and with all your mind; and your neighbor as yourself." And he said to him, "You have answered right; do this, and you will live."

But he, desiring to justify himself, said to Jesus, "And who is my neighbor?" Jesus replied, "A man was going down from Jerusalem to Jericho, and he fell among robbers, who stripped him and beat him, and departed, leaving him half dead. Now by chance a priest was going down that road; and when he saw him he passed by on the other side. So likewise a Levite, when he came to the place and saw him, passed by on the other side. But a Samaritan, as he journeyed, came to where he was; and when he saw him, he had compassion, and went to him and bound up his wounds, pouring on oil and wine; then he set him on his own beast and brought him to an inn, and took care of him. And the next day he took out two denarii and gave them to the innkeeper, saying, "Take care of him; and whatever more you spend, I will repay you when I come back." Which of these three, do you think, proved neighbor to the man who fell among the robbers?" He said,

"The one who showed mercy on him." And Jesus said to him, "Go and do likewise."

Luke 10:25–37

Our human nature is such that we often try to get out of giving more than we already have. We do all we can to justify our limits: why I do these things and why I don't do those things. We tend to put ourselves in the best light in the process—to justify our decisions or behavior or speech.

This lawyer is having one of those moments. He may be genuinely interested in what Jesus is saying, but he wants to make sure that pursuing this goal of eternal life is not going to demand more than he is prepared to give.

Jesus, wise teacher, answers his question with a question. And the lawyer is prepared: He knows the Law. Jesus commends him and tells him, in effect, just do what you yourself have said. But the lawyer is uncomfortable. There have to be limits to this neighbor business. So Jesus tells a story to illustrate His point.

The story is a powerful one. Two religious people pass by the injured man, choosing to put Israel's purity laws, which forbade them to touch the corpses of anyone but family members, above charity. One commentator says:

> These regulations were not meant to prevent people from helping the injured; they were designed for reasons of hygiene and respect for the dead. The aberration of the priest and the Levite in this parable consisted in this: they did not know for

sure whether the man who had been assaulted was dead or not, and they preferred to apply a wrong interpretation of a secondary, ritualistic precept of the Law rather than obey the more important commandment of loving one's neighbour and giving him whatever help one can.[1]

But the Samaritan, the enemy of the Jews, sees the injured person and makes an investment of time and money to see that the man is cared for. As we would say, he went above and beyond the call of duty. And he was serving someone who would have despised him under other circumstances.

The lawyer gets the point. And so should we. Whom do I exclude from my circle of friends and acquaintances? Why do I hold back from helping someone in need? It might be too hard, take too much time, cost too much. Or maybe I have other important things to do for God.

When I was about three, I was awakened one night by a noise. Curious, I crawled out of bed and went to my parents' room. No one was there, so I went on through the apartment. In the dining room I could see light coming from the kitchen. There stood a man with knife in hand. His wife, with a slash down her arm, was being held by my father and my mother. Peering between their legs unnoticed, I heard my dad say to this very drunk and angry man, "Joe, give me the knife." After much swearing and cursing, he did, and then he sat down and began to sob.

I don't know if my mother had ever witnessed such brutality, but both she and Dad befriended that couple over the three additional years we lived in that apartment building and many years after. The couple actually resolved their problems, and years later, on a visit home, I saw an announcement of their fiftieth wedding anniversary. I like to think my parents played a part by the way they loved their neighbor.

Neighbors can come in all sizes, races, religious backgrounds, personal strengths, weaknesses, failures, and sins. Can I love them? Yes, by the power that God gives me.

Who is your neighbor? All those for whom Christ died. If that is true, can you exclude anyone from your prayer, your service, your heart? Your compassion may be the gift that saves someone from death.

FURTHER REFLECTION

For this reason I bow my knees before the Father, from whom every family in heaven and on earth is named, that according to the riches of his glory he may grant you to be strengthened with might through his Spirit in the inner man, and that Christ may dwell in your hearts through faith; that you, being rooted and grounded in love, may have power to comprehend with all the saints what is the breadth and length and height and depth, and to know the love of Christ which surpasses knowledge, that you may be filled with all the fulness of God.

Ephesians 3:14–19

CHAPTER 13

The Good Portion

Now as they went on their way, he entered a village; and a woman named Martha received him into her house. And she had a sister called Mary, who sat at the Lord's feet and listened to his teaching. But Martha was distracted with much serving; and she went to him and said, "Lord, do you not care that my sister has left me to serve alone? Tell her then to help me." But the Lord answered her, "Martha, Martha, you are anxious and troubled about many things; one thing is needful. Mary has chosen the good portion, which shall not be taken away from her."

Luke 10:38–42

So often commentaries on this passage reflect on Mary as representing the contemplative life and Martha the active life. That is one interpretation. Most people I know who are familiar with these verses sigh and say, "Oh, I wish I were a contemplative; I envy them. But I've got a family, a business, a career." In other words, "I am about much serving; that's my life! I don't have time to spend in lengthy prayer."

I frankly don't think that such a division is what God has in mind. Each of us, as true Christians, have both calls. Some are called to emphasize one aspect or another by our state in life, but all of us are called to the praise and worship of God combined with attentive listening to His Word, and all of us are called to serve and care for those in need.

So how do we apply this Scripture to our daily lives?

Let's look at Mary's part first. As I said above, all of us, all baptized Christians, are called to the praise and worship of God. But in order for that to work well, every Christian has to make some decisions. Look at what Jesus said of Mary: "Mary has *chosen* the good portion," or, "the better part," as we read in some translations. Read the verse again: "Mary has *chosen*...."

If we want this absolutely essential part of the Christian life to work well for us, we need to *choose* to make it a priority, something we value. In today's world a time of quiet, of worship, of reflection each day, would seem to be at best a luxury and at worst a waste of time. But Jesus indicates that Mary made a *choice* to prioritize her life in such a way that God got her full attention as much as possible.

Martha, on the other hand, is working very hard to serve the Master. She loves Him, she has incredible faith in Him, and right now, in her mind, the most important thing is that He receive a good hot meal and some rest. Martha is spending herself to accomplish that and is frustrated that Mary isn't helping her in the necessary chores.

We all know people who are like Martha, and perhaps you identify with her. So let's take a step back. Your relationship with God is the most important one you have. You need to "tithe" your time, so that God receives what belongs to Him! Jesus desires to lead you, to counsel you, to impart the necessary wisdom for your day. He needs to have time with you, when you give Him your undivided attention.

Start with fifteen minutes. Praise Him with music or by reading the psalms (doing both is better), read the Gospel reading for the day, offer your day to Him, and ask Him for the help you need. Then throughout the day pause for a minute or two at a time, thank Him for the day so far, and ask for the help you need. Be still for a moment before your God. (Some people set an alarm on their watch or computer to remind them to stop and listen.)

God desires to be in communication with us, to be near us, to strengthen us, to guide us. So often we are just too busy to listen. Then we wonder why this or that went wrong! In the Gospel passage Mary made this attentive listening a part of her daily life, and we need to do the same.

Yes, we do want to get our jobs done, but if we are prayerful, if time with God is the obvious priority of our lives, then we can come to our tasks peacefully. We work hard, but there is an order and calm, even a joy, in the midst of even arduous labor. We end up serving one another in the process of accomplishing a service. How? Because God has been welcomed in our personal lives; we are ultimately serving Him in whatever task we do. God is glorified! There is no higher purpose in life than that.

So the conclusion? Most of us are called to be Mary *and* Martha or John *and* Joseph as the case may be. If you follow this plan, in whatever form works for you, I think you will find yourself growing in your personal relationship with God *and* genuinely helping to build His kingdom by your service.

Remember, Mary has chosen the better part, and it shall not be taken from her. May you make the same choice she did and be a blessing to all those around you.

FURTHER REFLECTION

Mary [Jesus' mother] said, "Behold, I am the handmaid of the Lord; let it be to me according to your word."

Luke 1:38

CHAPTER 14

Our Father

He was praying in a certain place, and when he ceased, one of his disciples said to him, "Lord, teach us to pray, as John taught his disciples." And he said to them, "When you pray, say:

"Father, hallowed be your name. Your kingdom come. Give us each day our daily bread; and forgive us our sins, for we ourselves forgive every one who is indebted to us; and lead us not into temptation."

And he said to them, "Which of you who has a friend will go to him at midnight and say to him, 'Friend, lend me three loaves; for a friend of mine has arrived on a journey, and I have nothing to set before him'; and he will answer from within, 'Do not bother me; the door is now shut, and my children are with me in bed; I cannot get up and give you anything'? I tell you, though he will not get up and give him anything because he is his friend, yet because of his importunity he will rise and give him whatever he needs. And I tell you, Ask, and it will be given you; seek, and you will find; knock, and it will be opened to you. For everyone who asks receives, and he who seeks finds, and to him who knocks it will be opened. What father among you, if his son asks for a fish, will instead of a fish give him a serpent; or if he asks for an egg, will give him a scorpion? If you then, who are evil, know how to give good

gifts to your children, how much more will the heavenly
Father give the Holy Spirit to those who ask him!"

Luke 11:1–13

Let's divide this Scripture reflection into two parts.

The Lord's Prayer

Some months ago I attended a conference where Fr. Larry
Richards, a diocesan priest from Erie, Pennsylvania, gave a talk on
the Lord's Prayer that made a deep impression on me. He said
that, for all the years of his priesthood, he has given only one
penance: to pray the Lord's Prayer slowly. Even people confessing
very serious sin receive from him the same penance: one Our
Father. They say to him: "Father, didn't you hear what I con-
fessed?" He assures them that he did and tells them why he gave
this penance: "One Our Father prayed with faith and devotion
will change you."

I have taken Father Larry's advice. One day in my own prayer,
a thought came into my head that I knew was not my own:
"When you pray to the Father, I [Jesus] pray that prayer with
you." I was dumbfounded and profoundly humbled and
inspired. How could I ever pray that prayer in a distracted fashion again!

Our Father, who art in heaven. Our! All of us who pray that
prayer in faith are my brothers and sisters; we are one family. Do
I pray often for and acknowledge my *whole* family, no matter of
what race or country or personality or politics?

Hallowed be thy name. Do I honor the name of God in thought and speech?

Thy kingdom come. Thy will be done. Thy, not my! Do I really work for the building of His kingdom in my family, my parish, my work place, my recreation? Do I try to know and follow God's will instead of my own?

Give us this day our daily bread. "Lord, I come to you confident that you know my needs and that you will supply—for this day—what I need to live and love and serve." Take it one day at a time. The Lord's grace is sufficient for the needs of this day. Trust Him!

Forgive us our trespasses as we forgive those who trespass against us. This is a very hard one, but God doesn't give us an out. Forgive as He has forgiven you! At every Mass you pray this prayer. Are you a man or woman of your word? God will supply the grace and wisdom if you supply the willingness.[1]

And lead us not into temptation. It's all around us, isn't it? Moment by moment we are tempted to take the easy way, avoid people, speak against them, dilute our business principles, lie, cheat, steal. Jesus teaches us to ask the Father for help, that we might be delivered from evil. God is faithful to His promises!

Ask, Seek, Knock

In the second part of this passage, Jesus uses an analogy to show us how the Father hears us and cares for us. He says that if a friend won't help you for the sake of friendship, he will give you what you need because of your persistent begging. And if human beings do that, how much more will your heavenly Father do for you who ask Him! So ask, seek, knock. These verbs are more accurately translated as "keep on seeking, keep on knocking, keep on asking." God will not turn a deaf ear.

God will give the ultimate gift to those who persevere in faith and petition. He will give us not just the things we ask for (if they are good for our eternal welfare) but even more the greatest gift—Himself, in His Spirit. With those who seek Him, God will share His very life, His very nature. You can live in deeper and deeper union with God. Be faithful, and keep on asking.

I wrote a small book on this kind of prayer for yourself and your loved ones, *Pray and Never Lose Heart* (Servant, 2001).[2]

FURTHER REFLECTION

Let love be genuine; hate what is evil, hold fast to what is good; love one another with brotherly affection; outdo one another in showing honor. Never flag in zeal, be aglow with the Spirit, serve the Lord. Rejoice in your hope, be patient in tribulation, be constant in prayer.

Romans 12:9-12

CHAPTER 15

What Is Your Treasure?

One of the multitude said to him, "Teacher, bid my brother divide the inheritance with me." But he said to him, "Man, who made me a judge or divider over you?" And he said to them, "Take heed, and beware of all covetousness; for a man's life does not consist in the abundance of his possessions." And he told them a parable saying, "The land of a rich man brought forth plentifully; and he thought to himself, 'What shall I do, for I have nowhere to store my crops?' And he said, 'I will do this: I will pull down my barns, and build larger ones; and there I will store all my grain and my goods. And I will say to my soul, Soul, you have ample goods laid up for many years; take your ease, eat, drink, be merry.' But God said to him, 'Fool! This night your soul is required of you; and the things you have prepared, whose will they be?' So is he who lays up treasure for himself, and is not rich toward God."

Luke 12:13–21

The first point we need to note here is that Jesus knows who He is and what His mission is. He makes it clear that He is not here to solve legal issues or be an arbiter in an inheritance dispute. He doesn't get sidetracked the way we can. He doesn't deviate from the mission given Him by the Father. He is here to help us know what will enable us to receive our eternal inheritance!

We would do well to ask for wisdom when we are asked to take on new things or solve some problem. Maybe we should, and maybe we shouldn't. If we take time to put the issue before the Lord and seek wisdom, we will avoid a lot of difficulty!

In verse 15 Jesus goes to the heart of the matter: Beware all covetousness, because a man's life does not consist in the abundance of possessions! The man in the parable builds bigger barns to house all the goods he possesses. This is what happens to man without God. A true Christian would look instead for those in need and share his good fortune.

Brothers and sisters, we in the United States (and probably the whole Western world) need to address this issue. Because we are losing our faith as a nation, people are more than ever looking for something to satisfy their deepest needs. They are rejecting the Lord, who is the fulfillment of our deepest desires, and accumulating more and more possessions. I was appalled recently to see, at a friend's house, a television program that tries to help people deal with the unnecessary purchases they have made and then dumped in room after room until their houses are no longer livable. What a tragedy!

I know a number of very wealthy people whose monies are being used to alleviate hunger and disease and to build homes, schools, and hospitals in many parts of the world. They give quietly and without fanfare. Their reward will be great in heaven.

For many of you things have worked pretty well financially: You have a job and a home, and maybe you can take a vacation. But in the last number of months, money is tighter, less certain; you may have taken a hit on retirement savings and been threatened by foreclosure. How does this Gospel apply to your circumstances right now?

We have a tendency, when going through difficult times, to think that we can't be concerned about anyone or anything else. But we are not exempt from our call as Christians to meet the needs of others less fortunate than we are. Look around you. Surely you have something you can share. When we are generous in the midst of our own needs, we will see that God will not be outdone in generosity

Not one of us knows the day or the hour when we will stand before God. Will we hear these words: "Come, O blessed of my Father.... I was hungry and you gave me to eat" (Matthew 25:34–35)?

God will not check your bank account, tally up your possessions, and judge you worthy on the basis of what you have. He will look at you and see if the image of His Son is shining in your heart and in your eyes. That will be determined, in great part, by how well you loved your neighbor, how much you were willing to sacrifice to meet the material and spiritual needs of those around you—at work, in your neighborhood, in the schools your children attend, in your parish, and so on.

When we stand before God, the possessions we acquired and treasured will count for nothing. What we did with them will count for a great deal!

add to this p. 62 - 63

FURTHER REFLECTION

Thus says the LORD:

Heaven is my throne

and the earth is my footstool;

what is the house which you would build for me,

and what is the place of my rest?

All these things my hand has made,

and so all these things are mine,

> says the LORD.

But this is the man to whom I will look,

he that is humble and contrite in spirit

and trembles at my word.

> Isaiah 66:1–2

CHAPTER 16

Faithful Stewards

"Fear not, little flock, for it is your Father's good pleasure to give you the kingdom. Sell your possessions, and give alms, provide yourselves with purses that do not grow old, with a treasure in the heavens that does not fail, where no thief approaches and no moth destroys. For where your treasure is, there will your heart be also.

"Let your loins be girded and your lamps burning, and be like men who are waiting for their master to come home from the marriage feast, so that they may open to him at once when he comes and knocks. Blessed are those servants whom the master finds awake when he comes; truly, I say to you, he will put on his apron and have them sit at table, and he will come and serve them. If he comes in the second watch or in the third, and finds them so, blessed are those servants! But know this, that if the householder had known at what hour the thief was coming, he would have been awake and would not have left his house to be broken into. You also must be ready; for the Son of man is coming at an hour you do not expect."

Peter said, "Lord, are you telling this parable for us or for all?" And the Lord said, "Who then is the faithful and wise steward, whom his master will set over his household, to give them their portion of food at the proper time? Blessed is that servant whom his master when he comes will find so doing. Truly, I tell you, he will set him over all his possessions. But if that servant says to himself, 'My master is delayed in coming,' and begins to beat the menservants and the maidservants, and to eat and drink and get drunk, the master of that servant will come on a day when he does not expect him and at an hour he does not know, and will punish him and put him with the unfaithful. And that servant who knew his master's will, but did not make ready or act according to his will, shall receive a severe beating. But he who did not know, and did what deserved a beating, shall receive a light beating. Every one to whom much is given, of him will much be required; and of him to whom men commit much they will demand the more."

Luke 12:32–48

Once again, through the readings the Church offers us this Sunday, our Lord and Savior is urging us to an alertness, a preparedness, a readiness for His return. Either He will come to bring us personally to Himself, or it will be the time of His second coming, when He will judge the living and the dead. Be ready! Be alert! Do not put off until tomorrow what you can do today!

Some years ago a young woman "set out to seek her fortune" in New York. Her new job didn't last long, and she was left with no money for food or rent. Confused and helpless, she went into a little diner and asked the man behind the counter if she could wash dishes for a sandwich.

The man looked at her and then proceeded to make her a very large sandwich. The young woman saw him take money from his pocket and put it in the cash register.

Fast forward about twenty-five years. This same woman, now the owner of a successful business in New York, was walking along the street one very cold winter day and saw a homeless man sitting on the pavement. She went up to him and offered to buy him a meal. The man cursed her, which drew the attention of a cop. After listening for a few minutes, the cop urged the poor man to take the woman's offer. He helped the woman pull the man into a nearby restaurant and seat him in a booth. The woman ordered a meal for him and coffee for the policeman.

The homeless man continued to berate the woman. "Nothing is ever free. What are you going to make me do? What do you want?"

The woman sat down across from him, looked him in the eye, and said, "Twenty-some years ago, when you worked in this restaurant, you befriended a young woman who had nothing. I was that woman. I promised myself that someday I would find you and try to repay you in some way for your generosity to me. I saw you pay for my sandwich out of your own pocket, and I have never forgotten."

With that she reached into her purse for a slip of paper and wrote a name and address on it. "Go to this address. You will meet a man there named Fred. We have need of a good worker in my office. He will take care of you and, with an advance, help you find a place to live."

Who has been good to you at difficult times in your life? Have you thanked that person? Have you returned the good deed in some fashion when possible?

Have you thanked those who taught you to love the Lord and

His Word? Have you thanked those who preached His Word so that it touched your heart? Have you expressed your gratitude for those who brought you the grace of the sacraments—especially the Eucharist and reconciliation?

What have you done with all these graces and blessings? Are you ready to render an account?

Do you have a grateful spirit, a grateful heart? Or are you closed minded, hard-hearted, unable to see all the graces and blessings offered you? Perhaps you are cynical because of some incident many years ago. God desires to heal and make new.

Once you become a good steward of the graces God has given you, then you are in a position to extend them to others. There is no better way to live your life. It will then be said of you, "Well done, good and faithful servant" (Matthew 25:21).

FURTHER REFLECTION

In the trials of life and in every temptation, the secret of victory lies in listening to the Word of truth and rejecting with determination falsehood and evil.

… [L]isten anew to the Gospel, the Word of the Lord, the word of truth, so that in every Christian, in every one of us, the understanding of the truth given to him, given to us, may be strengthened, so that we may live it and witness to it.[1]

Pope Benedict XVI

CHAPTER 17

The Assumption of the Blessed Mother

In those days Mary arose and went with haste into the hill country, to a city of Judah, and she entered the house of Zechariah and greeted Elizabeth. And when Elizabeth heard the greeting of Mary, the child leaped in her womb; and Elizabeth was filled with the Holy Spirit and she exclaimed with a loud cry, "Blessed are you among women, and blessed is the fruit of your womb! And why is this granted me, that the mother of my Lord should come to me? For behold, when the voice of your greeting came to my ears, the child in my womb leaped for joy. And blessed is she who believed that there would be a fulfillment of what was spoken to her from the Lord." And Mary said,

"My soul magnifies the Lord,
and my spirit rejoices in God my Savior,
for he has regarded the low estate of his handmaiden.
For behold, henceforth all generations will call me blessed;
for he who is mighty has done great things for me,
and holy is his name.
And his mercy is on those who fear him
from generation to generation.
He has shown strength with his arm,
he has scattered the proud in the imagination of their hearts,
he has put down the mighty from their thrones,
and exalted those of low degree;

he has filled the hungry with good things,

and the rich he has sent empty away.

He has helped his servant Israel,

in remembrance of his mercy,

as he spoke to our fathers,

to Abraham and to his posterity for ever."

And Mary remained with her about three months, and returned to her home.

Luke 1:39–56

In 2010 the Feast of the Assumption falls on a Sunday, so I have included this reading here. What a blessing it is to contemplate the life of our Blessed Mother!

One commentator wrote: "Luke's portrayal of the Virgin Mary is simply unparalleled in the [New Testament] for its beauty and sensitivity."[1] Luke is the only evangelist to tell us of Gabriel's announcement to Mary. He alone records Mary and Joseph's finding of the boy Jesus in the temple. He alone records the visit of Mary and Elizabeth and the Magnificat, the beautiful prayer that burst from Mary's lips.

Luke was a scholar, but his scholarship was coupled with a heart full of love for the Lord. That is an unbeatable combination. He often gives us an understanding of the prophetic words and actions of the Old Testament as they are fulfilled in the New Testament. I quote again from the commentator:

One tradition that Luke draws upon is from 2 Samuel. He intentionally sets up the subtle but significant parallels between

Mary's visitation with Elizabeth and David's effort to bring the Ark of the Covenant to Jerusalem narrated in 2 Samuel 6. When Luke tells us that Mary "arose and went" into the Judean hill country to visit her kinswoman (Luke 1:39), he reminds us of how David "arose and went" into the same region centuries earlier to retrieve the Ark (2 Sam 6:2). Upon Mary's arrival, Elizabeth is struck by the same sense of awe and unworthiness before Mary (Luke 1:43) that David felt standing before the Ark of the Covenant (2 Sam 6:9). Parallels continue as the joy surrounding this great encounter causes the infant John to leap with excitement (Luke 1:41), much as David danced with excitement before the Ark (2 Sam 6:16). Finally, Luke adds that Mary stayed in the "house of Zechariah" for "three months" (Luke 1:40, 56), recalling how the Ark of [the] Covenant was temporarily stationed in the "house of Obed-edom" for a waiting period of "three months" (2 Sam 6:11). Taken together, these parallels show us that Mary now assumes a role in salvation history that was once played by the Ark of the Covenant. Like this golden chest, she is a sacred vessel where the Lord's presence dwells intimately with his people.[2]

The Gospel reading for this feast of Mary recounts the visitation of Mary to her cousin Elizabeth. Think about Mary's act of great charity here: She leaves her own home for an extended period of time, makes that journey—no cars, no trains, but on a donkey— to serve her older relative, to put herself in second place at a time in her own life that must have felt like an earthquake had hit it. Think about the uncertainty she faced. What should she say, and to whom? What about Joseph? Other people? Provision for the child? The future? These are all normal human questions in the face of such momentous circumstances.

Mary was like us in very many ways: She, too, had to wrestle as she adjusted to a very new plan for her life. The difference: She took God at His word. She put *all* her faith and trust in Him, even though humanly she would not have understood how it would all work out. And she will pray for us, that we may grow in faith when we have to make major adjustments in our life's plan. Ask her for help! She is a true mother to us because Jesus asked her to be. When He gave His mother to the disciple John, she became our mother as well!

In the midst of uncertainty, Mary has no doubt about who God is, and she can praise Him. She dances in the darkness of unknowing: She does not know how all things will work out, but it is enough that God has asked, and she has said yes. God is her refuge and steadying anchor. She knows Him as a God of mercy and trusts Him. Can you?

Can you praise God wholeheartedly when there are still questions and uncertainty about some major change in your life? Praise Him because He is your Savior, because His love never fails, because you are convinced that He is utterly faithful to each person.

Mary said *yes!* The Greek word denotes more than mere passive acceptance; it indicates *desire*. Meditate on that for a while. Are your yeses reluctant? Are they grudging or conditional? Do you "compromise" sometimes with God: "I'll do what you ask, if ... or when ...?

On this feast when Mary was taken up to heaven, when she experienced the full reward of her yes, ask her to help you, to pray for you, that you might be more like her, that you might grow to love Jesus so much that you would withhold nothing from Him. Ask her help to make your yes a joyous yes, knowing that He who created you knows best how to bring you to that place of full surrender to God's plan for your life.

In the midst of life's storms, He is the refuge and the steadying anchor. Mary knows Him as a God of mercy and trusted Him with her whole life. So can we!

FURTHER REFLECTION

My soul keeps your testimonies;
I love them exceedingly.

Psalm 119:167

CHAPTER 18

The Narrow Door

He went on his way through towns and villages, teaching, and journeying toward Jerusalem. And some said to him, "Lord, will those who are saved be few?" And he said to them, "Strive to enter by the narrow door; for many, I tell you, will seek to enter and will not be able. When once the householder has risen up and shut the door, you will begin to stand outside and to knock at the door, saying, 'Lord, open to us.' He will answer you, 'I do not know where you come from.' Then you will begin to say, 'We ate and drank in your presence, and you taught in our streets.' But he will say, 'I tell you, I do not know where you come from; depart from me, all you workers of iniquity!' There you will weep and gnash your teeth, when you see Abraham and Isaac and Jacob and all the prophets in the kingdom of God and you yourselves thrust out. And men will come from east and west, and from north and south, and sit at table in the kingdom of God. And behold, some are last who will be first, and some are first who will be last."

Luke 13:22–30

This is a very important passage, particularly for us who live in the Western world. Why? Because we are particularly deceived into believing that appearances are everything. As long as we look good on the outside—with nice clothes, influential friends, possessions, bank accounts, status, and power—we tend to think we are successful.

Even more seriously, we can think that if we attend Mass every Sunday, serve on all kinds of Church committees, and give money to the Church and the poor, somehow these actions make us good Christians, and God will reward us. That is in effect what these people in the Gospel are saying. But if we have done these things for the sake of appearance or to earn a "merit badge," if we have prayed primarily to be seen and thought well of, then Jesus will say, "I never knew you" (Matthew 7:23).

Everything you have or use is there because of God's kindness, not your skill or ingenuity. You could not think one good thought or idea *without God's willing it*. You have faith and the opportunity to live eternal life because God died for you on the cross, because He forgave you your sins—not once but over and over and over. And what is more, every time you sincerely ask, He will continue to forgive.

Our good deeds in this life are to be expressions of *our gratitude* for what God has won for us! It takes humility to accept that truth. Our pride rears up, and we want to say, "I accomplished this," or, "I donated that," or, "Because of my blood, sweat, and tears…" Yes, you contributed those things, and God sees that. But none of those things would have any *eternal* value if not for Jesus' willingness to die for you.

Now, here's another essential point, and it has to do with worship. If we go to Mass weekly but are there only in body, going through the motions, it does not count as worship! Jesus warns people not to "heap up empty phrases as the Gentiles do" in their prayer (Matthew 6:7). That means just uttering empty words while your thoughts are far away. That is not acceptable worship! Empty worship is not heard before God's throne.

Now, before you despair, remember that God knows our weakness. He knows how hard it is to pay attention. And He forgives! But we have got to make some decision in our personal lives to do something about it!

Remember what Jesus says in this passage: Enter by the narrow door. That first of all involves humility—the humility to live a life of gratitude for God's work on my behalf in His Incarnation and death and Resurrection. I am not my own savior; He alone saves me!

Jesus is telling me to decide that the most important relationship to invest in is my relationship with God. I need to enter into and live in that relationship through my thoughts, words, deeds, and prayer as a son or daughter, yes, but also as a child, that is, one who is willing to be taught.

I need to remember with whom I am speaking when I pray; I need also to learn to listen to and obey His Word. As I do these things faithfully, I become more and more a genuine part of the family of God.

When I die Jesus will know me, and I will know Him. There will be no greater joy in heaven and on earth: to know and to be known.

Oh, brothers and sisters, let us decide today *not* to follow the standards of the world. Rather let us follow the standards of the gospel. The gate is narrow, but the grace of God is here for us in superabundance. Our choice has eternal consequences.

FURTHER REFLECTION

For this commandment which I command you this day is not too hard for you, neither is it far off. It is not in heaven, that you should say, "Who will go up for us to heaven, and bring it to us, that we may hear it and do it?" Neither is it beyond the sea, that you should say, "Who will go over the sea for us, and bring it to us, that we may hear it and do it?" But the word is very near you; it is in your mouth and in your heart, so that you can do it.

Deuteronomy 30:11–14

CHAPTER 19

The Best Repayment

Now he told a parable to those who were invited, when he marked how they chose the places of honor, saying to them, "When you are invited by any one to a marriage feast, do not sit down in a place of honor, lest a more eminent man than you be invited by him; and he who invited you both will come and say to you, 'Give place to this man,' and then you will begin with shame to take the lowest place. But when you are invited, go and sit in the lowest place, so that when your host comes he may say to you, 'Friend, go up higher'; then you will be honored in the presence of all who sit at table with you. For every one who exults himself will be humbled, and he who humbles himself will be exalted."

He said also to the man who had invited him, "When you give a dinner or a banquet, do not invite your friends or your brothers or your kinsmen or rich neighbors, lest they also invite you in return, and you be repaid. But when you give a feast, invite the poor, the maimed, the lame, the blind, and you will be blessed, because they cannot repay you. You will be repaid at the resurrection of the just."

Luke 14:7–14

One of the great difficulties we face in our world today is this sense of entitlement that seems to intrude on so many requests and demands. I'm owed this or that; I have a right to this exemption or this privilege; I'm entitled to this raise or promotion—even when I have done almost nothing to earn it.

Something is drastically wrong here. We are like children who never grew beyond a self-centered life. Somehow a poison has invaded our minds that says, "I am a free person, and freedom means if I want it, I am entitled to it."

That is not freedom; that is license! License can be defined as taking what you want when you want, regardless of others' ownership or needs. Uncontrolled it can lead to a lawless society, to chaos and self-destruction.

I am not overly dramatizing. We have all kinds of little seeds sprouting in our land that need to be pulled up by the roots. But we cannot undertake such a project until we have removed the destructive seeds that are, sometimes silently but no less lethally, working in our own minds and hearts.

Such as jealousy and envy. What happens to you when another is honored and you are not recognized, when another is complimented or blessed and you seem to be forgotten? What goes on in your spirit when someone is praised or an event is held in their honor and you can't rejoice and enter into the occasion because "nobody has ever done anything for me"?

Such battles can be won, but they will not be until we are convinced of who we are. We are sons and daughters of the living God. All rights and privileges accorded sons and daughters of the King are ours, once we have fully given our lives to Him. Acknowledge His lordship over you, promise to be His in thought and word and action.

When you begin to live this relationship, you begin to *want* to give to others a share in the blessings you have received. You rejoice to see others honored, because they are in truth your brothers and sisters. You seek to reach out to others and build them up. In short, you forget about yourself and begin to find yourself in Christ! God's reward is more than enough: "Well done, good and faithful servant" (Matthew 25:21).

This is not some Pollyanna mental trip. God draws very near to those who decide to live by the gospel.

Ask yourself, "What is it in me that makes me jealous, selfish? What keeps me from genuinely rejoicing in the blessings given to others? What don't I like about myself? What can I do to live more in God's grace and be open to change?"

Remember, you are so loved that if you were the only person on the face of the earth, God, in Christ, would have been willing to die for *you*. Live that truth, that love. Then you can reach out to all—rich and poor alike—with the love that flows through you by His Spirit. By forgetting yourself you will find yourself.

FURTHER REFLECTION

Let us therefore strive to enter that rest, that no one fall by the same sort of disobedience. For the word of God is living and active, sharper than any two-edged sword, piercing to the division of soul and spirit, of joints and marrow, and discerning the thoughts and intentions of the heart.

Hebrews 4:11–12

Are You a Disciple or a Camp Follower?

Now great multitudes accompanied him; and he turned and said to them, "If anyone comes to me and does not hate his own father and mother and wife and children and brothers and sisters, yes, and even his own life, he cannot be my disciple. Whoever does not bear his own cross and come after me, cannot be my disciple. For which of you, desiring to build a tower, does not first sit down and count the cost, whether he has enough to complete it? Otherwise, when he has laid a foundation, and is not able to finish, all who see it begin to mock him, saying, 'This man began to build, and was not able to finish.' Or what king, going to encounter another king in war, will not sit down first and take counsel whether he is able with ten thousand to meet him who comes against him with twenty thousand? And if not, while the other is yet a great way off, he sends an embassy and asks terms of peace. So therefore, whoever of you does not renounce all that he has cannot be my disciple."

Luke 14:25–33

When I was about twelve years old, our house—with my parents, my grandmother, and a brother and sister—was more than a bit crowded, and so my dad decided to refinish the attic and make two bedrooms there for my brother and me. I was excited! I would have my own room—with the emphasis on *my*, of course. I began to think about colors and curtains and bedspreads. My brother thought about a rack for his gun and a place to play his guitar. We each had our plans.

Meanwhile my mother and dad had to make plans of their own. How much would all the necessary wood and supplies cost, the additional wiring, the paint, the labor, and so on? One evening I found them huddled together at the dining room table trying to see how they could make things work financially. And they did, much to the delight of all of us! There were sacrifices on both their parts; my dad spent hours after work doing the construction himself. Yet I never heard either of them complain. They made the sacrifice because the result would be worth it.

All of you have probably made decisions that required planning, weighing options, and probably some interior wrestling. Well, this is what Jesus is asking of us in regard to being His disciples. And, brothers and sisters, you want to be a disciple, not a "camp follower."

A camp follower stays on the fringe—the edge of the event, battle, or encampment—and takes whatever he can get in terms of food and shelter. He's a hanger-on, with no commitment, no decision to serve, no desire to give himself to the project. A lot of Catholics are camp followers, not disciples. They carry the label of Catholic—they come to Mass and appear at parish events sometimes—but they are on the fringe: no upfront commitment, no dedication to growth in holiness, no service to the needs of others.

When in this passage Jesus sees the "great multitudes" who are following Him, He takes the opportunity to teach them and to teach us: If you are going to follow Me, you need to make some decisions. Are you following Me and listening because you want to be entertained? Are you following Me because you are curious? Are you following Me because of the miracle of the loaves and fishes, and you are hoping for more food for your body? Are you following Me because you are bored or out of habit?

Jesus asks us today, "Why are you following Me?" Brothers and sisters, we need to establish clarity in our relationship with Christ. We can't just keep doing what we have always done out of habit or out of a kind of passivity, that is, "nothing better to do."

Jesus wants to make disciples. He asks us to sit down and count the cost of what it would mean to become a genuine Catholic in thought, word, and deed. Your reading this book today is an avenue of grace for you, because this book is based on Scripture, which is alive. God's Word has power to change you if you open your heart, if you are willing to count the cost and make some decisions.

Write down, as you reflect: What needs to change in my personal life to make it truly conform to the gospel, to the commandments? What decisions do I need to make? What price am I going to have to pay in order to change? Am I willing? Do I believe that God is calling me to a more intimate relationship with Him? Do I believe that if I follow Him more closely, I will eventually know a joy and a peace beyond understanding? Am I willing to make a decision to change for the sake of my family, my loved ones, myself? What holds me back?

Take these questions and your answers—or lack of answers—to prayer. Take a week, reflect, pray, ask for grace. Then make at least a couple of concrete decisions. Begin or begin again, even for the tenth time—don't give up. Pray daily for the grace you need; do not depend on yourself.

I remember the day my brother and I occupied the third floor of our house. All of the family were celebrating, all so grateful. It was obvious from the faces of my parents that this was worth whatever sacrifice of time and money they had made. How much more will each of us rejoice when we definitively decide to put the Lord first in all things!

To "hate," as the Gospel calls us to do, is to count as nothing in preferring God and His will. Make the choice to put Him and His will before all else. Count the cost; ask for the grace to pay the price. God will never be outdone in generosity!

When we put His will, His way, before all else, we will find what we have been created for. Being a disciple will be our greatest honor. And then we will be empowered to *truly* love those God has given us.

FURTHER REFLECTION

Keep steady my steps according to your promise,
   and let no iniquity get dominion over me.
Redeem me from man's oppression,
   that I may keep your precepts.
Make your face shine upon your servant,

and teach me your statutes.
My eyes shed streams of tears,
  because men do not keep your law.

Psalm 119:133–136

CHAPTER 21

A Watchful Father

Now the tax collectors and sinners were all drawing near to hear him. And the Pharisees and the scribes murmured, saying, "This man receives sinners and eats with them."

So he told them this parable: "What man of you, having a hundred sheep, if he has lost one of them, does not leave the ninety-nine in the wilderness, and go after the one which is lost, until he finds it? And when he has found it, he lays it on his shoulders, rejoicing. And when he comes home, he calls together his friends and neighbors, saying to them, 'Rejoice with me, for I have found my sheep which was lost.' Just so, I tell you, there will be more joy in heaven over one sinner who repents than over ninety-nine righteous persons who need no repentance.

"Or what woman, having ten silver coins, if she loses one coin, does not light a lamp and sweep the house and seek diligently until she finds it? And when she has found it, she calls together her friends and neighbors, saying, 'Rejoice with me, for I have found the coin which I had lost.' Just so, I tell you, there is joy before the angels of God over one sinner who repents."

And he said, "There was a man who had two sons; and the younger of them said to his father, 'Father, give me the share of property that falls to me.' And he divided his living between them. Not many days later, the younger son gathered all he had and took his journey into a far country, and there he squandered his property in loose living. And when he had spent everything, a great famine arose in that country, and he began to be in want. So he went and joined himself to one of the citizens of that country, who sent him into his fields to feed swine. And he would gladly have fed on the pods that the swine ate; and no one gave him anything. But when he came to himself he said, 'How many of my father's hired servants have bread enough and to spare, but I perish here with hunger! I will arise and go to my father, and I will say to him, "Father, I have sinned against heaven and before you; I am no longer worthy to be called your son; treat me as one of your hired servants."' And he arose and came to his father. But while he was yet at a distance, his father saw him and had compassion, and ran and embraced him and kissed him. And the son said to him, 'Father, I have sinned against heaven and before you; I am no longer worthy to be called your son.' But the father said to his servants, 'Bring quickly the best robe, and put it on him; and put a ring on his hand, and shoes on his feet; and bring the fatted calf and kill it, and let us eat and make merry; for this my son was dead, and is alive again; he was lost, and is found.' And they began to make merry.

"Now his elder son was in the field; and as he came and drew near to the house, he heard music and dancing. And he called one of the servants and asked what this meant. And he said to him, 'Your brother has come, and your father has killed the fatted calf, because he has received him safe and sound.' But he was angry and refused to go in. His father came out and entreated him, but he answered his father, 'Behold, these many years I have served you, and I never disobeyed your command; yet you never gave me a kid, that I might make merry with my friends. But when this son of yours came, who has devoured your living with harlots, you killed for him the fatted calf!' And he said to him, 'Son, you are always with me, and all that is mine is yours. It was fitting to make merry and be glad, for this your brother was dead, and is alive; he was lost, and is found.'"

Luke 15:1–32

Luke's is the only Gospel that records this story of the Prodigal Son, yet more sermons have been given on it and it is more often quoted than most of the Gospel stories. That is because we can see ourselves in this story so clearly, and it touches the deepest chord in our hearts with the hope for forgiveness in our own lives.

Let's reflect on this passage through each of the three main characters.

The Father

How very many mothers and fathers can identify with this poor father. A son seeks to gain his inheritance prematurely. He wants it *now*, which in effect says, "I don't care about you; as far as I am concerned you are dead; and I want the money coming to me now, not after they bury you."

What that must have done to this father's heart: It probably broke it! But the father doesn't argue or express anger—which he could have done legitimately. Good father that he is, he knows his son, and he knows that this son will not respond positively to justifiable anger. So he gives this miserable youth what he has toiled hard to gain. Then, and this is the even more amazing part, the father waits and watches and longs for the son's return. Other fathers would have washed their hands of the son, but not this father.

And one day the son returns, humbled, and begs forgiveness. But the father doesn't even allow him to voice the speech he has prepared. He embraces him and restores to him all the symbols of being a son of the father: a robe and a ring (symbols of authority and honor) and sandals (servants went barefoot).

Jesus is telling this story to illustrate what kind of a Father each of us has. He is the Father who watches for our return, the one who knows our repentant heart and won't even allow us to get through our prepared speech of repentance, the one who forgives and forgets, the one who restores us to the privileged position of sons and daughters.

Do you know your heavenly Father? Ask the Holy Spirit to lead you into the fullness of truth about God *our* Father, *your* Father!

The Prodigal Son

Haven't we all known periods in our lives when we were so selfish, so shortsighted, so angry, we just grabbed whatever we could, by whatever sinful means were close at hand, and never gave a thought to those we might be offending or hurting? Our own perceived needs or desires can so blind us that we can't see beyond our own nose. So it was for this young man.

When the "party days" come to an end, as they inevitably do, the son "wakes up." Hungry and disillusioned, he knows nowhere else to go but home, where he will throw himself on his father's heart and beg forgiveness. All the way he practices his speech (don't we know what this feels like?), not knowing what the reception will be because of the terrible insult he gave his father. He literally throws himself on his father, and he is not disappointed. And on top of that, he is fully restored as son and heir! What a grateful son he must be.

The Elder Brother

Oh, my goodness! Can't you see yourself sometimes? "I've always been good; I've always done what you asked, but you never gave me anything." "He always gets this," "She always is chosen," "No one ever thanks me for all my labor and sacrifice," and so on and so on.

Oh, brothers and sisters, the elder brother is in all of us. Look out for him in your mind and spirit. He can make you mean, disgruntled, sour, and self-focused.

Ask the Holy Spirit for a renewal of your mind so that you can see things and situations as He does! Ask Him to purify your memory so that you forget all the slights, all the ways people failed to acknowledge and thank you for things you have done. Ask for the grace to begin again with a new heart and spirit, focused not on self but on the Lord, who sees and knows and will reward.

Hear me on this truth, and hear me loud and clear: Your heavenly Father sees all you do and all you give. Not one generous act goes unnoticed, and not one will go unrewarded in the kingdom of heaven, even if "this world" does not see all you do.

The Father is always watching for you; you will not be left out. Ask the Lord to deepen your faith and give you grace to rejoice in the goodness of your Father. Let Him teach you to trust Him!

FURTHER REFLECTION

Depart from me, you evildoers,
that I may keep the commandments of my God.
Uphold me according to your promise, that I may live,
and let me not be put to shame in my hope!
Hold me up, that I may be safe
and have regard for your statutes continually!

Psalm 119:115–117

CHAPTER 22

A Steward Renders an Account

He also said to the disciples, "There was a rich man who had a steward, and charges were brought to him that this man was wasting his goods. And he called him and said to him, 'What is this that I hear about you? Turn in the account of your stewardship, for you can no longer be steward.' And the steward said to himself, 'What shall I do, since my master is taking the stewardship away from me? I am not strong enough to dig, and I am ashamed to beg. I have decided what to do, so that people may receive me into their houses when I am put out of the stewardship.' So, summoning his master's debtors one by one, he said to the first, 'How much do you owe my master?' He said, 'A hundred measures of oil.' And he said to him, 'Take your bill, and sit down quickly and write fifty.' Then he said to another, 'And how much do you owe?' He said, 'A hundred measures of wheat.' He said to him, 'Take your bill and write eighty.' The master commended the dishonest steward for his prudence; for the sons of this world are wiser in their own generation than the sons of light. And I tell you, make friends for yourselves by means of unrighteous mammon, so that when it fails they may receive you into the eternal habitations.

"He who is faithful in a very little is faithful also in much; and he who is dishonest in very little is dishonest also in much. If then you have not been faithful in the unrighteous mammon, who will entrust to you the true riches? And if you have not been faithful in that which is another's, who will give you that which is your own? No servant can serve two masters; for either he will hate the one and love the other, or he will be devoted to the one and despise the other. You cannot serve God and mammon."

Luke 16:1–13

There are two very important lessons to be learned here. The first is about motive. Why do I do the things I do? Is it primarily out of love and a desire to serve others? Or is it primarily to be thought well of, to influence, to do favors for others so that I have "insurance" when I am in need?

Jesus is saying that the worldly person knows how to store up doing good to others while in reality he is serving himself. He may appear to be generous, but his motive is self-serving. The unjust steward doesn't really care about the person in debt; he just wants to be in a position to "call in the favors" when he is in difficulty. This is the world's way.

The lesson should be clear to each of us: Do the right things—generous acts—for *the right reasons*. Ask the Lord to purify your motive and intention. He will do it if you sincerely ask.

Second, are goods and money your idols? Do you compromise your conscience as this steward did—skimming off the top for his own profit? We often start out by doing little things, seemingly inconsequential things, with the office petty cash, for example. It's so little, it doesn't matter. But it does! Even little acts of dishonesty, over time, numb the conscience. We find ourselves less and less troubled by petty theft, and when the big temptations come, we have little resistance to them.

I know a man who worked at a company for many years. He was a solid, productive worker who was trusted. But when things became financially tight because of the economy, he began to take small pieces of equipment to use in a personal business he had started at home in order to make money he needed for the family. This was a good man, but fear and anxiety dulled his conscience to the point where he thought he could justify what he was doing. "It's only for a time; I'll return it all." And one day he had taken too much, and this became known.

Sometimes we can get ourselves into relationships with people who ask us to do them a favor that involves dishonesty. If we agree we forge an unholy alliance, and one day it will come back to smack us in the face.

A friend said to me, "I don't have many friends, but the friends I have are good ones." When I asked her what she meant, she said, "My friends are people who really want to see me get to heaven. When I am with them, I grow in faith and hope. They genuinely care what happens to me, so I want to do the same for them."

Such people are the real jewels, the true riches, of your life. Having such friends doesn't mean that all conversations and activities revolve around Church or prayer. They include such things, but they also include barbecues and sports events, good movies shared, leisurely meals or quick lunches, and coffee together for the sake of friendship and support.

Look for good friends, and count having even one such person in your life an exceptional treasure. When times are difficult for them or for you, you will not fail one another, and you will grow in the certainty of His presence and care. In effect, you become for one another good stewards of the gifts of God.

FURTHER REFLECTION

Your testimonies are my heritage for ever;
    yes, they are the joy of my heart.
I incline my heart to perform your statutes
    for ever, to the end.

Psalm 119:111–112

CHAPTER 23

Where Are the Poor?

There was a rich man, who was clothed in purple and fine linen and who feasted sumptuously every day. And at his gate lay a poor man named Lazarus, full of sores, who desired to be fed with what fell from the rich man's table; moreover the dogs came and licked his sores. The poor man died and was carried by the angels to Abraham's bosom. The rich man also died and was buried; and in Hades, being in torment, he lifted up his eyes, and saw Abraham far off and Lazarus in his bosom. And he called out, "Father Abraham, have mercy upon me, and send Lazarus to dip the end of his finger in water and cool my tongue; for I am in anguish in this flame." But Abraham said, "Son, remember that you in your lifetime received your good things and Lazarus in like manner evil things; but now he is comforted here, and you are in anguish. And besides all this, between us and you a great chasm has been fixed, in order that those who would pass from here to you may not be able, and none may cross from there to us." And he said, "Then, I beg you, father, to send him to my father's house, for I have five brothers, so that he may warn them, lest they also come into this place of torment." But Abraham said, "They have Moses and the prophets; let them hear them." And he said, "No, father Abraham; but if some one goes to them from the dead, they will repent." He said to him, "If they do not hear Moses

and the prophets, neither will they be convinced if some one
should rise from the dead."

Luke 16:19–31

God means what He says. If we want to know eternal life, then
we must care for others in some fashion, materially or spiritually.
Too often we think about it as an added extra: if or when I have
time. But the time never comes.

The poor beggar, rejected in this life, finds himself in the
bosom of Abraham—that is, he is safe in the presence of
Abraham, the forefather of Israel. The rich man had all the com-
forts of this world but shared none; as a result he suffers eternally.
Don't drift in this area; make one or two concrete decisions to
help the poor in your area. This has to be one of our priorities!

There is a mammoth garbage dump in Mexico where thousands of people—including families with small children—make
their home. Do you know about situations like this? You need to.
While we enjoy a home and food and some profitable work, there
are members of God's family, our family, who are severely
deprived.

One year a number of students from a local Catholic high
school participated in a weeklong mission trip to that garbage
dump. Most of the young people came from middle-class families. They had everything they needed—and sometimes more.
After five days in the dump, when they had an opportunity for an
evening off, they chose to use the money they had planned to
spend on themselves in a different way. They asked the adults

with them to take them to a store, and they spent that money on necessities and a few surprises for the children of the dump.

At the end of the week, when the students returned to the United States, most of them had only the clothes on their backs. They had voluntarily given everything else away.

There is a very good chance that this experience will brand these young people for life, and thank God for that. I don't think they will find themselves in the rich man's unenviable and eternal position. I think they will become aware of all the Lazaruses around them—the mentally, emotionally, intellectually, and materially poor.

God wants to teach us how to see the poor right in our own neighborhoods and families. Sometimes those are the hardest to see. To go on a mission trip is a very good thing to do, but God is after more. He wants us to have a *heart* for the poor, and that takes sensitivity and a willingness to take our eyes off ourselves in daily circumstances and look around.

Mother Teresa used to tell people who wanted to come to India to help that she would rather they first take a walk in their neighborhood and see what God sees. Find the poor in your extended family and your neighborhood, and help them. Don't let them pass by your door empty-handed.

Then you can go elsewhere and help others to see as Jesus does.

There is another lesson in the final verses of this passage: Make sure you are not *spiritually poor*. Do *you* believe that your Savior died and rose for *you*, that you might have eternal life? Does this miracle of love shape your life, your thinking, your convictions, and your decisions? Your eternal future depends on it!

I pray daily for faith and hope and love for all those who read my books and those who listen to my radio program, *Food for the Journey*.[1] I ask that God will give you the grace to grow in faith and be a sign of His presence to those who need to hear the Good News. Make this your prayer also.

FURTHER REFLECTION

The word is near you, on your lips and in your heart (that is, the word of faith which we preach); because, if you confess with your lips that Jesus is Lord and believe in your heart that God raised him from the dead, you will be saved.

Romans 10:8–9

CHAPTER 24

Increase Our Faith!

The apostles said to the Lord, "Increase our faith!" And the Lord said, "If you had faith as a grain of mustard seed, you could say to this sycamore tree, 'Be rooted up, and be planted in the sea,' and it would obey you.

"Will any one of you, who has a servant plowing or keeping sheep, say to him when he has come in from the field, 'Come at once and sit down at table'? Will he not rather say to him, 'Prepare supper for me and put on your apron and serve me, till I eat and drink; and afterward you shall eat and drink'? Does he thank the servant because he did what was commanded? So you also, when you have done all that is commanded you, say, 'We are unworthy servants; we have only done what was our duty.'"

Luke 17:5–10

Remember that I told you in an earlier reflection that when you read a passage from Scripture, it is always important to look at the context—that is, what immediately precedes it. Otherwise you can miss some of the significance of the teaching. This passage is a very good illustration of that principle.

Verse 5 begins with "The apostles said to the Lord, 'Increase our faith!'" It would be easy to gloss over that request because you have read it many times. But look more closely: The apostles are in real need. Theirs is not just a pious request. Note the exclamation point. What specifically led them to make this request?

To answer that question, look at the third and fourth verses of Luke 17. Jesus is calling the apostles to forgive—as many times as someone asks! The apostles are a bit shocked, and they realize that humanly they can't meet this request of Jesus—unless the Lord increases their faith. We can't be obedient to what You are asking without deeper faith in You, without the conviction that whatever You ask us to do, You provide the power for us to cooperate.

God never asks something of us for which He will not give the grace to carry it out *if we depend on Him* and not on our good will. All the good will in the world can't enable us to forgive some very grievous hurts. Only drinking from the heart of Christ, who forgave beyond our understanding, can enable us to cry out to forgive our enemies and so be true disciples. That is a great truth.

In salvation history it was a momentous step when people could agree to "an eye for an eye and a tooth for a tooth" (Matthew 5:38; see Exodus 21:24; Leviticus 24:20; Deuteronomy 19:21). That is, the punishment will equal the crime. We will not destroy those who have offended us but will demand only what is equal to what has been destroyed. Now Jesus calls his disciples —you and me—to an almost infinitely higher response when we are offended. If people ask to be forgiven, we are to forgive them fully, not just from the mouth but from the heart, from the center of our being. You say, "I can't." I understand; humanly it seems impossible. But in union with Christ, all things are possible! Lord, increase our faith![1]

One other point that I have mentioned in earlier books, which Pope John Paul II said it is important to remember: Forgiveness is not the opposite of justice. That is, if you need to pursue legal means in order to receive a necessary resolution to a very serious situation, you can do that, as long as you are willing to forgive. Restitution and forgiveness can go together.

Second, John Paul II did say, "Forgiveness is *the opposite of resentment and revenge.*"[2] When resentment and revenge fuel our motivation for seeking restitution, the person most poisoned is our own self. It never brings peace! "Lord, we cry, increase our faith!" And He will, as we persevere in prayer and acts of forgiveness.

Your faith might really feel like a mustard seed, so small that it looks as if it can't be the source of life for anything. But water it with God's grace in frequent confession and reception of the Eucharist. Lay your heart bare before God. Decide to obey His command to forgive, and one day you will realize the new life flourishing inside you. You will become a source of hope for many.

Jesus tells us that because we are His servants, His disciples, we need to be ready to obey. When we do obey, thank Him for His grace; don't get stuck in another mire, the mire of pride, patting yourself on the back and saying, "Look how I forgave; look how I am obeying God's Word. I am really becoming holy. I hope others notice!"

Brothers and sisters, obey out of love. "I forgive, Lord, because You have forgiven me so much. I forgive because You have asked me to do it. I forgive this person because I want to be more like You!"

Keep your eyes fixed on the eternal reward: "What no eye has seen, nor ear heard, nor the heart of man conceived, what God has prepared for those who love him" (1 Corinthians 2:9; see Isaiah 64:4).

FURTHER REFLECTION

Your commandment makes me wiser than my enemies,
> for it is ever with me.
I have more understanding than all my teachers,
> for your testimonies are my meditation.
I understand more than the aged,
> for I keep your precepts.
I hold back my feet from every evil way,
> in order to keep your word.

Psalm 119:98–101

CHAPTER 25

Thank You

On the way to Jerusalem he was passing along between
Samaria and Galilee. And as he entered a village, he was met
by ten lepers, who stood at a distance and lifted up their voices
and said, "Jesus, Master, have mercy on us." When he saw
them he said to them, "Go and show yourselves to the priests."
And as they went they were cleansed. Then one of them, when
he saw that he was healed, turned back, praising God with a
loud voice; and he fell on his face at Jesus' feet, giving him
thanks. Now he was a Samaritan. Then said Jesus, "Were not
ten cleansed? Where are the nine? Was no one found to return
and give praise to God except this foreigner?" And he said to
him, "Rise and go your way; your faith has made you well."

Luke 17:11–19

This is a well-known passage of Scripture, but is the lesson well-
known? Is it part of your life and mine? This passage has a great
deal to teach us about charity and gratitude.

Let's set the scene. Ten men cry out from a distance to Jesus as
He enters the city. They are lepers: Their disease, by Jewish law,
renders them unclean, so they can have no contact with anyone,
including family. They can attend no religious services; they
cannot work; they have to sleep outside the city limits, with no

accommodations and no safety. They are, in a way, condemned to a living death.

Now, one of the men is a Samaritan. The Jews saw Samaritans as those who had chosen to marry foreign women and embrace pagan customs and beliefs. Samaritans were idolaters: They had betrayed the one true God. The Jews would have nothing to do with them.

So these ten men, one a Samaritan, cry out to Jesus from a distance, "Please, have mercy on us." They are desperate. And Jesus doesn't reject them. He simply tells them to do what Jewish law requires: Go show yourselves to the priests so they can verify that you are healed. Healing will mean they can be restored to their families, can work, can interact with people again, can pray with others. They will no longer experience that crushing, isolating loneliness.

We don't know the thoughts of these ten men. The Samaritan could be fearing that Jesus will reject him because of his heritage or that someone will hear the commotion and cast him out. But Jesus can read men's hearts, and He gives healing and freedom and restoration to all ten.

The men realize their good fortune. In their joy nine of them forget about Jesus and run off to the priest to get the necessary permission to be restored to the family of Israel. They probably shout and rejoice, clap one another on the back, celebrate with family. But they never return to the source of all healing to give thanks.

The Samaritan, the foreigner, the "enemy," is also caught up in the incredible blessing he has just experienced. But he returns immediately to the source, throws himself at the feet of Jesus, and acknowledges with gratitude God's blessing. Perhaps he is converted. At any rate he knows the right thing to do, and nothing diverts him from carrying it out—not even the delirious joy that must almost overwhelm him.

Jesus comments on this. He wants to emphasize the importance of gratitude in our relationship with God and with others.

What part does gratitude play in your life? Are you a grateful person? Do you acknowledge the daily "small" blessings that come from the hand of God? Are you thankful to others for the small favors as well as the big ones? We can get so caught up in what is not working on any given day that we are blind and deaf to the gracious acts of God on our behalf. Are you able to find joy in God's abundant kindness to you moment by moment?

When I was a sophomore in high school, a girl joined our class who was blind from birth. She took notes in Braille, and all her textbooks were in Braille. She was bright and courageous. But the lesson I have carried all my life from this girl is her genuine thankfulness for everything. She who had so many losses and obstacles to overcome daily, sometimes hourly, could *always* find something—morning, noon, and night—for which to be grateful. When I was around her, my problems seemed less. Hope and confidence burned brightly in her presence. Even at fifteen and sixteen, her classmates recognized this and counted this young woman a blessing.

What about your life? Do you acknowledge God's goodness to you specifically *every* day? You should begin if you haven't. It is wonderful to put on glasses of gratitude. Your vision will never be better!

FURTHER REFLECTION

Let the word of Christ dwell in you richly, as you teach and admonish one another in all wisdom, and as you sing psalms and hymns and spiritual songs with thankfulness in your hearts to God.

Colossians 3:16

CHAPTER 26

Never Lose Heart

And he told them a parable, to the effect that they ought always to pray and not lose heart. He said, "In a certain city there was a judge who neither feared God nor regarded man; and there was a widow in that city who kept coming to him and saying, 'Vindicate me against my adversary.' For a while he refused; but afterward he said to himself, 'Though I neither fear God nor regard man, yet because this widow bothers me, I will vindicate her, or she will wear me out by her continual coming.'" And the Lord said, "Hear what the unrighteous judge says. And will not God vindicate his elect, who cry to him day and night? Will he delay long over them? I tell you, he will vindicate them speedily. Nevertheless, when the Son of man comes, will he find faith on earth?"

Luke 18:1–8

I would like you to look in your Bible at several passages: Matthew 6:25–33; John 15:1–17; 16:1–24. These passages plus the one above give us some very important lessons about prayer.

Many people are looking for a formula that will guarantee a sought-for result. But Jesus doesn't want to teach us correct formulas: He wants us to enter into a very deep and personal relationship with Him, whereby we really begin to understand how

He thinks, what His priorities are, and what fruit He wishes to see in our lives and in the lives of those whom we love.

We can never fully comprehend the infinity that is God, but He does bless those who sincerely seek an intimacy of friendship, which is available to all who will approach Him on His terms. Why His terms? Because God created us; He knows us and our inner workings far more than we could possibly understand ourselves. Because He created us and because He knows us through and through, He knows what we most need for our eternal salvation and what others close to us need as well.

He tells us in a remarkable promise: "Whatever you ask in my name, I will do it" (John 14:13). You can say, "Well, I ask and ask, and nothing happens. I give up. Either God doesn't care, and this is all a farce, or God doesn't love me."

Notice, Jesus tells us *to ask in His name.* What does that mean? In the world, when you need a favor and you have access to someone who could help to grant it, you might say, "I am a friend of so-and-so, and this is my need. My friend told me I could use his name when asking for this favor." The other person then knows that his friend is implicitly recommending this person's request.

When we ask for something in the name of Jesus, that means Jesus sees our request as pleasing to the heart of the Father. So whenever you pray for something or for someone, ask the Lord Jesus, "Is this according to Your will? Will this bring someone closer to You? Will this contribute to this person's salvation? Is there anything about my request that would not be in conformity to Your will?"

Certainly we can't fully know the answers to these questions, but we don't want to ask God for things that might put the eternal life of people we love in jeopardy. In short, we want our prayers and our fasting for our needs and those of others to be as fully conformed to God's will as we can know. And though we do not know perfectly God's will, we know that with our right intention God will act in His mercy on our behalf.

God always wants repentance for sin, deeper conversion, greater love and hope, and an increase of faith. God wants eternal life for the people you love. So when you pray, put *first* in your prayer what is first in God's heart: What is most important to God needs to become most important to us.

Let me also say here, when we pray for ourselves and others, know that God is concerned for their health, their relationships, their work, a living wage, the addictions they might have, and particular challenges. God is as concerned as we are for all these things and even more. But as you pray for these human needs, widen your prayer to something like "God, if what I am asking will contribute to an increase of their faith, a deeper repentance for their sin, their hope of eternal life, and so on, please hear my prayer." And God will, because you are now praying for not only their human needs but for what is first in God's heart—that they share eternal life with Him! What good would it be to have every prayer answered for human satisfaction in this life and end up in hell?

Finally, hear what Jesus is emphasizing: Do not stop praying, even if your requests are not answered immediately, even if situations for which you are praying seem to get worse. God honors persistence. He will either show you how to adjust your petition or answer it, because He sees a faith that will not be deterred. Never give up![1]

FURTHER REFLECTION

It is good for me that I was afflicted,
   that I might learn your statutes.
The law of your mouth is better to me
   than thousands of gold and silver pieces.

Psalm 119:71–72

CHAPTER 27

Be Merciful to Me

He also told this parable to some who trusted in themselves that they were righteous and despised others: "Two men went up into the temple to pray, one a Pharisee and the other a tax collector. The Pharisee stood and prayed thus with himself, 'God, I thank you that I am not like other men, extortioners, unjust, adulterers, or even like this tax collector. I fast twice a week, I give tithes of all that I get.' But the tax collector, standing far off, would not even lift up his eyes to heaven, but beat his breast, saying, 'God, be merciful to me a sinner!' I tell you, this man went down to his house justified rather than the other; for every one who exults himself will be humbled, but he who humbles himself will be exalted."

Luke 18:9–14

There is a message regarding humility here that is repeated often in one form or another. The repetition can cause us to gloss over the passage, to say, "Yes, yes, I know all that," and end up reading God's Word only superficially. Don't do that! The Lord repeats His wisdom and advice and warning to us because we need it! You need it! I need it!

The Pharisee's problem here is that he uses his prayer time to tell God how great he is in obedience to the Law and then over and above the Law. He has become absolutely dependent on external conformity to the rules as his ticket to heaven. He even uses his prayer time to talk about himself.

The tax collector, on the other hand, is hated and despised because he collaborates with the Romans in collecting taxes. Already judged and rejected by others, he prays a prayer that is simple and pure and humble. And God hears it.

There's an old Irish saying, "Pride dies twenty minutes after you do." The older I get, the more I believe it is true—at least for me. From the two-year-old's "Me do it" to the elderly person's efforts to do something he or she should not try, pride is a deep river that runs through all of us. I am not speaking against a necessary part of human growth in the two-year-old nor the courage in the elderly to keep trying to serve, to give of themselves, to make a contribution. I am saying that we need to look clearly into our own hearts and ask, "Am I trying to save myself rather than letting God be my Savior?" In other words:

- Do I do good deeds to earn brownie points with God? Be honest!
- Do I serve in order to be recognized by others?
- Do I think that generous acts will make up for my sins?
- Do I pray in public places in order to be seen?

Stop here and examine your own conscience. See where you have fallen into these traps of pride, and ask God to make you sensitive to false motivations.

Then very simply ask God to purify your motivations. "Lord, I want to do this for your glory." "Lord, I offer these acts of generosity in *reparation* for my sin." "Lord, please forgive me! I choose You, Lord, for my Savior! Forgive me for trying to save myself. It is only Your death on the cross that made possible my salvation. I want to spend my life doing good and growing closer to You as an act of thanksgiving for what You have done for me." Ask the Holy Spirit to convert your mind.

You see, humility is truth, the truth of who you are and the truth of who God is. When that truth is operative in your personal life, a huge burden lifts from you. "I can't save myself. God didn't create me to save myself. He will do the saving; I do the cooperating."

Two lessons:

1. We are in need of being saved every moment of every day. God will do it for us if we depend on Him and acknowledge His saving power in our lives, day in and day out.

2. Our willingness to live in the truth of who we are and who God is, and our willingness not to judge the motivations and intentions of others, will bring us to a place of joy and confidence and peace. "The truth will make you free," Jesus promised (John 8:32).

FURTHER REFLECTION

> With my whole heart I seek you;
>> let me not wander from your commandments!
> I have laid up your word in my heart,
>> that I might not sin against you.

Psalm 119:10–11

CHAPTER 28

Conversion of Heart

He entered Jericho and was passing through. And there was a man named Zacchaeus; he was a chief tax collector, and rich. And he sought to see who Jesus was, but could not, on account of the crowd, because he was small of stature. So he ran on ahead and climbed up into a sycamore tree to see him, for he was to pass that way. And when Jesus came to the place, he looked up and said to him, "Zacchaeus, make haste and come down; for I must stay at your house today." So he made haste and came down, and received him joyfully. And when they saw it they all murmured, "He has gone in to be the guest of a man who is a sinner." And Zacchaeus stood and said to the Lord, "Behold, Lord, the half of my goods, I give to the poor; and if I have defrauded any one of anything, I restore it fourfold." And Jesus said to him, "Today salvation has come to this house, since he also is a son of Abraham. For the Son of man came to seek and to save the lost."

Luke 19:1–10

There are times when I think God wakes me in the middle of the night to pray for those who are lost; those who are so mired in sin that they think their situation is hopeless; those who have no idea that God would forgive them completely if they but asked; those who are lost in addictions, bound by a hunger and thirst they cannot satisfy; those who have no clue as to the meaning of life and just give themselves day by day to whatever the world offers; those so abused by life and by evil people that they have no idea how to love or be loved; those who have handled the pain in life by cynicism and stubbornness and anger, bitterness and hatred; those who have never heard of Jesus because no one has told them. These are the lost for whom Jesus came to bring hope and love and salvation.

Do you believe? Have you seen Jesus save you or someone you love? Pray for the lost, that Jesus' mercy may reach them and they can accept it when it comes. Remember, Jesus said that this is why He came!

Jesus came to Zacchaeus. The Scripture tells us that Jericho was not His destination, but as He was passing through, His heart was open and searching for those willing to be saved. And surprise! It was not one of the "religious" people but Zacchaeus.

Who was Zacchaeus? A tax collector—one hated by the Jews for collaborating with the enemy. He charged high taxes so he could skim off his share before giving money to the Romans. He was cheating his own people.

Yet there was some unnamed inspiration in Zacchaeus's heart to see Jesus. This desire was so great that he put his pride in his pocket, so to speak, ran ahead of Jesus, and climbed a tree so he could see him. Zacchaeus was a little man, and so he must have had experience in finding vantage points when he was in a crowd.

And there was a large crowd with Jesus. But Jesus looked up when He passed the tree. Amid all the noise and requests for cures and other help, Jesus was searching for the heart crying out in its sin. "Zacchaeus, come down; I must stay at your house today."

Can you imagine Zacchaeus's surprise? "He knows my name, and He called me, and He wants to come to my house!"

I am sure that word *house* meant more to Jesus than a physical dwelling. In effect Jesus was saying, "I want to live in your heart, Zaccheus; invite Me in."

Zacchaeus scrambled down the tree and joyfully, says the Scripture, received Him into his home. And even though the crowd labeled Zacchaeus a sinner and questioned Jesus for going to his house, Jesus was not deterred, and neither was Zacchaeus. Jesus was seeking the lost, and Zacchaeus received the grace of conversion. They were both overjoyed; the condemning cries of the crowd fell on deaf ears.

Now, notice what the conversion led Zacchaeus to do. He stood up and declared, I will give half of all I own to the poor; and if I have defrauded anyone, I will return it fourfold. His publicly declared decisions went above and beyond what the law required as recompense for cheating: that he pay back in full what he took and then double the amount; Zacchaeus quadrupled it!

This is real conversion! To *convert* means to turn away from what you have been doing and turn toward a whole new way of living, toward the person of Christ.

When Christ captures your heart, you respond spiritually and often materially or in some concrete fashion, with far more than what is required. Why? Because the King is now enthroned in your heart, and your desire is to see Him loved in those around you. You find yourself becoming generous in time and talent and treasure, beyond what you normally would have parted with, because you know you are loved with a love that will not fail!

Zacchaeus, the sinner, found new life. So can you!

FURTHER REFLECTION

My soul melts away for sorrow;
strengthen me according to your word!

. . .

This is my comfort in my affliction
that your promise gives me life.

Psalm 119:28, 50

CHAPTER 29

Every Tear Wiped Away

There came to him some Sadducees, those who say that there is no resurrection, and they asked him a question, saying, "Teacher, Moses wrote for us that if a man's brother dies, having a wife but no children, the man must take the wife and raise up children for his brother. Now there were seven brothers; the first took a wife and died without children; and the second and the third took her, and likewise all seven left no children and died. Afterward the woman also died. In the resurrection, therefore, whose wife will the woman be? For the seven had her as wife."

And Jesus said to them, "The sons of this age marry and are given in marriage; but those who are accounted worthy to attain to that age and to the resurrection from the dead neither marry nor are given in marriage; for they cannot die any more, because they are equal to angels and are sons of God, being sons of the resurrection. But that the dead are raised, even Moses showed, in the passage about the bush [see Exodus 3:6], where he calls the Lord the God of Abraham and the God of Isaac and the God of Jacob. Now he is not God of the dead, but of the living; for all live to him."

Luke 20:27–38

The Sadducees, as it tells us in the first verse of this passage, do not believe in the resurrection. They are challenged by Jesus' belief, and they do what most threatened people do: They come up with a ludicrous example to try and prove their point. They are sure Jesus will not have an answer for their unlikely example. They think they have Jesus trapped.

But Jesus, instead of reacting (as we might) to their exaggerated example, gives a very clear response: In this life we marry and are given in marriage, but those who die will enter a life where "no eye has seen, nor ear heard, nor the heart of man conceived, what God has prepared for those who love him" (1 Corinthians 2:9). We enter into a totally new life—an infinite life where "he will wipe away every tear from their eyes, and death shall be no more, neither shall there be mourning nor crying or pain any more" (Revelation 21:4). We will enter into union with Love Himself.

Our bodies will be restored to us after the Final Judgment, and they will have all the characteristics that Jesus' body exhibited after the Resurrection—no limitations, no barriers, no suffering (for starters). Please take time to read the section on heaven in the *Catechism of the Catholic Church* (# 1023–1029). You will get a wonderful education, and your faith will be made far more secure in the goodness of God.

The life of glory is hard for us to imagine because we are finite, and to imagine the infinite is beyond our ability. But we can dispose ourselves to receive the Holy Spirit's gifts of wisdom and understanding. Ask that the graces you received in confirmation, the gifts of the Holy Spirit, be more fully released in your life. Pray humbly for this.

I also think you might be encouraged to read what the saints had to say about heaven. Ralph Martin, in his book *Fulfillment of All Desire*, summarizes what God our Father told Saint Catherine of Siena and quotes directly from Saint Catherine:

> The union with and love of God that begin in this life and grow as the spiritual journey progresses will be gloriously manifested and perfected in heaven. But so also will the union and love that we have had with one another in this life be gloriously manifested and perfected in heaven. The Father tells Catherine that the particular relationships we had on earth, insofar as they were in the Lord, will actually increase in depth of intimacy and love in heaven. Friendships and marriages that were lived in and with Jesus will be "saved" and indeed prove to be a love that is truly "forever." The time for biological procreation will have come to an end—our bodies now transformed in glory, made ready for an eternity of celebration —but the love, in Christ, that was built up in true Christian relationships will last forever. We will not only know and recognize one another in heaven, but know and love each other even more!

> They are hungry and satisfied, satisfied yet hungry—but they are far from bored with satiety or pained in their hunger.... They are established in love for me and for their neighbors. And they are all united in general and special love, both of which come from one and the same charity. They rejoice and exult, sharing each other's goodness with loving affection, besides that universal good which they all possess together. They rejoice and exult with the angels, and they find

their places among the saints according to the different virtues in which they excelled in the world.

And though they are all joined in the bond of charity, they know a special kind of sharing with those whom they loved most closely with a special love in the world, a love through which they grew in grace and virtue. They helped each other proclaim the glory and praise of my name in themselves and in their neighbors. So now in everlasting life they have not lost that love; no, they still love and share with each other even more closely and fully, adding their love to the good of all.... When a soul reaches eternal life, all share in her good and she in theirs.[1]

FURTHER REFLECTION

Blessed is the man who trusts in the LORD,
    whose trust is the LORD.
He is like a tree planted by water,
    that sends out its roots by the stream,
and does not fear when heat comes,
    for its leaves remain green,
and is not anxious in the year of drought,
    for it does not cease to bear fruit.

Jeremiah 17:7–8

Endurance Will Bring Life

And as some spoke of the temple, how it was adorned with noble stones and offerings, he said, "As for these things which you see, the days will come when there shall not be left here one stone upon another that will not be thrown down." And they asked him, "Teacher, when will this be, and what will be the sign when this is about to take place?" And he said, "Take heed that you are not led astray; for many will come in my name, saying, 'I am he!' and, 'The time is at hand!' Do not go after them. And when you hear of wars and tumults, do not be terrified; for this must first take place, but the end will not be at once."

  Then he said to them, "Nation will rise against nation, and kingdom against kingdom; there will be great earthquakes, and in various places famines and pestilences; and there will be terrors and signs from heaven. But before all this they will lay their hands on you and persecute you, delivering you up to the synagogues and prisons, and you will be brought before kings and governors for my name's sake. This will be a time for you to bear testimony. Settle it therefore in your minds, not to meditate beforehand how to answer; for I will give you a mouth and wisdom, which none of your adversaries will be able to withstand or contradict. You will be delivered up even by parents and brothers and kinsmen and friends, and some of you they will put to death; you will be hated by all for my name's sake. But not a hair of your head will perish. By your endurance you will gain your lives.

Luke 21:5–19

First, a little historical context: Jesus prophesied before His death, as recorded here in Scripture, that Jerusalem and the temple would be destroyed by the Romans—so thoroughly destroyed that not one stone would be left upon another. This took place, as Jesus said it would, around AD 70.

We are nearing the end of the Church year, and the readings remind us that this is not our final home. If we want our final home to be heaven, then we need to make certain choices—all that I have been encouraging through this little book of reflections. We also need to be very clear that being a disciple of Christ involves some hard things, and we need to be ready for them. Just as Jesus set his face toward Jerusalem (committed to the Father's will to face whatever was needed to save us), so do we, by the graces of baptism and the Eucharist and confirmation, need to be fortified to clearly witness the truth and love of Christ in all circumstances.

Most of us want to shrink from that, and some of our brothers and sisters, it is true, have lived in peaceful times, when they were not called to witness to Christ with their physical lives. But did you know that more people were martyred for Christ in the twentieth century than in all others put together? That should give you some very necessary perspective.

I am not saying that you and I will die a physical death for the sake of Christ. I do not know that! But I do know that part of being Christ's disciple is the willingness to do whatever Christ asks of us. We need to grow in faith enough to give Him a blank check. He can fill in the amount that we are to give for the sake of ourselves and others.

Love for Christ makes that possible—nothing else. I have met heroes and heroines who are willing to pay the price. They have not had to give up their lives, but they are willing to risk their own personal safety to save the lives of others. If that kind of courage is present in some very good human beings, how much more courage and wisdom and hope will Christ give His followers who ask Him for grace to follow in His footsteps, whatever the cost. Jesus for our sake was "scorned by men, and despised by the people" (Psalm 22:6). Can we, His disciples, embrace the form of the cross we are asked to bear?

Some time ago I had the opportunity to serve some of our brothers and sisters in China. I was humbled by their willingness to bear great hardship for the sake of the gospel, to meet the needs of others whatever the cost to themselves. One young priest said, "Sister, I would be honored to shed my blood that the faith might be spread in China. Gladly would I give my life for my people."

Sometimes we are called to sacrifice our lives as did Maximilian Kolbe and Edith Stein, two martyrs of the twentieth century. Sometimes we are called to sacrifice our lives as did Mother Teresa and Pope John Paul II. The point is not to try and figure all that out beforehand. Most times we don't know until the decision is upon us. But we can heed our Lord's words and be ready for whatever He asks of us.

For further reflection: There is a story told among the desert fathers that certainly has the ring of truth. A very young monk went to a desert father and told him that he wanted to be holy. "I keep my little fast," he said, "and I pray the little prayers, and I strive to keep the little Rule. What more can I do?"

The old father raised his hands and arms to heaven, and as he prayed, his fingers became like ten torches. "My son," he said, "why not be totally changed into fire!"

This is a graphic image of a man consumed by the love of God. So God will do with us as we turn more and more of our lives over to Him by the power of His Spirit.

FURTHER REFLECTION

We must be sure that however burdensome and tempestuous the trials that await us may be, we will never be left on our own, we will never fall out of the Lord's hands, those hands that created us and now sustain us on our journey through life (Ps 138:8).[1]

Pope Benedict XVI

CHAPTER 31

Christ the King

And the people stood by, watching; but the rulers scoffed at him, saying, "He saved others; let him save himself, if he is the Christ of God, his Chosen One!" The soldiers also mocked him, coming up and offering him vinegar, and saying, "If you are the King of the Jews, save yourself!" There was also an inscription over him, "This is the King of the Jews."

One of the criminals who were hanged railed at him, saying, "Are you not the Christ? Save yourself and us!" But the other rebuked him, saying, "Do you not fear God, since you are under the same sentence of condemnation? And we indeed justly; for we are receiving the due reward of our deeds; but this man has done nothing wrong." And he said, "Jesus, remember me when you come into your kingly power." And he said to him, "Truly, I say to you, today you will be with me in Paradise."

Luke 23:35–43

The last Sunday of the Church year is the Feast of Christ the King. Surprising Gospel, isn't it, for this great feast? And yet how very, very appropriate!

Our King is not like any earthly king. His dominion, as far as earthly eyes could see, was highly limited—Bethlehem and

Nazareth, Galilee and Jerusalem and Calvary. The throne from which he won victory was the cross of shame and death. His scepter was a reed; His crown, thorns. His kingly power seemed impotent in the scourging, the trial, the carrying of the cross. His disciples lost hope: Many fled, leaving Him almost alone in His time of greatest trial. What kind of a king is this who cannot command and elicit loyalty?

If you had stood that day on Calvary and witnessed the crucifixion, would you have continued to believe? Or is He your king only when His cause seems victorious? Is He your king when you are asked to acknowledge Him? Or do you seek to distance yourself from any kind of affiliation when the cause is not popular?

The heavens acknowledge that He is King of all kings and Lord of all lords. Does your voice resound with the myriads upon myriads of heavenly voices who night and day, without ceasing, acknowledge His kingship? (Read Revelation 4 and 5.)

Right now—in your living room, in the car, on the street, wherever you can—acknowledge His kingship over you and in spirit join your voice to the invisible but very real chorus of angels and saints who worship Him without ceasing. "Holy, holy, holy" (Revelation 4:8).

Often in our world Jesus is an unpopular king. His policies and decrees seem impossible, crazy, outmoded. We pick and choose, trying to "balance" His commands with the world's siren call. As a result we end up in the unenviable position of straddling the world and the kingdom of God. That's a very unsafe place to be.

Do I find myself in this position sometimes? What can I do about it?

The two thieves were both condemned to death. The one thief, in his agony, chose to reject a moment of grace and instead rant and rave in despair. The other acknowledged the justice of his sentence and was touched by the innocence of Jesus. He opened his heart to God's mercy and to the incredible promise God made to him: "*Today* you will be with me in Paradise."

What Jesus did for the good thief, He desires to do for you! What you read in this passage is an expression of the mercy and love that Jesus has for you and for everyone who turns to Him sincerely and with repentance. No sin is too big for forgiveness: That is the mercy of your King! We don't deserve heaven, and we never will, but we can ask our King for mercy. He will give it to those who sincerely seek Him. He desires to be King of your life and to bring you one day to that place of eternal happiness.

As we celebrate Jesus' kingship this Sunday, don't let it be lip service. "This day … I have set before you life and death, blessing and curse; therefore choose life, that you and your descendants may live, loving the LORD your God, obeying his voice, and clinging to him" (Deuteronomy 30:19–20). Choose life! Choose to follow Him! Choose to come under His authority and know the joy of obedience that sets you free.

FURTHER REFLECTION

Have this mind among yourselves, which was in Christ Jesus, who, though he was in the form of God, did not count equality with God something to be grasped, but emptied himself, taking the form of a servant, being born in the likeness of men. And being found in human form he humbled himself and became obedient unto death, even death on a cross. Therefore God has highly exalted him and bestowed on him the name above every name, that at the name of Jesus every knee should bow, in heaven and on earth and under the earth, and every tongue confess that Jesus Christ is Lord, to the glory of God the Father.

Philippians 2:5–11

The grass withers, the flower fades;

    but the word of our God will stand forever.

Isaiah 40:8

One truth stood out for me in the months of prayer and of writing this book: Unless we know who we are and to whom we personally belong, we will not have the motivation to live a life according to God's Word.

Pope Benedict XVI wrote some years ago, when he was Cardinal Joseph Ratzinger:

> God created each of us according to his will, and this will is our prime origin. It is not just a remote and general will, but a particular will for each one of us. However it may seem when viewed from outside, no one exists solely by chance. Each one has been willed by God and has his own proper place in life. There is, for each one, a meaning and a role in the universe, and our lives will be all the more replete and happy, the more we realize this meaning, the more we incorporate this will into our lives and are one with it. Hence there arises the next question: "What kind of will is this?" What concept does God see fulfilled in the human race? For one thing, we can say that he has his own design for each person; each one is something special, not merely one example of a product

reproduced by the million. Each one is unique, never to be repeated, and willed by God precisely as he is. That is why we say that God calls each of us by name—not just by a concept, but by a name that only this one individual knows and that belongs solely to him. For each one there is a special call. And only if we live attentively in conversation and dialogue with God can we know why he needs us in such an apparently insignificant position and why we are, precisely in that position, so immeasurably important. We need only recall that individuals who were apparently the most forgotten and insignificant in the world—a young woman in Nazareth, fishermen on the Lake of Genessaret—became immeasurably significant. It is not always so evident, yet God wants each one of us, he needs each one of us, so that his world may become what he wants it to be.[1]

These words have echoed in my mind as I wrote and have inspired me when the day was long and hard. May they do the same for you. May they inspire you, as a beloved son or daughter of God, to persevere in feeding on His word, night and day, until you see His face.

BIBLIOGRAPHY

Benedict XVI. *Spiritual Thoughts: In the First Year of His Papacy*. Washington, D.C.: United States Conference of Catholic Bishops, 2007.

Catechism of the Catholic Church. Washington, D.C.: United States Catholic Conference, 1997.

Hahn, Scott, and Curtis Mitch. *Ignatius Catholic Study Bible, The Gospel of Luke*, second Catholic ed. San Francisco: Ignatius, 2000.

Holy Bible, New Revised Standard Version. Catholic ed. Grand Rapids: Zondervan, 1998.

Holy Bible, Revised Standard Version. 2nd Catholic ed. San Francisco: Ignatius, 2006.

Ratzinger, Cardinal Joseph. Unpublished homily, 88th *Deutschen Katholikentag* [German Catholic Day], July 5, 1984, in *Co-workers of the Truth: Meditations for Every Day of the Year*. San Francisco: Ignatius, 1992, p. 222.

University of Navarre, *Navarre Bible: St. Luke*, 3rd ed. (New York: Scepter, 2005).

Vatican Council II, *Dei Verbum*, Dogmatic Constitution on Divine Revelation, in Austin Flannery, ed. *Vatican Council II, Volume 1: The Conciliar and Post Conciliar Documents*, rev. ed. New York: Costello, 1998, pp. 750–765.

An Open Letter to Readers

1. Pope Benedict XVI, Angelus Reflection, November 6, 2005, available at www.vatican.va.
2. Archbishop Charles Chaput, "God's Word Has the Power to Change Hearts and History," Keynote Address, Catholic Bible Conference, Denver, Colorado, June 26, 2009, available at www.zenit.org.
3. Scott Hahn and Curtis Mitch, *Ignatius Catholic Study Bible: The Gospel of Luke* (San Francisco: Ignatius, 2001), pp. 13–14.

Chapter Three: How Deep Is Your Faith?

1. See Hahn and Mitch, p. 17.

Chapter Seven: Love Your Enemies

1. My booklet *Why Forgive?* can be helpful in learning how to forgive when you have been seriously wounded or even when the hurts are the daily small ones. Your first copy is free; additional copies are $2.00. Order through Renewal Ministries, P.O. Box 1426, Ann Arbor, MI 48106.

Chapter Nine: Who Do You Say I Am?

1. See Ann Shields, *Deeper Conversion: Extraordinary Grace for Ordinary Time* (Cincinnati: Servant, 2008), pp. 65–67.

Chapter Ten: Follow Me

1. University of Navarre, *The Navarre Bible, St. Luke*, 3rd ed. (New York: Scepter, 2005), p. 103.

Chapter Twelve: Go and Do Likewise

1. *Navarre Bible, St. Luke*, p. 111.

Chapter Fourteen: Our Father

1. In *Why Forgive?* I explain all the tools that help us receive God's grace and carry out His will in this area.
2. Order *Pray and Never Lose Heart* by Sister Ann Shields from Renewal Ministries, P.O. Box 1426, Ann Arbor, MI 48106, or at renewalministries.net. Cost is $10.00, which includes shipping and handling within the United States.

Chapter Sixteen: Faithful Stewards

1. Pope Benedict XVI, General Audience, March 1, 2006, available at www.vatican.va.

Chapter Seventeen: The Assumption of the Blessed Mother

1. Hahn and Mitch, p. 14.
2. Hahn and Mitch, p. 21.

Chapter Twenty-Three: Where Are the Poor?

1. You can listen to episodes of *Food for the Journey* online at www.renewalministries.net. Click on the "TV/Radio" link on the left side of the home page.

Chapter Twenty-Four: Increase Our Faith!

1. Again I suggest you read my booklet *Why Forgive?*
2. Pope John Paul II, Message for the World Day of Peace 2002, no. 3, January 1, 2002, available at www.vatican.va.

Chapter Twenty-Six: Never Lose Heart

1. For a fuller treatment of this topic, see my book *Pray and Never Lose Heart* (Servant, 2001). Order information is in chapter fourteen note.

Chapter Twenty-Nine: Every Tear Wiped Away

1. Ralph Martin, *The Fulfillment of All Desire: A Guidebook for the Journey to God Based on the Wisdom of the Saints* (Steubenville, Ohio: Emmaus Road, 2006), pp. 57–58, quoting Catherine of Siena, *The Dialogue*, p. 83.

Chapter Thirty: Endurance Will Bring Life

1. Pope Benedict XVI, General Audience, December 7, 2005, as quoted in *Spiritual Thoughts: In the First Year of His Papacy* (Washington, D.C: United States Conference of Catholic Bishops, 2007), p. 69.

Conclusion

1. From an unpublished homily given at the 88th *Deutschen Katholikentag* [German Catholic Day], July 5, 1984, as quoted in Cardinal Joseph Ratzinger, *Co-Workers of the Truth: Meditations for Every Day of the Year* (San Francisco: Ignatius, 1992), p. 222.

ABOUT THE AUTHOR

SISTER ANN SHIELDS, S.G.L., is an internationally known evangelist and the host of the daily evangelistic and inspirational radio program, *Food for the Journey*. She is the author of several books, including *Deeper Conversion: Extraordinary Grace for Ordinary Times, Pray and Never Lose Heart* and *Fire in My Heart*. Sister Ann is a member of the Servants of God's Love, a charismatic religious community based in Ann Arbor, Michigan.